THE CHICKASAW RANCHER

THE CHICKASAW RANCHER
REVISED EDITION

BY Neil R. Johnson
EDITED BY C. Neil Kingsley
FOREWORD BY Dr. Arrell M. Gibson

University Press of Colorado

© 2001 by the University Press of Colorado

Published by the University Press of Colorado
5589 Arapahoe Avenue, Suite 206C
Boulder, Colorado 80303

The University Press of Colorado is a cooperative publishing enterprise supported, in part, by Adams State College, Colorado State University, Fort Lewis College, Mesa State College, Metropolitan State College of Denver, University of Colorado, University of Northern Colorado, University of Southern Colorado, and Western State College of Colorado.

The paper used in this publication meets the minimum requirements of the American National Standard for Information Sciences–Permanence of Paper for Printed Library Materials. ANSI Z39.48-1992

Library of Congress Cataloging-in-Publication Data

Johnson, Neil R., 1893–1970.
    The Chickasaw rancher / by Neil R. Johnson.–Rev. ed. / by C. Neil Kingsley ; foreword by Arrell M. Gibson.
        p. cm.
Includes bibliographical references (p.) and index.
    ISBN 0-87081-634-9 (hardcover : alk. paper)–ISBN 0-87081-635-7 (pbk. : alk. paper)
    1. Johnson, Montford T., 1843-1896. 2. Pioneers–Oklahoma–Biography. 3. Ranchers–Oklahoma–Biography. 4. Frontier and pioneer life–Oklahoma. 5. Ranch life–Oklahoma–History–19th century. 6. Oklahoma–Social life and customs–19th century. 7. Chickasaw Nation–History–19th century. I. Kingsley, C. Neil, 1948– II. Title.

F697.J6 J62 2001
976.6'03'092–dc21

Design by Daniel Pratt

2001002734

To my mother Elise (Johnson) McCartt
and my Great Aunt, Arline (Johnson) LeFlore

Contents

Foreword

The American West continues to captivate the popular fancy, and while this enduring public interest puzzles many social critics, actually an explanation is not too difficult to come by. The West was a savage, dangerous land, and the challenge it hurled to the men who would conquer it was deadly certain and exacting. Survival, ever a clear and constant question, required endurance and initiative, resourcefulness, and above all courage. The very uncertainties of existence induced an admirably reckless daring. The West was an outlet for individualism, a land of strong personalities. And the region produced a coarse nobility, esteemed by contemporaries, and understandably admired in a nauseously secure, tamed age. Devotees of the West are well acquainted with the likes of Charles Goodnight, John Clay, Richard King, and Ab Blocker. *The Chickasaw Rancher* introduces to the world a worthy confederate for these range aristocrats—Montford Johnson.

The epic of the Chickasaw rancher is based on the memoirs of Montford Johnson and his son Edward. Neil Johnson, grandson of Montford and son of Edward, has fused these parental recollections into a candid, instructive, and exciting narrative.

The Chickasaw Rancher is a multidimensional story, for besides its primary focus—that of supplying a detailed view of ranching in the Chickasaw Nation—it provides a description of life among the Five Civilized Tribes before, during, and after removal to the Indian Territory. The catalyst that provoked these five nations—the Choctaws, Chickasaws, Cherokees, Creeks, and Seminoles—to remarkable advances in the Anglo civilization was the mixed-blood family formed from the liaisons of inter-married white traders, missionaries, and frontiersmen. Just as the Ridge, Hicks, Lowry, and Ross lines, initiated among the Cherokees even be-fore American independence, were producing leaders to sustain this tribe's high-level economic and political life down to the government-enforced dissolution of tribal existence around 1900, a similar development was taking place among the other four nations. The Grayson, McIntosh, McGillivray, and Porter mixed-blood families were preeminent in Creek affairs, as were the Brown and Davis lines among the Seminoles, and the Folsoms, LeFlores, McCurtains, and Pitchlynns for the Choctaws.

Outstanding mixed-blood families developed in the Chickasaw Na-tion too, and none was more esteemed than the issue of Charles Johnson. English-born Johnson came to the United States at the age of nineteen, and after a brief stint as an itinerant actor, he became a trader in the Chickasaw Nation. By his marriage to a Chickasaw girl, Rebekah Courtney, Johnson became a citizen of the tribe and accompanied the Chickasaws west over their "Trail of Tears" to a new home in the Indian Territory. Beginning in 1837 and for nearly twenty years, the Chickasaws lived with their linguistic brethren, the Choctaws. The independent Chickasaws grew dissatisfied with this arrangement, and finally in 1855, after years of complaint, were permitted to separate from the Choctaws and were assigned a national domain of their own, its boundaries as finally established extending west from the Choctaw line to the ninety-eighth meridian, bounded on the north by the Canadian River, on the south by the Red River.

Several important developments took place in the Johnson family before the Chickasaws received their new home west of the Choctaws. In 1843, Montford Johnson, the future Chickasaw rancher, was born; shortly his mother died, and Charley Johnson returned to the East, leav-ing his two children, Adelaide and Montford, with Indian relatives. Montford grew to young manhood in the shadow of Fort Arbuckle, and from his recollections we are furnished with a glimpse of pioneer life on the western rim of the Chickasaw Nation, where, as on other American frontiers, social status was based more on courage, honor, dependabil-ity, and hospitality, and less on considerations of birth and wealth. Fur-ther, *The Chickasaw Rancher* contains an intimate account of the hard-ships and heartaches, the successes and failures of the hardy settlers who tamed this howling wilderness. This is timely since up until now, except for scant references found in such impersonal sources as the annual re-ports of the Commissioner of Indian Affairs, little has been known of the region and its people.

The only whites permitted in the Indian nations in these times were licensed traders, agency employees, and military personnel and their

families. While loneliness must have been the common lot of most of
the families stationed at Fort Arbuckle, *The Chickasaw Rancher* reveals
how this loneliness was eased by visiting among the Indian families of
the community that grew up near the post. This blending of Indian and
Anglo cultures produced a colorful social life—the dances, play parties,
and Sunday dinners of the military families reciprocated by the Indian
festivals and horse races. Some interesting social interaction took place
too. Sons of military personnel stationed at Fort Arbuckle courted
Chickasaw girls, and Chickasaw boys courted daughters from the post.
Michael, a son of Sergeant Charles Campbell, married Montford's sister, Adelaide, and Montford wooed and won one of the Campbell girls,
Mary Elizabeth.

Interestingly, *The Chickasaw Rancher* brings to light a curious aspect
of the Civil War in the Indian Territory. From reading Colonel W. H.
Emory's reports, one receives the impression that, during the spring of
1861, there was a total evacuation of Indian Territory posts, and that the
United States troops and their families rushed north to Fort Leavenworth
to escape capture by invading Texas Confederate forces. Sergeant
Campbell did leave with Emory's column and subsequently he participated in several Union Army campaigns against the Confederacy. His
wife, Mary Campbell, was a slaveholder of sorts, having a Negro cook,
and she refused to leave Fort Arbuckle. Her children remained with her,
and one of her sons, Michael, was appointed major in a Confederate
Chickasaw battalion.

Among other things, *The Chickasaw Rancher* is a sort of frontier "how
to" book, and many questions heretofore puzzling researchers and the
curious on early life in the West are answered in satisfying detail. This is
especially true concerning food and medicine. As a matter of fact *The
Chickasaw Rancher* comprises a primitive *materia medica*, describing the
step-by-step method of "cupping"; the general remedies for colds, toothache, and snakebite; the annual round of sulphur and molasses; and the
successor to this damnable blood-purge—sassafras tea. These practitio-
ners of frontier medicine were inventive too; witness Mary Elizabeth
Johnson losing her second infant son. To relieve the pain of the mother's
full breasts, Aunt Eliza successfully used a hungry greyhound pup for a
breast pump.

This book reveals that cattlemen in the Chickasaw Nation did not
disdain farming, but were remarkably self-sufficient, and actually raised
most of their food. Montford took almost as much pride in his vegetable
patches, grain fields, and orchards as he did in his sleek livestock herds,
and his musical recollection of ox-pulled plows slipping "through the
matted grass roots . . . ripped like the tearing of a piece of cloth" sounds
off-beat and anomalous for a cattleman. Salt and soap making, hunting

the bee tree, stalking wild game, and grinding corn all conjure nostalgic raptures. The uses corn was put to by these people is a further tribute to their ingenuity—besides an important feed for stock, corn was ground into the meal that produced the staff of life for these hardy folk, was used as a cleaner for chapped and dirty hands, and with lard or tallow and wick made a long-burning light. And corn doubled for coffee too. In times of scarcity, a savory substitute could be had by parching a quantity of corn in a Dutch oven, adding molasses, hydrating, and grinding coffee-fine.

With all its frontier lore, *The Chickasaw Rancher* is primarily a book about ranching, and though Montford's interests were varied, he was first and foremost a stock raiser. And while his remarkable success as a ranchman was due in no small way to creditable personal qualities—abundant energy and drive, a remarkably strong constitution, personal courage, and imagination—Montford, it must be admitted, enjoyed several advantages over stock raisers in other sections of the West.

First of all, Montford did not have to face the constant threat of range curtailment suffered by cattlemen in other parts. Basic to a successful ranch operation in the open-range days were vast areas of unfettered grassland. The ranchman's struggle for land, grass, and water was a recurring epic in the history of the West. In Texas, where the range-cattle industry got its start, the state was able to manage its own land policy, and thereby developed a generous range settlement program to encourage stock raising. Cattle drives from Texas to markets in the Kansas cow towns after the Civil War resulted in a discovery of the grazing possibilities of open public-domain pastures of the states and territories of the central and northern Plains.

As the range-cattle industry expanded into America's first billion-dollar industry, these upper grasslands were quickly occupied by Texas ranchmen and cattle corporations formed by capitalists in the eastern United States and Europe. The westward surge of agricultural settlement encouraged by the Homestead Act, Preemption Act, Timber Culture Act, and Desert Land Act, whereby a single farmer might gather up in fee simple nearly 1,200 acres, quickly reduced the open range and posed a severe threat to stock raising. Through these troubled years, when most cattlemen were having to fight in a very literal sense to hold any grass at all, Montford Johnson had no land problems.

As a mixed-blood Chickasaw, he was entitled to share in the land bounty of his tribe. The tribes of the Indian Territory held their lands in common. Title was vested in the tribes. An Indian, or intermarried white, who was thereby a tribal citizen (witness Caddo Bill Williams, Montford's neighbor on the west), could settle any place in his respective nation as long as he did not encroach on a neighbor's holdings. He could erect improvements and use the land for his lifetime and pass on to his heirs, not the land, but the preempted right of use, plus his improvements. Anytime a sale of land is mentioned in the Indian nations before allotment in severalty, it means sale of right of use of a particular tract and improvements. Since the Chickasaws were not allotted until around 1900, Montford prospered land-wise.

Not only did the common land system favor Montford's rise as a leading cattleman in the Southwest, but in addition, he was favored by the pattern of Chickasaw settlement. The government had been prodigious in assigning nations and reservations to the tribes of the Indian Territory. Like most of the other tribes, the Chickasaws had a population density of considerably less than five persons per square mile. The Chickasaw communities were concentrated for the most part in the eastern portion of the national domain. The western half was shunned by most tribal citizens for years because of their fear of attack from the fierce Kiowa and Comanche who neighbored on the west. Thus, this section of the nation was virtually uninhabited in 1861 when Montford started ranching.

Montford Johnson seemed peculiarly blessed at every turn, for besides having virtually the entire western half of the Chickasaw Nation to select a center for his projected stock-raising enterprise, he managed, through an old friend, Jesse Chisholm, to establish a modus operandi with the chief obstacle to settlement in the western Chickasaw Nation, the hostile Kiowa and Comanche. The courageous Jesse Chisholm, a mixed-blood Cherokee, his name commemorated in western history by the greatest of all cattle highways—the Chisholm Trail—had served on the southwestern frontier for years as a guide and trader. Through his far-flung chain of trading posts in the western Chickasaw Nation and into the old Leased District, the home of the Kiowa and Comanche, and because of his reputation for fair dealing, Chisholm was esteemed and respected by the chiefs and headmen of the frontier tribes.

Montford had started ranching on a small scale around Fort Arbuckle, a relatively protected area, in 1861. By 1865, his herd had increased to the point that he needed more grass. While hunting buffalo with Jesse Chisholm on the Canadian River, the northern borderland of the Chickasaw Nation, Montford became enthusiastic about the range value of these Canadian pastures. When he confided to Chisholm that aside from the buffalo and wild Indians these grasslands would be a ranchman's paradise, Jesse assured that he could arrange with the chiefs to permit Montford to bring in his cattle, and that periodic patrols by Montford's riders would keep the cattle separated from the migrating buffalo herds. It is interesting that Chisholm warned that as an Indian he, Montford, would have the indulgence of the Kiowa and Comanche only as long as he refrained from using white men as riders, Texans especially being resented by these tribes. The ethnic sensitivity of these savage peoples is intriguing—Montford could use Indians, Negroes, and Mexicans as cowboys to patrol his range.

True to his promise, Chisholm spoke to the Kiowa and Comanche chiefs on Montford's behalf and gained their assent. In view of the many treaties and agreements made between these tribes and the United States and the regular violation of terms by both parties, it is all the more amazing that the Chickasaw rancher and his family could live and prosper on the northwestern borderland, astride the buffalo range coursed by these savage people, enjoying almost complete immunity from depredations.

With few exceptions, Montford kept his word to the Kiowa and Comanche regarding use of white riders. When pressed for help during roundup, he hired range crews from a colony of Mexicans near Fort Sill. These descendants of Indian captives, brought in by the Kiowa and Comanche from south of the Rio Grande, had been employed by Jesse Chisholm from time to time to freight in supplies and work about his trading posts. For routine operations, Montford relied on Negroes and Indians. He divided his Canadian range into designated ranches and settled Negro and Indian families on them and operated on a partnership basis, giving each tenant every fourth calf and colt. While this was a curious way to run a ranching empire, his pledge to the Kiowa and Comanche not to use Anglo riders drove him to it, and the system worked. Thus Jack Brown was set up at the Walnut Creek Ranch, and Grandma Vicey at Council Grove. Adopting the orphaned Chickasaws Chubb Moore brought in added to his labor force. His son Edward, a strong, hardworking youth, had become by the age of twelve a skilled cowman in his own right. And of course Montford worked hard himself.

As a stock raiser, Montford worked at improving his herds. At first his ranges were stocked with animals descended from Chickasaw cattle brought in from Mississippi during the "Trail of Tears," and according to Montford "they were all colors but much superior to the Texas longhorns" that passed through the Chickasaw Nation northward to the cow towns of Kansas. Montford pioneered in importing Durham bulls to upgrade his range stock, and his sleek horse herds were the envy of stock raisers all over the Southwest.

During the 1880s, the Kiowa-Comanche menace having been eliminated, cattlemen from Texas began entering the Chickasaw Nation and leasing ranchland from the tribal government. This reduced the periphery of Montford's operations, but ever resourceful, the Chickasaw rancher developed a sensible range management program that prevented overgrazing on his choice pastures, and assured longer life for the Canadian grasslands; and by raising feed and hay and using winter feeding he was assured more marketable animals and stronger breeding herds.

The intricate descriptions contained in *The Chickasaw Rancher* on handling calves, trapping wild horses and cattle, using milk cows to decoy the wild ones, and setting salt lures and traps on early roundups leave little to be desired in the way of detail on early-day ranching. And Montford's recollections disclose that the rancher's life was more than riding, roping, branding, and a periodic spree in town; that it had an unromantic side too, with such routines as screwworm treatment, wolf control, castrating bulls, and building fence.

There is a fresh quality about *The Chickasaw Rancher,* and it may well be able to claim to bring to readers and collectors of Western Americana several new angles. One of these concerns handling outlaw steers. Charley Siringo and other cowboys have described throwing uncooperative animals, sewing their eyelids together, thus blinding the creatures and making them easier to handle. The Chickasaw rancher used what may have been an original device on incorrigibles—two-inch sticks, flat on one side, which were placed perpendicularly under the eyelids, thus serving as a sort of blinder.

The Indian Territory became, after 1865, a great cattle highway for several million Texas longhorns bound for the Kansas cow town markets. The East Shawnee, West Shawnee, Chisholm, and Dodge City or Great Western Trails are the names most commonly used to identify the leading roads to Kansas. Specific location is another matter. As an example, the Shawnee Trail, with its two branches, has been identified in at least six different locales. Historians have marked the Shawnee Trail as crossing into the Indian Territory at Colbert's Ferry on Red River, thence north to Boggy Depot, the eastern branch bending to the forks of the Canadian, northward through the Cherokee Nation to Baxter Springs, Kansas, with the western arm branching at Boggy Depot and extending northwest toward Wichita.

The Chickasaw Rancher identifies a more westerly course for the Shawnee Trail, and it would seem from the different locations given for this trail alone, that while common names prevailed, trail drivers often cut their own lines of march, determined by, besides custom, local conditions of grass, water, and fords on the rivers. The herds fed en route, and a commonly used trail, heavily grazed on its margins by preceding drives, could force a swing to the east or west by the latecomers.

Speaking of cattle trails, *The Chickasaw Rancher* accounts for a curious development in trail driving—the resumption of use of the central courses, the so-called Shawnee and Chisholm Trails, which gave rise to the cow towns of south central Kansas. Hunnewell and Caldwell continued to do a substantial cattle shipping business long after the evolution of Dodge

City. According to Montford, this was due to Texas Panhandle ranchers' associations levying grazing fees and fines on the drovers for crossing their ranges to Dodge City. Hunnewell and Caldwell were closer for many ranchmen and the drovers' fee charged by the Indian nations was less exorbitant.

While Montford generally sold his steers to cattlemen up from Texas on their way north, once in a while he would organize his own trail drive. He shared the problems common to all trail drivers and has described them in satisfying detail, and one of these drives, supervised by Edward Johnson, depicts the "bullin' steer." *The Chickasaw Rancher* details the anomaly of this critter, the disturbance he caused in the trail herd, and the artifices used in an attempt to overcome his sex appeal. Liberal applications of axle grease sprinkled with cayenne pepper had the opposite effect, for instead of reducing, this measure seemed to increase his appeal.

The pace of *The Chickasaw Rancher* is broken from time to time by accounts of tragedy (such as the prairie fire incident), excitement (when Edward and his riders recovered their stock from the Fort Reno cavalry patrol), and it is laced with enough humor to reduce the grimness and prodigious effort required of the Chickasaw rancher and his clan in carving out their range empire. Some of this humor is direct, like the cookstove incident. And some is the more subtle sort, notably the machinations of Boggy Johnson when he learned of the prosperity of his abandoned son, Montford.

Here and there enough traits are evident that one can glean a characterization of the Chickasaw rancher. Besides his ingenuity, resourcefulness, and courage, Montford was ambitious without being viciously so. And Montford was adaptable, for once the country opened to settlement, Edward and he were active in developing towns, banks, and stores. The humanity of this frontier patriarch is shown in his enduring concern for relatives, outsiders such as Grandma Vicey, and his adoption of the wagonload of Chickasaw orphans brought in by Chubb Moore. Montford even took time to visit the Indian prisoners in the federal prison at Saint Augustine, Florida, and was instrumental in gaining their freedom. That Montford's influence and prestige extended beyond the Chickasaw Nation is evidenced by the Tom Wassom episode. Wassom, one of Montford's most trusted riders, lived under a shadow of supposed guilt for crimes charged to him. Montford induced Wassom to carry his letter of introduction and explanation to the "hanging judge" of Fort Smith, Isaac Parker. Wassom returned to the Chickasaw Nation a free man. Montford dabbled in Chickasaw Nation politics for the purpose of ramming through the tribal legislature a fence law to better protect his own interests, but in most cases, like other cattle barons of the West, Montford was a law unto himself; by vigorous enforcement of his own code, the Chickasaw rancher maintained his own brand of law and order on the frontier of the Canadian.

—ARRELL M. GIBSON

Preface to the Revised Edition

It has been over forty years since Neil R. Johnson first published *The Chickasaw Rancher*. Six more generations have walked the soil of Oklahoma since Montford T. Johnson and his contemporaries first roamed the Chickasaw Nation. Many of the landmarks that these pioneers used for finding their way or marking off their ranges have long since been paved over and are gone forever. In the hustle and bustle of our modern world we pass by these historic places, unnoticed, as we race against the demands that our increasingly complex society puts on all of us. Admittedly, this is but one small bud off the heavily flowered historic tree of Oklahoma, yet I still think it merits a look.

From time to time people stop me on the street and ask me if anyone plans to reprint my grandfather's book. For years I thought that someone else would do just that, but I eventually realized that if I wanted the book published, I would have to be that someone.

It had also been pointed out to me, especially by the late John Womack, that there were a few mistakes that should be corrected if a new edition were to be published, and that some photographs or maps would compliment this expansive story. Well if the truth be known, Neil Johnson did have a number of illustrations when he first submitted the book to the University of Oklahoma Press. Unfortunately, when the Press declined to publish his book in the mid 1950s, his manuscript was returned, but all his photographs and maps were gone, never to be found again (at least not from this source). In the late 1960s, the Press was planning to publish a third printing of the book (Redlands Press in Stillwater, Oklahoma, had done the first two printings in 1960 and 1961). Neil Johnson asked Savoie Lottinville to look again for his misplaced illustrations. Savoie wrote back to Neil saying, "We have turned this place inside out and have found nothing." The University of Oklahoma Press did sign a contract with Neil and then later, after his death, with his surviving brothers to publish the book when the Press had the surplus funds. After some fifteen years in limbo, the book, still not reprinted, was given back to Neil Johnson's family and ended up in my arms.

So my mission was threefold: correct the errors that I could, corroborating family history with Indian Territory and Oklahoma history; fill in a little more history of the family's Chickasaw heritage and their pioneer neighbors; and lastly search out photographs, maps, and other illustrations that would illuminate the book's contents. In the age of video bombardment and shortened attention spans, these illustrations seemed a vital necessity.

I've gone through the original edition of *The Chickasaw Rancher* and augmented it from many sources. Fortunately for me, I found a great many sources to help fulfill these goals. The primary ones are "Memoirs of M. T. Johnson" by Edward B. Johnson, "Going West" by Mary Elizabeth (Mollie) Johnson, the memoirs of Edward B. Johnson Jr. and Montford T. Johnson (two of Neil R. Johnson's younger brothers), as well as the *Chronicles of Oklahoma*, which has published many articles with related and sometimes integrated themes to those in *The Chickasaw Rancher* during the forty-one years since the book was originally published.

Additionally, here is a list of institutions and, more importantly, people I am most grateful to. In Norman, Phyllis and Ron Murray, W. D. McIntosh, Norma White of the Church of the Latter Day Saints' Genealogy Library, John Lovett and his staff at the Western History Collection at the University of Oklahoma, Karen Kerr, my sister, Sandy McPherson, Alan Moring for the updated map of Silver City and Jana Moring for indexing the book, Wayne and Joan Rowe for their editing help, Michael Lovegrove, Jim and Jere Agar, Frank Parman, Bonnie Speer, Jim Briscoe, William (Bill) Savage Jr., Connie Platt, Paula Allen, the late John Womack, Susan Miller, Steve Davies and Valerie Moore, Darrell Rachael, Richard Adkins, Patricia Furnish, Louis LeFlore, Glenn and Reba Solomon, the Cleveland County Genealogical Library, Cleveland County Historical Museum, Linda Lockett and her staff at Colorchrome Labs, the *Norman Transcript*, the staff at Borders Store no. 108, and the Norman Public Library. In Purcell, Joyce A. Rex, Edna (Pat) Strickland (Chisholm), the late Vernon Mitchell and Charles Breeden, Freida Hicks, and the McClain County Historical Society. In El Reno, Jean Gardiner at the Canadian County Historical Museum. In the Oklahoma City area, the Oklahoma Historical Society, Chester Cowen, Judith Michener, Bill Welge and their great staff of volunteers, Dande Evans, Chickasaw tribal historian Richard Green, Mary Ann Blochowiak, Phil Bartlett, Arline (Johnson) LeFlore, Louis LeFlore, Mary (LeFlore) and Richard Clements, Naldia Blair, and Dorothy Jean Kostka. In the Tuttle-Minco area, Cheryl Paxton and her late mother, Norma Jean Gambill, Chincie and Dick Ross, Charlie Guthery and his sister Annie. In Chickasha, Jane H. Bond, Catherine (Bond) Wootten, Myron Bond, Mary H. Bailey, David and Kami Ratcliff, Irvin and Margaret Munn, Bill Davis, Mavis Clark, and the Grady County Historical Society. In Texas, Elise (Johnson) McCartt and her sisters Janet Duncan, Joan Shelton, and Jean Brander. In Tulsa, Elaine (Johnson) Edwards, Margaret (Johnson) Herring, Julie (Johnson) Casey, Monty Johnson, M. T. Johnson Jr., and in Wichita Falls, the late James T. Montgomery and Mrs. Paul (Barbara) Crumpler. In Sulphur, Judy Reeder, park ranger at the Chickasaw National Recreation Area. In Ada at the Chickasaw Nation's Headquarters, Glenda Galvin, museum curator and manager at the Chickasaw Nation's Museum and Pauline Walker, Chickasaw elder. At Fort Sill, Director Towana Spivey and his staff at the Fort Sill Museum. In Connecticut, Wendy St. Jean. In New York, John Mooney. Lou Stancori at the National Museum of the American Indian, the U.S. Army Military Institute in Carlisle, Pennsylvania, and the Florida State Archives in Tallahassee, Florida. And finally, Darrin Pratt, Laura Furney, Daniel Pratt, Dave Archer, Scott Vickers, and Luther Wilson at the University Press of Colorado.

I would like to give special thanks to Greg Burns for his talent, generosity, and friendship in creating the great scene with Montford and his cowboys for the front cover.

Although a great deal of additional material has been merged into this revised edition of *The Chickasaw Rancher*, I have tried to stay faithful to the general feel and direction of the book. The original material was written between fifty and eighty years ago, and much of that was taken from firsthand accounts dating back as far as one hundred and thirty years ago. With that in mind, I hope the reader will understand that some of what today would be considered offensive or pejorative terms— Negro, nigger, Indian, squaw, Red Man, savage, etc.—have been left intact to preserve the authenticity of the original work. No disrespect was or is intended.

In April 2000, unexpectedly after a thirty-year wait, Neil R. Johnson's missing boxes of reference material showed up. These boxes contained a lot of original material pertaining to the book, including letters, photographs, one of the Silver City ledger books, and much of E. B. Johnson's firsthand accounts of the events that happened to the Johnsons in the Chickasaw Nation. These have all be incorporated into the present edition.

As a final note, Neil Johnson, expecting to reprint the book before he died, also wanted to acknowledge D. L. Larsh, Isaac and George Graham, Joe Colbert, John T. Stibbins, along with his parents, Mollie Elizabeth and E. B. (Ed) Johnson.

—C. NEIL KINGSLEY

Preface 1960

There are several reasons or excuses for writing *The Chickasaw Rancher*. Most people have a false idea that the civilization of Oklahoma did not begin until the opening of Oklahoma for settlement by the Run in 1889. The truth of the matter is that Montford T. Johnson, the Chickasaw rancher, with his family and friends, brought civilization to this particular section of Oklahoma in 1868, just twenty-one years before the opening. He moved into the northern part of the Chickasaw Nation with the wild Prairie Indian tribes as neighbors. He lived peacefully with them until after the opening of Oklahoma.

The white settlers, who observed and heard of his fine well-bred livestock, his farming, his fine racehorses, and his plantation type of home and way of living, were attracted to the country and wanted to share it. Montford's son, Edward B. Johnson, who lived and experienced and saw the beginning and the changes that took place in the Chickasaw Nation, shortly before his death wrote the "Memoirs of Montford T. Johnson."

Edward B. Johnson's wife, Mollie, after reading the "Memoirs of Montford T. Johnson," wrote of her early-day experiences as a wife of a Chickasaw rancher.

Several years after the death of Edward B. Johnson, I was asked by an Oklahoma University student if I knew anything about the "early day ranching" in the Chickasaw Nation. It was then I decided to write *The Chickasaw Rancher* so that future generations might know the facts.

I wrote this from the viewpoint of the Chickasaw Indian and endeavored to show what effect the changing conditions had on the life of the Indian, who was given these lands.

I am extremely grateful that the "Memoirs of Montford T. Johnson" were written, which gave me an outline of the events that took place. I also am thankful for the information furnished by many of the early settlers who knew, worked for, and admired Montford T. Johnson. I was also helped by records found in the State Historical Society at Oklahoma City, in the Phillips Collection in the library of the University of Oklahoma, and in the library at Fort Sill, Oklahoma.

I trust that my children and theirs may read and learn how Montford T. Johnson, the Chickasaw rancher, lived and civilized this part of Oklahoma.

–NEIL R. JOHNSON

List of Cattle Brands

The Flying H
*Montford Johnson and
Granny Vicey Harmon*

The Hat
*Montford Johnson (eventually
became his family's primary
brand)*

The Hookety-Hook
Montford Johnson

The Figure-Eight
Montford Johnson

The Heart with X
*Montford Johnson with Jones
and Cruckshank*

The Pointed H
*Montford and Granny Vicey
Harmon*

The Diamond Link
Montford Johnson

The AB
Johnson and Clayton

The Fleur-de-lis
Charlie Campbell

BC or 7BC
C. B. Campbell

The Seventy-four Bar
Newton (Nute) Burney

Two Up and Two Down
Goldsmith brand

Eliza Brown's
Jack Brown

The 7C
Bill McClure

The Half-Moon
W. G. Williams

2 and 4 Connected
Sallie (Thompson) Walker

EC or 7EC
Ella Campbell

The Circle-A
Montford's sister Adelaide

JB Brand
James Bond

Perry Froman

W. P. Leeper

THE CHICKASAW RANCHER

Chickasaws in Mississippi

On July 4, 1837, a large cavalcade of Chickasaw Indians passed through the town of Memphis, Tennessee, and headed toward the bluffs overlooking the Mississippi River. Most of the Indians–men, women and children–were mounted on ponies, and followed by a train of wagons and packhorses carrying their household belongings. The Chickasaws were beginning their part in the "Trail of Tears," the forced removal from their native homelands that all "Five Civilized Tribes" were forced to make to the Indian Territory. There was much anxiety within the tribe, and most of them were sad, for they were about to set forth on a great pioneering expedition forced on them by the rapid settlement of white men on their homelands in Mississippi. What Alexis de Toqueville, the French traveler and writer, wrote about the Choctaws as he watched them entering that same river on a cold day six years earlier, would apply just as well to the Chickasaws on this day: "Never will that solemn spectacle fade from my remembrance. No cry, no sob, was heard among the assembled crowd; all were silent."[1]

In 1540 Hernando De Soto with his Spanish expedition started up the Mississippi River, finding the Chickasaw Indians living on lands east of the river in the northern part of what is now the state of Mississippi. The Chickasaws were living in well-built log cabins, constructed of poles or rails placed upright in the ground. These poles were plastered over with a mortar made of clay and grass mixed with water. The roofs of the cabins were also made of poles that extended from the walls to a short ridgepole. A thick layer of mortar was spread over these poles, making the roof thoroughly waterproof. The only opening was a door, covered with skins. During the warm months, the Indians did not sleep in their cabins, but pitched camps under trees or under brush arbors.

The cooking was done in the open or under an arbor. After the fire was started, ends of large logs placed like spokes in a wheel were thrust to the edge of the fire. To keep the fire going, the logs were shoved toward the central point as the ends burned. At this time the Chickasaws did not have tables or chairs; when they gathered to eat, they sat tailor-fashion on the ground or on a skin spread out, or perched on the ends of the logs away from the fire. The cooking utensils consisted chiefly of a wooden mortar and pestle with which they pounded and broke their corn into meal. The chaff from the corn was blown away by the wind as they poured the meal from the mortar into a tightly woven basket. They had in addition a few pots and bowls that were fashioned out of clay and baked.

Although the Chickasaws held their lands in common, each cabin had a small garden patch where each spring they planted beans, peas, squash, corn, maize, and some other varieties of vegetables. The women and children, aided at times by the old men, did most of the work around the cabins and gardens. The younger men did the hunting, fishing, and fighting. Later in the spring sweet potatoes were set out. In the fall, these crops were harvested and stored. The sweet potatoes were an important staple food. After being sorted, they were placed in a heap near the house and then covered with cornstalks and dry grass. A boxlike opening was made with brush, so that the potatoes could be reached as needed. A coating of earth and mud was spread over the mound to keep out the air.

The Chickasaws were a proud and independent tribe who basically just wanted to be left alone. De Soto and his men had been an imposition on the tribe all winter and the tribe's patience was wearing thin. Having heard reports about De Soto's expedition from other tribes long before they reached Chickasaw country, the tribe was quite wary of the Spanish, knowing that they had taken other Indians as slaves. In early March 1541, when De Soto demanded that the Chickasaw chiefs supply him with two hundred of their young warriors to act as bearers for him, the warriors felt their tribal honor insulted. This suggestion that they do manual labor, and other misunderstandings, induced the Chickasaw warriors to attack De Soto's camps. In these raids, the Chickasaws stampeded his hogs, which he had brought along for food. These hogs, which were never recovered, ran wild, multiplied, and fattened on the mast in the forests. The Chickasaws would soon learn to domesticate these hogs, and thus began the business of hog raising.

The French explorer Robert Cavalier de la Salle was the next European to make contact with the Chickasaws in 1682, and by 1698 the

British were also trading regularly with the tribe. From 1703 on, the Chickasaws grew steadily more aligned with the British, while the Choctaws and French gradually became allies. The first war with the French began in 1720. These hostilities raged on until the French and British ended their own Seven Years War with the signing of the Peace of Paris treaty in 1763, with the British being the victorious party.

In an early battle with the French, the Chickasaws thought the French, dressed in white robes, might be midnight ghosts or wizards, since the Indians' bullets seemed to have no effect on the wizards' chests. As the chiefs' council was beginning to think these spirits unbeatable in battle, the French began their attack on the fort, throwing hand grenades over the walls with long-burning fuses on them. With the help of their trader allies, the Chickasaws were soon pulling out the fuses or throwing these grenades back at their attackers. The Chickasaws quickly realized that these so-called phantoms were only common Frenchmen covered with woolpack, which had made their breasts invulnerable to all their well-aimed bullets. The Chickasaws now turned out of the fort, fell on, and fired at the Frenchmen's legs, bringing down many of them, scalping them, and driving the others off with considerable losses. The remaining French forces ran off to the neighboring hills, where the trembling army had posted themselves out of danger. In the midst of the night they decamped and saved themselves by a well-timed retreat, leaving the Chickasaws triumphant and inspiring them with the fierceness of so many tigers.[2] The French never could conquer the Chickasaws, no matter who or what tribe they allied themselves with.

As early as 1736, English visitors to the Chickasaw country reported many sleek cattle and horses grazing in their beautiful and fertile valleys. Major Rogers, on a tour of their domain in 1758, noted among other things the remarkable beauty of the Chickasaw women. He described them as tall and handsome, very attractive, with sunny dispositions; they were very friendly, yet virtuous as well. The character of the women accounts, no doubt, for the fact that four times as many whites intermarried with the Chickasaws as they did with any of the other Five Civilized Tribes. The relations with the British for the most part stayed very positive. The Chickasaws always felt that the British traders were much fairer to the tribe in their dealings than were the French.

Outside of battles with the Europeans, the Chickasaws had to constantly defend their large land base from intrusion from other Indian tribes. The Chickasaws and Cherokees had teamed up together in 1715 and again in 1745 to defeat the Shawnees, but they turned on each other in 1769. The Chickasaws had spread back out to the east to their former lands at the Chickasaw Old Fields. The Cherokees did not like this intrusion and attacked, but the Chickasaws walked away the winners.

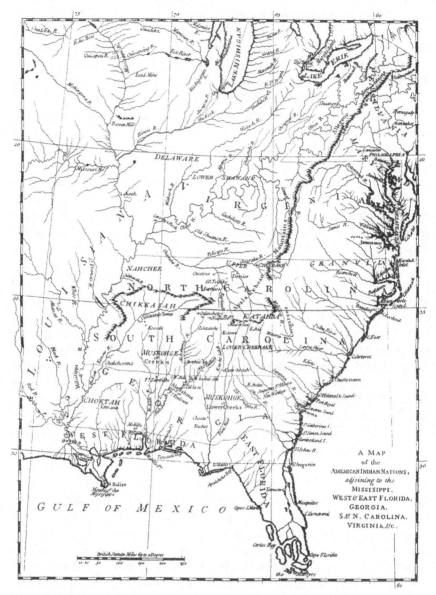

Map of American Indian Nations, 1815. The History of the American Indian, *James Adair, [1775] 1930, Johnson City, TN: Watauga Press.*

In 1786, official relations with the United States began when the Treaty of Hopewell fixed the Chickasaws' northern boundary at the Ohio River. They went to war against the Creeks from 1793 to 1795, but by this time the pressure from the encroaching white settlers was increasingly becoming their biggest problem. Another treaty that opened up the floodgates of travel through the Chickasaw Nation was the treaty permitting the Natchez Trace road in 1801. This road soon became the most heavily traveled road in the southwestern part of the United States. Of course as travel was made easier, that many more settlers came, increasing the need for more roads and in turn creating more pressure to remove the Indians. This also allowed more and more traders into the Indian lands. Then, consistent with government policy starting with Thomas Jefferson, the Indians could gradually be traded into greater and greater debt. This increased pressure began to pay off as the government convinced the Chickasaws to give successive land cessions in 1805, 1816, 1818, and 1832. Using economic hardship and constant pressure from the increasing numbers of settlers made it unnecessary for the United States government to go to war against the Indians to relocate them.

The years 1786 to 1818 were the most crucial in the history of the Chickasaw Nation. It was in this period that the erosion of Chickasaw independence and the corruption of their old tribal ways was begun by the purposeful influence of the Spanish, French, and British. The slow, steady, and insidious destruction was completed by the Americans, eventually making the Chickasaws and the other Five Civilized Tribes wards of the government.

Speculation in lands lying west of the Appalachians began as early as 1800. These lands were sold on credit and, for those times, at what was considered a very high price. After the panic of 1819, the credit system was abolished. A flat price of one dollar and a quarter an acre was agreed upon. Compromises were made with the defaulters, and they were given title to as much land as they could pay cash for. At about the same time, the idea of free land for homesteaders developed, and free land was demanded as a right for men who would settle on it and improve it. Soon speculators and homesteaders were crowding out toward northern Mississippi, where the Chickasaws had had their homes for hundreds of years. And now the government asked them to give up their homeland, to leave their houses, their burial grounds, and the very forests and valleys, steeped in their traditions, and to find themselves a new land beyond the great river.

In the year 1820, there were 2.5 million people living west of the Allegheny Mountains; by 1830 the number had increased another million. Most of these people were Native Americans who had moved from the Atlantic seaboard, pushed, and at last forced out by the large plantation owners. To most sections of the western country, these frontiersmen moved slowly, but along the Mississippi River travel was easy, and the river became the highway on which moved not only the honest men seeking new homes and lands, but also roving bands of adventurers ranging from schemers and tricksters to robbers and outlaws. Among the easy victims of these adventurers were the Indians living along the great river. Not understanding the white man's notion of the rights of property, the Indians could easily be persuaded to sell or lease their lands and homes, which they had never been conscious of owning. Claims and counterclaims were made—sometimes between the swindled Indians and the tricksters, sometimes between the Indians and innocent men who believed they had a right to the property they had bought from the tricksters.

In 1830 the frontiersmen, who had helped elect Andrew Jackson as president, began demanding the lands occupied by the Five Civilized Tribes—that is, the Chickasaws, Cherokees, Choctaws, Creeks, and Seminoles. In June of that year Congress, on the recommendation of President Jackson, passed the Indian Removal Act, which provided for the removal of the Indians east of the Mississippi River to lands in the West. The federal government assured the Indians that these new homelands were to remain exclusively Indian country. No doubt the government also had in mind the advantage of having the more peaceful Five Civilized Tribes as a buffer state between the settled white communities and the wild tribes of the Plains. The legislatures of both Mississippi and Alabama passed acts that erased all tribal laws and made all Indians subject to state law.

During this time, of course, the laws prohibited the introduction of whiskey into Indian country by any trader or traveler; however the government "[had] reserved the right to itself to use liquor in its negotiations with the Indians. For the employment of liquor equally with bribery of the responsible members of the tribes became part of governmental policy in dealing with the Indians east of the Mississippi River."[3] Further, "the Indians were gorged with meat and the smartest and most influential of them were treated freely to liquor and in return for signing the desired papers, returning home with money in their pockets."[4] Earlier in 1830 at Franklin, Tennessee, President Jackson had come down from Washington, D.C., to lend his prestige to hammering out the Franklin Treaty with the Chickasaws and Choctaws. He said:

> Laws will be passed and enforced by white men that will be unsuitable for you, and that you will not understand. You will be unhappy and finally overwhelmed. Cross the Mississippi River and enter into a new country. As chief representative of the white man's Government, the great United States of America, I pledge to you that this new country shall be yours and your children's as long as the grass shall grow and the water shall run. Upon this solemn pledge, I ask you to give up your homes, cross the great river, and take up your homes in the West.[5]

Persuaded by President Jackson and pressured by United States treaty commissioners John Eaton and John Coffee, using "the old government trick of withholding the Chickasaw annuity," the Chickasaws entered into this treaty with the government.[6]

This treaty was made as between independent peoples, for the United States has, from earliest times, treated each Indian tribe within the borders of their respective nations as distinct communities over which the United States exercised control and guardianship. Boundary lines between states and Indian nations were designated and established, and agreements were made with as much care and precision as between the United States and a foreign country. Among other agreements in this treaty was one giving the Chickasaws an "out" if they could not find land suitable to their needs. This clause read, "If, after proper examination, a country suitable to their wants and conditions can not be found; then, it is stipulated and agreed, that this treaty, and all its provisions, shall be considered null and void."[7]

The first move was to find a suitable place west of the Mississippi in which to settle the Indians. Captain Bonneville was sent out in September 1830 from Fort Gibson, located in the eastern part of what is now Oklahoma, to examine the territory adjacent to the Canadian River. Upon his return, Bonneville forwarded to Washington a report and map of the country he had inspected. This map included the headwaters of the Little River. Bonneville described the country through which he had passed as a barren waste. He did not find any game, any timber suitable for use, or any land fit for cultivation.

From the report it is quite obvious that the government thought that these lands would never be of use to white settlers and that in giving them to the Indians, the government was making a good bargain. Yet the Indians who came to this barren waste managed to survive and to develop the country; it happens that the western limit of Captain Bonneville's travels was on the eastern line of what thirty years later would become the range of Montford T. Johnson. On September 27, 1830, the Choctaws signed the Treaty of Dancing Rabbit Creek and finally agreed to their removal to the Indian Territory.

The white settlers continued to overrun the Chickasaw lands in Mississippi and Alabama, with each state passing laws to extend its jurisdiction over the Chickasaw Nation, further pressuring the tribe to agree to its own removal. In October 1832, the Chickasaws signed the Ponotoc Treaty with the federal government and finally agreed to remove themselves from the increasing oppression from both the federal and state levels of government. A Chickasaw delegation of twenty chiefs and citizens returned to Washington, D.C., in 1833, attempting to convince federal officials to alter the Pontotoc Treaty on the grounds that the tribe had been ruthlessly exploited during the negotiations because Levi Colbert, their principal spokesman, was deathly ill and had been unable to speak for the tribe during the original negotiations. Tensions were high as President Jackson told them that the white men would continue to encroach upon their country.

The Chickasaws agreed to cede to the United States all their lands east of the Mississippi, provided that they found a suitable country in the western area that they could purchase. A committee of Chickasaws made three trips to the Choctaw country in the Indian Territory. They went first in 1828, again in the fall of 1830, both times rejecting any land they saw as unsatisfactory. In the summer of 1834 Levi Colbert died; up to that time he was the most powerful Chickasaw against the removal. However, once the Chickasaws' Mississippi homeland was actually being surveyed in anticipation of their removal, Chickasaw explorers in 1835 and 1836 finally found land suitable to their needs and made an agreement with the Choctaws for a part of their central and western country.

The Choctaws had been led to believe that they could be the leaders in creating an Indian United States in Indian Territory. Now they saw an opportunity to place the Chickasaws, whom they feared and respected as warriors, between themselves and the wild Plains Indians. In 1834, a new treaty was negotiated with the Chickasaws to amend the Ponotoc Treaty, but it was late in 1836 before they found land suitable for their needs. Finally, on January 17, 1837, the Chickasaws signed the Treaty of Doaksville near Fort Towson, with the Chickasaws to buy the western and central part of the Choctaws' territory.[8] The Chickasaws could now bring themselves to leave their tribal homes and begin the journey to the new country. It took another seven years to complete the move. In part, the treaty provided that the Chickasaws should have the privilege of forming their own district within the limits of the Choctaw country, which would be held in common by the Chickasaws and the Choctaws. The Chickasaws were to have equal representation in the Choctaws' general council and were also supposed to take an active part in the Choctaw government. The truth was, however, that the Chickasaw Nation was being absorbed by the Choctaws, or as the Choctaws put it, purchasing the right to share in the benefit of Choctaw citizenship. Independently, each tribe reserved the sole right for their respective tribe to share in the residual funds that were left from the sale of each other's land.

The Chickasaws agreed to pay the Choctaws $530,000 for their western district in Indian Territory. This district includes about two-thirds of the lands located between the South Canadian and Red Rivers in the present state of Oklahoma. It was later learned that part of the territory originally described lay in Texas, at that time an independent republic, and therefore beyond the limits of the United States. Clearing title to this land eventually cost the Chickasaws an additional $50,000.

The Treaty of 1855 between the United States and the Chickasaw and Choctaw tribes more clearly designated the land limits of the Treaty of Doaksville, stating that the Chickasaws and Choctaws quitclaim and relinquish to the United States any rights to lands lying west of the one-hundredth meridian. Between the Treaty of Doaksville and that of 1855, Texas had been admitted to the Union. Since there had been some question about the boundaries of the new state, the Treaty of 1855 recognized, in effect, the claims of Texas to this large territory west of the meridian. The treaty further provided that the United States might lease all that portion of the common territory of the Chickasaws and Choctaws, west of the ninety-eighth meridian for the settlement of the Wichitas and other Indians; provided, however, that the territory so leased should always remain open to settlement by the Chickasaws and Choctaws. For this "Leased District" the eastern border ran just a few miles (ninety-eighth meridian) west of the present-day mainline of the Rock Island Railroad, bounded on the north by the South Canadian River, on the south by the Red River, and on the west by the present western boundary of Oklahoma (hundredth meridian). The Chickasaws and Choctaws received as lease money $800,000, which was split 200/600 respectively. A final canny provision of the treaty stipulated that the lands should all revert to the United States in case the Indians should become extinct or if they should abandon the land.

Among the government agents who assisted in making the treaty, and later in enrolling the Chickasaws for removal, was Charles B. Johnson. He was born in England, probably about 1819, and came from a family that had long been connected with the theater as actors and musicians. When he was nineteen, he and his brother visited America. Both of these young men had been trained as Shakespearean actors, and while they were in Philadelphia, Charles joined a small stock company that was to make a tour of the South. His brother soon returned to England and later became a popular and successful London physician.

Charles's family lost touch with him for several years. When they next heard from him, he had married a young Chickasaw girl and was running a small Indian trading post in Mississippi. This trading post was located near the banks of the Mississippi River and deep in the Chickasaw country. Here the Chickasaws gathered to trade, relax, and visit. They discussed the plight of their tribe with the sympathetic young trader who had courted and married a beautiful, blue-eyed, half-breed Chickasaw girl, Rebekah (Becky) Courtney. Her father was a Scotsman, Peter Courtney, and her mother, Sallie Wolf, was a full-blood Chickasaw of the house of Intel-le-bo,[9] who later married a Chickasaw named Tarntubby

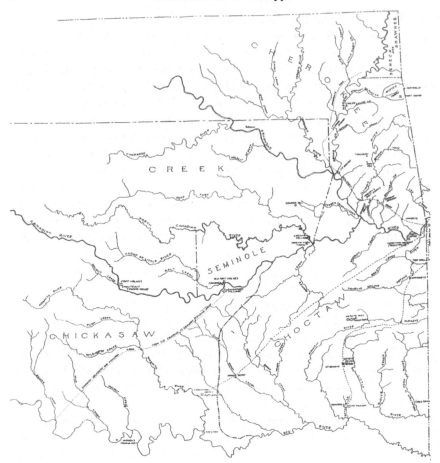

Map of Indian Territory, 1842. A Trader in Indian Territory, Journal of Ethan Allen Hitchcock, *edited and annotated by Grant Forman, Norman: University of Oklahoma Press, 1930, 1958, 1996.*

(Tahnetubby or, most likely, Tontubby).[10] Rebekah had a younger brother named Peter, but he died before marrying and left no children.

After the Chickasaws were enrolled, Becky sold her Chickasaw land,[11] and Charles Johnson sold his interest in the trading post and joined in with his adopted tribe in their migration to their new homes. He helped them as they gathered together their personal property, which included their Negro slaves, horses, grain, cattle, hogs, chickens, turkeys, and household utensils. At last they were ready, and after a last sad look around at their homes and burial grounds, they set out toward Memphis where they and their heavily loaded horses and wagons could be ferried across the Mississippi.

The story goes that, while camped on the bluffs overlooking the river, Rebekah and many of the other young men and women spent much of their time swimming back and forth across the Mississippi while the boats were being loaded. De Soto reported that all the Chickasaws could swim like ducks, and this ability was handed down from one generation to another.

After considerable time and difficulty, the crossing of the river was made. Soon the Indians and their belongings were drenched with almost incessant rains. Several heavily loaded horses, after crossing the river, were bogged down and lost; the swamps, lagoons, and marshes of Arkansas became impassable. The Chickasaws threatened to rebel and return to their Mississippi homes, which they had so reluctantly given up. In a long council, and after much debate, Charles Johnson helped convince the Indians that they were going to a virgin country that was much better than the land they had left. He organized the men into small companies. They cut down saplings, and spreading these poles across the route, they built a corduroy road through the swamps, and with this more secure footing managed to get through. Because of Charles Johnson's ingenuity in persevering with them through this boggy country, the Chickasaws, in Indian fashion, gave him the name "Boggy," which he used for the rest of his life.

Most of the early emigrants first camped in and around Fort Coffee. Once a viable road was constructed, many moved further south to the Boggy and Blue River area, where a government depot was established for the issuance of supplies and rations. This place they called Boggy Depot. This particular group of Chickasaws settled around Boggy Depot on Boggy Creek in this new Indian Territory. Incidently, "Boggy" Johnson's nickname had nothing to do with their proximity to Boggy Depot. The Johnson family built a home near the Blue Creek/Blue River area, a few miles north of Tishomingo near Connerville and Belton's Crossing, and Boggy opened a small trading post up the new road at Fort Coffee.

Several other groups of Chickasaws were brought to the new country by agents employed for that purpose; many small groups came of their own accord and at their own expense. Sometimes the sick had to be carried on homemade litters. While they were passing through Arkansas, horse thieves, whiskey peddlers and pariahs of all kinds followed their trail. Many of the Indians' horses were stolen. These trail parasites took full advantage of the migrating Indians, taking every opportunity, delaying and hindering their march westward even more. Shortly after the Indians arrived in their new homeland, an epidemic of smallpox broke out, and between five and six hundred of them died; the rest of them were saved by vaccination. Those who survived did not have time to put out crops that first year. It looked as if they might all die of starvation that first year if no additional help came. In February a few half-starved hogs were driven into Boggy Depot and sold at the high price of twenty-five cents a pound, many times the going rate. A short time later, some urgent requests for additional rations were made by the Indian agent, William Armstrong: "The situation of the Chickasaws require immediate action to save them from starvation," and ". . . the Chickasaws settled on Blue and Boggy Creeks are in danger of great suffering, there is neither cattle or hogs in the country."[12] Fortunately, Congress authorized an additional issue of rations for seven months. This supplement was essential in helping the Chickasaws get through their first year in the Indian Territory. The more wealthy ones bought the improvements of the Choctaws and settled in the fertile valley of the Red River. Many had large numbers of slaves, and the following year they began raising cotton. All told, the Chickasaws and Choctaws and their Negro slaves in the Indian Territory numbered about fifteen thousand.

To make matters worse for the Chickasaws and the other displaced tribes, enormous fraud was perpetrated on them by individuals and companies who furnished the provisions during the removal. These problems became so widespread, that the secretary of war, J. C. Spencer, sent Major Ethan Allen Hitchcock to Indian Territory to investigate them. In one example, he found that "spoiled rations to the value of $200,000 had been sold to the Chickasaws," and that they were charged for rations valued at over $700,000 that were never delivered. He also found reason to look into the "shockingly high" transportation charges made against the Chickasaw emigration fund. One example involved a Captain Buckner who wished to be certified for 125 tons of baggage on his ship. Colonel Guy, the contractor, refused and finally dickered down to 75 tons, although other observers estimated the 260 people and their baggage at no more than 20 tons.[13] Hitchcock also ran into a "conceited young fop" named Johnson in February 1842, who appeared to be the issuer at Fort Coffee—"Boggy" perhaps?[14]

Bribery, perjury, and forgery were the chief instruments employed in these infamous transactions investigated by Major Hitchcock. Due bills were issued by contractors to the Indians and then bought back at a fraction of their value. Short weights, issues of spoiled meat and grain, and every conceivable subterfuge was employed by designing white men on ignorant Indians. After the investigation was made, Major Hitchcock prepared a report with one hundred exhibits attached that he filed with the secretary of war. Committees in the U.S. Congress tried vainly to have it submitted to them so that appropriate action could be taken, but it was stated that too many friends of the administration were involved to permit the report to become public. It disappeared from the files and no trace of it is to be found in the voluminous correspondence on this subject now in the files of the Office of Indian Affairs.[15]

Notes

1. Faulkner, W. 1971. "Chickasaw Queen." *Chronicles of Oklahoma*, Oklahoma Historical Society. Vol. 49, p. 339.
2. Adair, James. [1775] 1930. *The History of the American Indian.* Johnson City, TN: Watanga Press, p. 356.
3. Foreman, Grant. 1934. "Century of Prohibition." *Chronicles of Oklahoma*, Oklahoma Historical Society. Vol. 12, p.133.
4. Ibid., p. 134.
5. Foreman, Grant. [1932] 1972. *Indian Removal.* Norman: University of Oklahoma Press, p. 193.
6. Gibson, Arrell M. 1971. *The Chickasaws.* Norman: University of Oklahoma Press, p. 175.
7. Ibid., p. 173.
8. Ibid., p.178.
9. O'beirne, Harry F. 1891. *Leaders and Leading Men of Indian Territories,* vol. 1, *Choctaws and Chickasaws.* Chicago: American Publishers Association, p. 284.
10. Bond, Adelaide (Johnson). Questionnaire from 1927 interview. E. B. Johnson Collection. Western History Collection. University of Oklahoma, Norman, OK.
11. Carroll, William. 1837. "Mississippi Chickasaw Orphan Land Sales–1837," edited by Kerry M. Armstrong. Chickasaw Historical Research Page. (Http://home.flash.net/~kma/index.htm)
12. Foreman, Grant, ed. 1930. *Commissioner of Indian Affairs.* Vol. 2. Foreman transcripts. Oklahoma Historical Society. p. 124.
13. Foreman, Grant. 1934. *Five Civilized Tribes.* Norman: University of Oklahoma Press, p. 213.
14. Hitchcock, Ethan A. [1930] 1996. *Traveler in Indian Territory.* Noman: University of Oklahoma Press, pp.175, 179.
15. Green, Michael D. [1930] 1996. "Introduction" to *Traveler in Indian Territory*, by Ethan Allen Hitchcock. Norman: University of Oklahoma Press, p. 12.

Building a Life in Indian Territory

On Christmas Day in 1841, Rebekah Johnson gave birth to a girl whom her parents named Adelaide. Almost two years later in November, a son, Montford T. Johnson was born, possibly named after Governor Montford Stokes, a Revolutionary War hero who served for a time as the Cherokee Indian agent in Fort Gibson, where "Boggy" Johnson worked, up until their removal with the rest of the Chickasaws. Montford Stokes died on November 4, 1842, and was buried at or near Fort Gibson, the only Revolutionary War veteran buried in Oklahoma.[1] Two years later, in late 1843 or early 1844, Rebekah died of pneumonia. She was buried near the family home, and a small log house was placed over her grave to keep the varmints from digging it up.

After the loss of his wife, "Boggy" Johnson grew dissatisfied with life in the Indian Country and began preparing to take his children back East with him. Rebekah's mother, Sallie Tarntubby (Tontubby), objected adamantly. According to Adelaide in a discussion years later, she recalled her Chickasaw grandmother's words as, "If you take these children away from here, my people will follow you and kill you." Among the Chickasaws it was a common practice to take into their homes motherless children and bring them up as their own. So a teary-eyed "Boggy" left Adelaide and Montford in the care of their grandmother and returned to the East without his children. This would be the last contact Adelaide and Montford would have with their father for thirty-three years. Adelaide also stated that their father never made any provision for the care and support of his two orphaned children. Needless to say, this situation left the two children, especially Montford, quite bitter toward their father.

Growing up with his grandmother's family, Montford learned to take care of a few milk cows, chickens, ponies, hogs, and turkeys. In looking after these animals, Montford got his early training as a stockman, for all the land was held in common, and all of the stock ran on the open range. As he grew older, Montford became a great hunter and fisherman, and in this way helped supply the family with food. Most of his hunting was done with a bow and arrow, the common weapon used by Indian boys of his age.

Living as a Chickasaw boy, Montford developed the character of his mother's and grandmother's people rather than the pompousness of his Shakespearean-actor father. He was taught strict obedience, but was never whipped. Spending many hours alone while he herded his mother's stock, he grew into a serenity of mind and temper that enabled him to face disappointment without fretting and to accept misfortune as he did wind and rain, the result of forces beyond his control.

By the time Montford had come to school age, a number of things were happening to the Chickasaws. In the treaty made with the Five Civilized Tribes, the government had agreed to protect them from the wild Indians. Up to 1850, the government had done nothing to provide this protection, but now that white men were making for California during the gold rush, something had to be done. The route of the prospectors lay through the Chickasaw country and into the Plains Indians' territory beyond. In 1850, Captain R. B. Marcy was sent out to establish a camp and stockade on the Canadian River. His first site was about two miles northwest of the present town of Byars, a few hundred yards west of where Montford would later settle; this camp he named Camp Arbuckle. During the first winter in this camp, many of the soldiers became ill with malaria. In the period from 1839 to 1855 in the twenty-two military regions in the United States, only the soldiers on the Gulf Coast suffered more from malaria than the men at the Oklahoma forts.[2] This may be a contributing factor for Montford's chronic health problems and his early death. Before the wooden barracks were completed, Captain Marcy received orders to hunt a new and hopefully healthier location further west, but was unable to until the following spring. In April 1851 the detachment moved south of the Washita River and finally located near a spring at the headwaters of a stream emptying into Wild Horse Creek. Here a permanent fort was established, displacing a Kickapoo Indian village some seven miles west of the town of Davis, Oklahoma, and named Fort Arbuckle.

During these years, the Chickasaws were becoming more and more dissatisfied with the treaty of 1837 made between themselves and the

Drawing of old Camp Arbuckle, home of Captain Black Beaver's Delaware Band, August 19, 1853, by H. H. Whipple. [Site was abandoned during the Civil War, became Johnsonville after Montford Johnson and his family moved there in 1869– C.N.K.] Courtesy, Oklahoma Historical Society, 9256-OD32, Archives and Manuscripts Division.

Choctaws, since they found themselves outnumbered and with very little voice in their own government. The Chickasaws drafted and adopted their first constitution in 1846 at Boiling Springs, near Fort Washita. Two years later the tribe approved a more formal document for their constitution at their convention. Edmund Pickens was the first Chickasaw chief in the Indian Territory under this new constitution. The last stumbling block to the separation of the two tribes was the establishment of the boundary lines between the two nations. Agent Douglas H. Cooper was brought in to arbitrate this dispute. He hired Captain R. L. Cooper to resurvey and establish this boundary. Following this survey, Agent Cooper arranged a conference between the two tribes, and this last stumbling block was dispensed with.[3]

Shortly thereafter, a new treaty was prepared in June 1855 granting the Chickasaws the right to set up their own form of government. Soon afterward, the Chickasaws drafted a new constitution, which was signed and ratified on August 30, 1856. This constitution was republican in form, contained a bill of rights, and guaranteed trial by jury. The chief executive, called the governor, was elected by the popular vote for a term of two years, and eligible to hold office only four years out of any six. The legislature was composed of two branches, a senate and a house of representatives. There were twelve senators, who served for two years; three were elected from each of the four senatorial districts: Panola, Pickens, Pontotoc, and Tishomingo. Eight representatives were also elected annually. The judicial branch was made up of a supreme court, circuit courts, and county courts. A sheriff and other necessary county officers were elected to serve for two years. A superintendent of public instruction was elected by the legislature to serve four years; he in turn appointed school trustees for the various neighborhood schools. Cyrus Harris was elected the first Chickasaw governor in 1856.

In 1855 some of the Plains Indians had been placed on a reservation in Texas; but as the Five Civilized Tribes had been harassed by the white settlers east of the Mississippi River, so these Indians were oppressed by the Texans. The favorite trick of the Texans was to make raids on ranches near the reservation, and then throw the blame onto the Indians. Stolen animals were driven toward the reservation, leaving a trail that could be easily followed. The raiders dropped arrows, moccasins, and other articles, previously purchased from the Indians, which would point the finger of guilt at the Indians. The irate ranchers, in hot pursuit, finding the telltale evidence along the route, filed complaints with the Indian agents. Such raids exasperated the agents, the Indians, and the settlers. Finally, in 1859, about fourteen hundred Indians, representing a dozen tribes, were brought to and settled on the Chickasaw lease.

Two years after their removal from Texas, the governor of Texas, admitting that a great injustice had been done these Indians, and realizing that with their departure the state had lost its protection against the wild Indians, asked them to return. The Indians refused, and in the years that followed Texas paid dearly for their blunder in raids against the ranchers that were carried out by some of the wilder Plains Indians.

Later, acting on the provisions of the Treaty of 1866, the government moved a number of these tribes to the Leased District area, lying between the Washita and South Canadian Rivers. At late as 1872, Thomas C. Battey, a Quaker schoolteacher among the Plains Indians, said, "On one occasion the sheriff of one of the northwestern counties of Texas informed me that twice in his official capacity, he had called out a portion of the militia to put down Indian depredations in his county, and in the ensuing skirmish, one or two of the raiders had been killed. The slain individuals proved to be white men; so thoroughly were they disguised with false hair, masks, and Indian equipment, as to be readily mistaken for Indians."[4]

While these events were taking place outside the Chickasaw Nation, Montford and Adelaide Johnson were being sent to school, Adelaide to Rock Academy and Montford to the Chickasaw Manual Labor Academy. This school was located about twelve miles northwest of Fort Washita. Montford's name appears on the roll of the school in 1858 as "Monford" Johnson, the name by which he was known throughout his life. At other times, he was noted or referred to as "Mumford." This may have been the Indian way of pronouncing his name. It is evident that he did not learn the proper spelling of his name until he met his father again in 1877. Perhaps this is the reason that he always objected to the shortening of names and nicknames. Everyone called his son Tilford, "Till"; Robert, "Bob"; Edward, "Ed" or "E. B."; Henry, "H. B."; Benjamin, "Ben"; but Montford always addressed his children by their full God-given names.

Montford and Adelaide attended school for about three years. Montford was not strong and missed many days through illness; he did, however, learn to read and write and to work simple arithmetic. In addition to this, Montford had at the school practical instruction in farming. Each year the school planted about fifty acres in wheat, seventy-five acres in corn, forty acres in oats, and eight acres in sugar cane. Barns and sheds housed the cattle, hogs, and sheep. The students were taught the use of simple farm machinery, which included the reaper, the corn sheller, the cultivator, and the roller. One thing of importance Montford learned at school: the ground must be broken deep and be well worked if a good crop is to be made. Many Indians just scratched the ground, plowing to the depth of an inch or two before planting. If the season was excellent, they raised a small crop, but if it turned dry during the growing season, the crops soon withered and died. He also learned that oxen, though slow, are best suited for breaking heavily turfed sod. He was content to walk behind the slowly plodding oxen as they pulled the plow through the matted grass roots, which ripped like the tearing of a heavy piece of cloth.

Montford turned fifteen in 1858, the same year that his grandmother Sallie died. She requested that they bury her under her log cabin so that the wolves and panthers would not disturb her body. At the end of the school period in that year, the two children were passed on to the nearest of kin who were able to take care of them. That summer they moved to the home of their grandmother's half-brother, Captain Townsend Hothliche, who lived on the Washita River about fifteen miles south of Fort Arbuckle. Not long after their arrival at his homestead, Captain Hothliche took Adelaide with him on one of his trips to Fort Arbuckle for supplies. While making purchases in the sutler's, or government-sponsored store, Sergeant Charles Campbell's wife, Mary, and daughter, Mary Elizabeth, came in. They were attracted by the shy, beautiful Indian girl. Mary Elizabeth's mother was a large, pleasant Irish woman who made friends easily. She spoke to Adelaide and was agreeably surprised when Adelaide replied in broken English. Mary Elizabeth joined in the discussion, and the girls soon became close friends.

Life around the fort was lonely for Mary, who had no companions except her four brothers. Mrs. Campbell saw in Adelaide a girl companion for her daughter and asked Captain Hothliche to permit Adelaide to stay with her for a short visit. He consented, and in this way a friendship began between the two girls that lasted as long as they lived. While visiting Mary, Adelaide fell in love with Michael Campbell, Mary's oldest

Montford T. Johnson and his widowed sister Adelaide Campbell, circa 1870. Neil Kingsley Collection.

Montford's and Mary's first home (nearly finished) at Camp Arbuckle/Johnsonville, circa 1869. Neil Kingsley Collection.

brother. After a short courtship, they were married; the ceremony took place in Tishomingo in the fall of 1859. After her marriage, Adelaide moved to the fort where Michael and his three brothers lived with their father, Sergeant Campbell. The boys had brought with them several head of cattle from their father's last station in Texas, and they herded these cattle near the fort. Soon after Adelaide moved to the fort, Montford followed her. Through the assistance and influence of the Campbells, Montford obtained the contract to carry the mail between Fort Arbuckle and Fort Washita. For this route of about fifty miles, he purchased two small riding mules, which stood up to the hardships caused by the rocky terrain better than horses and required less food. By the late 1850s life seemed to be getting better for the Johnsons and Campbells as well as for the Chickasaw Nation as a whole. Unfortunately, the Civil War was just around the corner and everything the Chickasaws had gained would be wiped away.[5]

In the fall of 1860, Captain Hothliche was robbed and murdered while on his way home after collecting his Chickasaw annuity at Post Oak Grove, near Fort Washita. His home place was given to Adelaide. Shortly after this tragedy, Montford helped Adelaide and her husband, Michael Campbell, move from the fort to the Captain's place, which was on the south bank of the Washita River, near the mouth of Oily

Spring Creek. Under Montford's supervision, two fields were cleared and broken. The one in the river bottom contained ten acres; the other one, a flat piece of land near the cabin, contained six. The two men gathered together about thirty head of Michael's best cows that were running loose in the mountains, and located them on the range near their cabins. This small herd was affectionately called "the milk pen bunch." Besides these cows, Michael owned three horses, two of them condemned government horses bought at auction, the third, a blind mare. He also had five yoke of oxen, an ox wagon, and a few farming tools.

The young people had a hard time that fall and winter because of the severe drought of the preceding summer. Feed for the cattle was scarce, and the corn planted the spring before by Captain Hothliche withered to nothing. Aside from any help from the in-laws, food for the family became a problem, and before the winter was over they were reduced to eating acorn meal, the acorns being gathered and ground to take the place of corn. Toward the end of this especially hard winter, Adelaide gave birth to her first child, a son, Charles Bryant Campbell, on January 28, 1861.

But worse troubles were in store for the family, and for all the Chickasaws. For some time rumors of war had been drifting through the country, and in 1861 these rumors became a reality. Before war was declared, the Texas secessionists had made contact with the Chickasaws. Shortly after war was declared, a force of Texas volunteers crossed the Red River and attacked Fort Washita, which soon fell into their hands. They proceeded to Fort Arbuckle, which was abandoned by the federal troops on May 5, 1861. The federals, including Sergeant Campbell, retreated to Fort Cobb; soon after, Colonel Emory, with the assistance of Black Beaver, the highly regarded Delaware Indian scout, united all the federal troops and retreated to Fort Leavenworth, Kansas. The country around Fort Arbuckle was left in the hands of the Confederacy, and local troops were organized and took over the forts. Michael Campbell and his brothers joined sides with the Confederacy. Michael became a major in the Chickasaw battalion stationed at Fort Arbuckle. At this time, Michael moved his mother, Mary Campbell, his sister, Mary Elizabeth, and his mother's Negro cook down to live with Adelaide.

On July 12, 1861, Albert Pike, representing the Confederacy, made a treaty with the Chickasaws. Among other things, the treaty provided in Article VIII: "The Confederate States of America do hereby solemnly guarantee to the Choctaw and Chickasaw Nations, to be held by them to their own use and behoof in fee simple forever."[6] This was to last as long as the grass should grow and the water should run. The treaty further stated: "That no state or territory shall ever pass laws for the government of the Indians; that no part of their country shall be annexed by any other territory or province; that the tribes have the unsolicited right to erect a territory or state out of their domain; that jointly they shall be entitled to a delegate to represent them in Congress. If later they desire to enter into the Confederacy as a state, they shall enter on equal terms as one of the original states."[7] This treaty was one of the most fair and liberal ever made with the Indians. The Union forces, on the other hand, did nothing to hold this Indian country. During the campaign of 1860, William H. Seward said: "The Indian Territory south of Kansas must be vacated by the Indians."[8] The attitude expressed in this statement, and the fact that many of the Chickasaws were owners of slaves, accounts for the fact that both they and the Choctaws joined the Confederacy.

Some Chickasaws, mostly full-bloods, disapproved of the treaty made with the Confederacy and took their families north for the duration of the war. The majority of these neutrals lived in Le Roy, Kansas. There they were joined by refugees from the Creek, Cherokee, and Seminole Nations to wait out the war. The Cherokees did not participate in the Confederate treaties. Thousands of other Indians fled south to escape the war, many of whom ended up in the Chickasaw Nation living off the generosity of the remaining Chickasaw families.[9]

The Chickasaw battalion was kept busy acquiring and issuing rations for the Indians and for the Confederate Army. As early as December 1862, beef was selling in Fort Arbuckle for six cents a pound. Michael sold a large number of cattle to W. Benjamin Savage, who had the beef contract. Payment for these cattle was made in Confederate dollars, which Michael delivered to Adelaide when he visited his family from time to time.

With the fall of Fort Arbuckle to the Confederates, Montford lost his mail route. According to one source, Montford then served a time with Frashier McLish's militia and for three of those months rode express between the headquarters of the Chickasaw battalion and the Texas troops stationed at the mouth of Mud Creek where it joined the Red River.[10] With Michael now spending most of his time at the Fort or on the march, Montford, upon his release, took over the management of Michael's stock and property. Montford, at least for the time being, was now head of the household until the end of the war.

By the start of the war, Montford had accumulated for himself fifteen head of cows and calves, a few yearlings, a pair of year-old steers, and a yoke of oxen that Captain Hothliche had given him. He had six mares and colts, several saddle ponies, and about three hundred head of hogs. One old negro man helped him with the farming. Montford was anxious to get more heavily involved in the stock business, so he and his brother-in-law, Michael, had agreed to become partners with Charley Eastman. Sadly, the war destroyed these plans along with many others. More than

five years would pass before Montford would try again to become the
cowman he aspired to be.

During the time he had helped Adelaide settle on the Hothliche
place, Montford came to know Michael's younger sister, Mary, quite
well. Now that he was looking after Michael's affairs, he saw more and
more of her and their friendship gradually ripened into love. Mary's
father had not been too keen on Montford's courtship of his daughter,
but by this time Sergeant Charles Campbell had long since departed the
area with the rest of the Union Army to Kansas. In the fall of 1862,
Montford and Mary Elizabeth were married with the blessing of her
mother. As soon as he could, Montford, with the help of his farmhands
and slaves, set out to build a new home for his family. On the junction of
Henry House and Caddo Creeks, about seven miles north of present-
day Lone Grove, Oklahoma, he built a simple two-room log house on
the north side of Caddo Creek. A few miles further west on the Hickory
Creek and Caddo Creek junction were a few more settlers. Some of
Montford's neighbors in the area included Frazier McLish, Ed Colbert,
and the Humphrey family.[11] The house itself was fourteen by sixteen
feet, the two small rooms being separated by a hallway in the middle of
the house. The roof was made of clapboards held in place by ridgepoles.
Under the puncheon floor of one room a small cellar was dug. The
fireplace was made of logs and sticks coated over with clay. Montford cut
notches in the outside logs of the chimney because it sometimes caught
fire when too large a fire was built. These notches were used as steps that
he could climb up, carrying a bucket of water to pour down the inside of
the chimney when it caught fire. After some experience, they learned
just how large a fire they could build without starting the chimney
burning.

On October 1, 1863, Edward Bryant, or "E. B.", Montford's first son,
was born. Mary Bryant Campbell, the Sergeant's wife, and her Negro,
Aunt Eliza, attended to her daughter, Mary Elizabeth, in her confinement. They named the baby Edward for one of her four brothers.
Montford was greatly pleased that his first child was a healthy boy.

While Michael Campbell was stationed at Fort Arbuckle, he often
rode home to spend the night. The road winding south of the river was a
long, rough, and rocky route, so he usually rode straight south from the
fort, crossing the winding Washita many times. He always felt quite safe
taking this route because his big sorrel bald-faced horse, which he called
Old Baldy, was an excellent swimmer. Late one afternoon in the summer of 1864, Michael started for home. When he reached Henry Colbert's
place, about six miles south of the fort, he found the Washita up and the
stream bank full. Colbert advised him that it would be safer to take the
route across the mountain, but Michael laughed and said, "Old Baldy

can swim the Atlantic Ocean." Waving to Colbert, he rode his horse into the river just east of the house at what was called the Thomas Crossing. Below this ford the river made several bends that Michael had to cross before he reached home. Old Baldy took the first two crossings in his usual stride, but by the time Michael reached Hothliche Crossing, it was so dark that he could not see the ford. Taking extra precautions, he removed his boots and clothes and tied them behind the saddle. Then, trusting to Baldy's keen sense of direction to locate the ford, he plunged in.

Later that night Old Baldy, with Michael's clothes tied to the saddle, arrived riderless at his home. At Baldy's whinny, the dogs began to bark. Nute (Newton) Burney, a Negro farmhand, went out to investigate and found the riderless horse, and reported to Adelaide Campbell. She was frantic with grief and worry, and after gathering up the members of her household, they rushed down to the crossing. Although they screamed and shouted Michael's name as they searched the riverbanks, they got no reply. Finally they gave up the search and came back to the house to wait for daylight. Jack Brown, another of the Campbell's slaves, was sent to tell Montford. He came as quickly as he could, bringing with him Jack and Mary Campbell. Adelaide paced the floor the rest of that long night.

As soon as it was light enough to see, Montford set out, backtracking Old Baldy to the river. The tracks came out about fifty yards below the regular crossing. Riding along the bank toward the ford, he found the place where the horse, missing the ford, had tried to come out of the river at a place where the bank was steep and slick. By the marks of the horse's hoofs in the red mud, it looked as if he had tried to get out but could not make it. Since the tracks did not lead back into the river, it was evident that the horse had fallen backwards into the stream. Montford, swimming his horse across the river, found the place where Michael Campbell had dismounted and removed his clothes, and in this way established a point from which to begin a search. Two days later, with searchers working both sides of the river, the badly swollen body of Michael was found caught in a mass of driftwood. His body was wrapped in a blanket and brought on to be buried near Montford Johnson's home. Michael's widow, Adelaide, and her three small children, C. B., Katherine, and Ella, went to live with Montford and became part of his family.

Finally in 1865 the war ended, and the men who had survived came home. They found little to cheer about when they returned home. These veterans were worn out and penniless when they returned to their homes. Their country was disorganized. Cattle, their chief possession, had for the most part gone wild. During the latter years of the war, it was not safe to have cattle on hand for fear they would be taken by foraging details of Confederate Indian soldiers and refugees of the other civilized tribes. In

Mrs. Montford T. (Mary Elizabeth Campbell) Johnson, early to mid-1870s. Courtesy, Oklahoma Historical Society, #1725 OHS, Archives and Manuscripts Division.

Montford T. Johnson (Chickasaw), circa early to mid-1870s. Courtesy, Oklahoma Historical Society, #1726 OHS, Archives and Manuscripts Division.

an attempt to save some of them, the women and others left in charge
had driven them off into the mountains where they were scattered and
considered lost.

Montford Johnson, at the age of twenty-two, had become the pro-
vider for his own family and for the widowed, and very pregnant, Adelaide
Campbell and her children. It was a good thing that his early training
had made him strong and self-reliant, and that he was generous and
kindly by nature. Many years later Montford learned that his father,
Boggy Johnson, had been near him during this hard time. During the
war he had been at Sherman, Texas, acting as commissary officer for the
Confederate Army. He is also mentioned in 1866 in connection with the
removal of some Indian tribes from Texas. He apparently made no attempt to find or communicate with his children during this period.

The end of the war found the Chickasaws in a sad plight. As a nation, their tribal government had shut down and their governor, Winchester Colbert, had fled to Texas to wait out the end of the war. All of
their schools and academies had been closed down and were being used
as barracks or hospitals. It was not until the mid-1870s that the Chickasaw
educational system was up and running again at full speed.[12]

In July 1865, the Chickasaws officially surrendered and the fall of the
Confederacy was complete. The Chickasaws were the last to surrender.
The money the Chickasaws and Choctaws had received for their cattle
and produce during the war was worthless. "Caddo Bill" Williams, one
of Montford's good friends and Charley Eastman's son-in-law, had over
eighteen thousand dollars of this Confederate money that he had received for his cattle; now he was broke and had to start all over again.
Adelaide Campbell had over three thousand dollars of this worthless
money, which Michael had given her, but the only thing she had of real
value was a twenty-dollar gold piece that she kept in reserve for doctor
bills.

All the Indians in the Indian Territories lost men, much of their livestock, their slaves, and their money during the war. They never really recovered from the devastation caused by the war.[13] As Chiefs Opothleyahola
and Ok-ta-ha-hassee, two Creek Indian leaders, had stated in 1861 in a
letter to President Lincoln, pleading with him to remove the white man's
war, referred to as "the wolf," from Indian Territory: "Now I write to the
President our Great Father who removed us to our present homes, and
made a treaty, and you said that in our new homes we should be de-
fended from all interference from any people and that no white people
in the whole world should ever molest us unless they come from the sky
but the land should be ours as long as grass grew or waters run, and
should we be injured by anybody you would come with your soldiers
and punish them, but now the wolf has come, men who are strangers

tread our soil, our children are frightened and the mothers cannot sleep for fear. This is our situation now."[14]

The wolf had indeed come to the Indian Territory and taken or destroyed everything that the Indians possessed. The Chickasaws and the rest of the Five Civilized Tribes took up the wrong side and suffered the devastating consequences.

Notes

1. Thoburn, Joseph B. 1916. *Standard History of Oklahoma.* Chicago and New York: American Historical Society, p. 146.
2. Kalisch, Phillip A., and Beatrice J. Kalisch. 1970. "Indian Territory Forts: Charnel Houses of the Frontier, 1839–1855." *Chronicles of Oklahoma,* Oklahoma Historical Society. Vol. 50, p. 73.
3. Foreman, Grant.1934. *Five Civilized Tribes.* Norman: University of Oklahoma Press, pp. 121, 122, 130.
4. Steele, Aubrey L. 1944. "Lawrie Tatum's Indian Policy." *Chronicles of Oklahoma,* Oklahoma Historical Society. Vol. 22, p. 84.
5. Foreman, Grant. 1934. *Five Civilized Tribes.* Norman: University of Oklahoma Press, p. 144.
6. *War of the Rebellion.* 1900. Government printing office, Washington, D. C. p. 447.
7. Ibid., pp. 447–453.
8. Abel, Annie H. 1915. *The American Indian as Slaveholder and Secessionist.* Cleveland: Arthur C. Clarke Co., p. 58.
9. Hale, Duane K., and Arnell M. Gibson. 1991. *The Chickasaw.* New York: Chelsea House Publishers, pp. 77–78.
10. O'beirne, Harry F. 1891. *Leaders and Leading Men of Indian Territories,* vol. 1, *Choctaws and Chickasaws.* Chicago: American Publishers Association, p. 284.
11. Bynum. 1870s government survey map. Oklahoma City: Oklahoma Genealogical Society. Vol. 39, no. 2.
12. Gibson, Arrell. M. 1971. *The Chickasaws.* Norman: University of Oklahoma Press, pp. 280–281.
13. Abel, Annie H. 1915. *The American Indian as Slaveholder and Secessionist.* Cleveland: Arthur C. Clarke Co., pp. 245–246.
14. Ibid., pp. 245, 246.

Treaty of 1866

dding to the misfortunes that the Civil War brought upon the Chickasaws, the federal government, as victor, forced a new treaty upon the tribe as a whole. According to the terms of this treaty, the Chickasaws, in consideration of the sum of $300,000, ceded to the government all their territory lying west of the ninety-eighth meridian. Although the treaty did use the word *cede*, the Chickasaws were under the impression that they were only leasing the land to the government, and have always referred to it as the "Leased Districts." The treaty also gave the former slaves, or Chickasaw freedmen, all the rights, privileges, and immunities, including the right of suffrage, that the rest of the Chickasaws had. Further, the treaty also provided that the government should hold the $300,000 as a forfeit until the Chickasaws adopted the freed slaves as citizens of the tribe. However, if the Chickasaws refused to adopt these Negroes or freedmen within two years, the government agreed to remove the Negroes within ninety days from the Chickasaw territory and give the forfeit money to the Negroes. Neither of these solutions were ever executed.

In Article 6 of the treaty there was also a provision for the granting of rights-of-way to railway companies to build railroads across the Chickasaw and Choctaw Nations from north to south and east to west. In other words, it would bring in more encroachment by the hordes of white settlers and non-Indians waiting to enter the Indian Territory via other states.

Another important clause of the Treaty of 1866 attempted to change the tenure of land in the Chickasaw and Choctaw country from a holding in common by each nation to a holding in severalty by the individual Indians. A further provision allowed the government to remove

from Kansas ten thousand Indians to the Chickasaw and Choctaw country. These new Indians were to have the same rights as citizens as the
present members of the two tribes.

Although the Chickasaw leadership was composed primarily of
mixed-bloods by the end of the Civil War, the Chickasaws refused to
adopt the Negroes as citizens in 1866, and later, in 1876 and 1885. The
other four civilized tribes did finally adopt their respective Negroes.[1] The
federal government however, continued to ignore the inaction of the
Chickasaws and never, as the treaty stated, removed the Negroes from
the Chickasaws' territory. The matter only got worse as time went by. In
the 1890 census of Indian Territory, 91 percent was non-Indian, and by
1900 there were over five thousand resident Negroes claiming to be
Chickasaw freedmen when there had been barely one thousand at the
end of the Civil War.[2] The number of Chickasaws had remained fairly
constant at slightly less than forty-five hundred.[3] This action, and what
seemed to them the confiscation of some 6 million acres of land at about
five cents an acre, had seemed to the Chickasaws a grave injustice.

As the head of the family, Montford assumed the responsibility of
consolidating the Johnson-Campbell resources. Besides Michael,
Montford's wife had lost two other brothers—Frederick, a commissioned
captain in the Confederate Army, who died in the Second Battle of Bull
Run in 1862, and Edward B. Campbell, also a Confederate, who after
surviving a serious wound at the Battle of Glorietta, vanished in 1864.
Charley, the youngest brother, survived the war and stayed in the area.
He got the nickname "Turkey Egg Charley" because of his light com-
plexion and a face covered with freckles. Charley's mother never cared
for that nickname and she was overheard one day while looking at a
bucket of turkey eggs and muttered to herself, "Turkey Egg Charley—a
hell of a name for my baby boy." Charley Campbell later married Sallie
Humphreys, a Chickasaw and a sister of Henry Colbert's wife.

According to Bill Chisholm's daughter, Mary, Charlie Campbell worked
for her father at the Johnsonville store before Montford's acquisition of it.[4]
At some point, Charley and his wife moved to Tishomingo and went into
the hotel business. He took the contract to board the Indian children who
attended the Harley Male Academy. Years later, in 1874, he moved back to
Johnsonville, taking with him a Mr. Hebison, one of the teachers in the
academy who had boarded with him. When the legislature finally appro-
priated the money to pay for the board of the Indian students, Mr. Hebison
went to the capital to get the pay warrants. When he returned, he persuaded Charley he could double his money if he would use the warrants to
buy hides in the Seminole Nation. Charley Campbell endorsed the warrants to Hebison and sent him off to buy hides. That was the last Charley
ever saw of Mr. Hebison.

Montford's sister, Adelaide Campbell, her children, and Grandmother Campbell were now making their home with Montford. To keep
everything businesslike, Montford bought from Grandmother Campbell,
Adelaide, and Charley their interest in the Campbell cattle and brand,
the figure eight. Then Montford made an agreement with the other men
on the neighboring farms to round up the cattle that had been driven up
into the mountains. Because the families' former slaves had kept close
tabs on them, Montford still had a good many hogs. These he arranged
to trade to Charley Eastman for his cattle, with the understanding that
Montford would round up all the loose cattle in the mountains. With the
other neighbors, he made a verbal agreement that he should have the
option of buying cattle bearing their brands at the following prices: ten
dollars a head for the bulls and cows, seven dollars for the two-year-old
heifers, and five dollars for the yearlings. As pay for rounding up these
cattle, Montford was to have all the unbranded ones he caught.

Having made similar trades with two other cowmen, Holmes Colbert
and Captain Robertson, who had also turned cattle loose in the mountains, Montford began rounding up these wild cattle. His first move was
to drive his milk cows up into the mountains where the wild cattle were
in the habit of bedding down for the night. These cows were herded
under the watchful eyes of Montford and some of his neighbors. At dawn
they started the "milk pen bunch" toward the bedding ground of the
wild cattle, letting them drift into the wild ones at their own pace. As
soon as the two bunches came together, they started bawling and fighting. While this gang fight was going on, Montford and his crew surrounded them. The tame cattle were whipped in a short time and headed
for the safety of their home corrals. As they left the scene of battle, the
wild cattle were driven along with them. When they arrived at the pen,
the whole bunch was driven inside, the gates fastened, and salt placed
around in the corrals for the cattle to lick. The wild cattle craved salt, and
this made it easy to get them into the pens. They were kept in the corrals
until they were dry from lack of water; then they were turned out to
drink and graze. In the evening they were driven back to the pens. This
constant handling gradually calmed them down. These wild mountain
cattle were soon as easy to handle as their domestic herd.

Seeing that the wild cattle were craving salt, Montford thought it
might be easy to catch large numbers by establishing salt licks near their
accustomed watering places. He placed salt at certain drinking places
and then tried to hold the cattle as they came upon the watering hole.
Unfortunately, this scheme did not work because the cattle drifted into
the water in small numbers; the others were frightened away by the presence of the riders who were trying to hold in the first small bunch that
had arrived to water. Learning by this mistake, Montford decided to

build traps around the salt licks that would hold some of the cattle without disturbing the others. These traps were pens with an entrance and exit chute. The entrance chute was made of poles, wide at the outside but narrowing down so that a cow could just manage to squeeze through at the inner end. The inner ends of the poles were sharpened so that pointed ends would stick into the shoulders of the cows when they attempted to exit out of the opening they had come in. As they entered the shoot, the cattle could spring apart the poles as they pushed along, but when the poles sprang back into place, the opening was too narrow to let the cows go back. On the other side of the pen was constructed an exit chute, so that the cattle could force their way out just as they had forced their way in.

After the trap was built, salt was placed inside and the men went home, leaving the cattle to use the pen without fear. After giving the cattle time to get accustomed to the trap, Montford went out and placed poles across the exit chute so that the pen was closed on that side. Then he went home and waited about three days for the trap to fill up. When he went back to the trap, he drove before him a small group of domesticated cattle that he drove into the trap. He then rode in himself and drove the whole bunch around the corral until they became accustomed to being handled. As soon as he thought they were tame enough to handle, he turned the whole bunch out and drove them to the home corral. Montford and his men were pleased with the success of these traps and decided to celebrate.

Most of his helpers had been in the Confederate Army, and they told Montford that during the war they used to sit around their campfires at night and dream of getting back to the free open country where they could hunt and fish for the rest of their lives. Since they had been good helpers, and because Montford liked the idea himself, he allowed himself to be persuaded to take time out for a buffalo hunt with these men and his friend Jesse Chisholm.

Two things had to be done before Montford was ready to go. First, he went home to leave instructions with his freedmen farmhands to keep plenty of salt in the traps while he was gone. This salt he got from a salty spring near Henry Colbert's place. Charley Cohee, one of Colbert's former slaves, was the principal salt maker for their Caddo Creek area. He had built two rock walls just far enough apart that large iron kettles would rest between the tops of the walls. He had seven of these kettles, which he filled with the salty water from the spring. Under the kettles he built a fire to speed the evaporation. When the water boiled away, each kettle yielded a gallon of pure salt.

With the salt and traps taken care of, Montford and his party—Sam Garvin, Sam and Bill Moncrief, Caddo Bill Williams, and Jerry Carson—

went to a ledge of lead in the mountains where the Indians had been
going for years to get lead for their bullets. They chopped out chunks of
this lead and prepared plenty of balls for their guns and pistols. Then
they packed their horses and headed for Jesse Chisholm's store near the
old Camp Arbuckle site.

Jesse was glad to see this hunting party arrive and sent word to his
son, Bill Chisholm, who lived down the river, to come up and join them.
He also decided to have his teamster, Dick Cuttle, rig up some wagons
to bring back the hides. After buying some supplies, the hunters, joined
by Jesse and Bill Chisholm, headed up the South Canadian River. Soon
after they passed the point where the Canadian turns up to the north,
they came upon a large creek joining the Canadian on its west bank.
They rode up the creek about eight miles, and camped for the night in a
walnut grove. Next morning, with Jesse in charge, they rode up a small
draw that extended north into the flats. By staying in the draw, the hunters were able to ride up without being seen and, as the wind was in the
north, their scent was not carried to the buffalo grazing on the flats.
When they arrived near the head of the draw, Jesse dismounted and
went ahead on foot to reconnoiter. He came back and reported that a
small herd of buffalo was grazing peacefully in the morning sun a little to
the north and east of them.

At a given signal, the hunters, riding at full speed, burst forth from
the draw. They were on top of the buffalos before they could get away.
As they began to run, the cows and calves, being the swiftest, took the
lead. The bulls, with their tails hoisted and twisting in the air and their
eyes darting back and forth, were the first to be overtaken. Each hunter
picked out a victim, rode alongside him, and shot him down. As soon as
he was sure he had brought him down, he rode on to another. All the
hunters were credited with one or more buffalo, and everyone was pleased
with the success of the hunt. As the small herd took up its flight, they
were joined by others, and soon it appeared as if the whole country was
moving. The thundering of the buffalo hooves shook the ground like an
earthquake, and clouds of dust hung like a pall of smoke.

When the chase was over, the hunters returned to see that the buffalo were all dead, and then began skinning them. After the hides were
removed, they cut out the tongues, the humps off the backs, and several
sides of ribs; these choice pieces they spread out on the hides. Two of the
men went back to camp to start the cooking while the rest remained to
finish the skinning. Finally, Dick Cuttle and his wagons arrived; the hides
and the rest of the beef were loaded on them and taken back to camp. In
the afternoon, the men began jerking the meat Indian-style. The meat
was cut in long thin strips and hung on stretched rawhide ropes to dry in
the sun.

Later that evening, while the men lounged around the camp smoking, talking, and dreaming of the future, Montford remarked that this country they were in "would make for a wonderful cow country if it weren't for the buffalo and the wild Indians." Jesse told Montford that the cattle could be herded and the buffalo frightened away. He said, too, that he could arrange with the Indian chiefs not to bother Montford and his cattle. Jesse had been too ill to attend the Medicine Lodge Council, but he had learned that the wild Indians were going to be placed on reservations. These reservations included the lands west of the ninety-eighth meridian leased from the Chickasaws and Choctaws under the Treaties of 1855 and 1866. They also included certain lands north of the reservation where the Wichitas and other Texas tribes had been placed. These lands lay between the North and South Canadian Rivers. The Cheyenne and Arapahoe Indians were to be placed to the north and west of the Wichitas, and the Kiowa, Comanche, and Apache Indians were to be south of them. Jesse said he believed that the frontier settlers would be safe from attack if the government kept the whites and the buffalo hunters out of the Indian Country.

Over five thousand Indians, including the principal chiefs, had attended the Medicine Lodge Council. Some of the chiefs did not want to retire to reservations; all they wanted was to be left alone. But Jesse said he was confident that the government would place them on reservations whether they liked it or not. According to the terms offered by the government, the Indians were to retire to designated areas in the western part of the Indian Territory. The Indians agreed to stop raiding the settlements; the government agreed to keep immigrants and buffalo hunters out of the Indian Country. Churches, schools, and farming implements were to be furnished to the Indians so that they could learn the white man's ways. In addition, the government was to furnish certain annuities. Jesse said it had not been expressly stated, but he believed that the government would have to issue food to the Indians, as he thought that was what the Indians understood by annuities. As long as they were well fed, Jesse thought, the Indians would not cause much trouble. And even if the Medicine Lodge Treaty didn't work out, Jesse said he felt sure he could arrange it so that Montford could establish his ranch. On the way home from the hunt, Jesse kept discussing the plans for Montford's new ranch. He insisted that Montford move from the south side of the Arbuckle Mountains to the former Camp Arbuckle site so that he could live near his new ranching operations and only be a short ride from Jesse's place to the east. The hunting party soon dropped off Jesse and Bill at Jesse's trading post so that they could prepare for the fall trading with the Indians. The rest of the hunting party headed back south to their homes. Jesse's suggestion that Montford could put a ranch on this

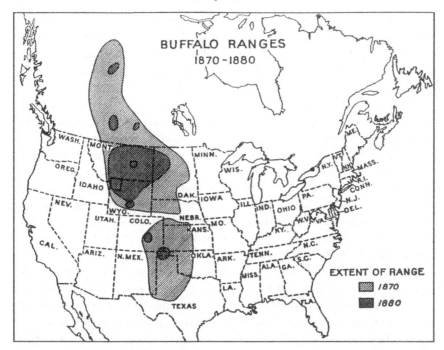

Buffalo Ranges 1870–1880. The Range Cattle Industry, *Edward D. Dale, University of Oklahoma Press, 1930.*

untamed land really lit a fire in him and Montford could not shake the idea of a ranch in that open rolling countryside out of his mind.

Ten years later in 1878, shortly before Montford moved to Silver City, he and a number of friends joined Bill Chisholm to participate in hunting the last buffalos in the Pottowatomie country. The group gathered at Bill's double log cabin located about a mile south of present-day Asher. After spending the night there, they headed north across the South Canadian River for about seven miles to the south bank of Salt Creek. The following morning they commenced the hunt, in which Bill Chisholm was credited with killing the last of the herd. (This story ran in the column, "Localized History of Pottawatomie County," by Charles Mooney, in the *Escort* magazine, included in the *Sunday Oklahoman,* August 31, 1969.)

The vast buffalo herds vanished from the Plains long before anyone thought possible. By 1880 the American buffalo were virtually gone from the Southwest, and by 1884 buffalo hunting as a business had come to an end. For example, the total amount taken in from buffalo robes sold to traders through the Kiowa-Comanche agency went from $70,400 in 1870 to $5,068 in 1879.[5] This slaughter of the buffalo was primarily a problem caused by the white hunters, who killed the animals by the thousands for their hide and left the rest of the animal to rot. The Indians killed the buffalo for basic needs and, wasting nothing, utilized literally every part of the animal. As Frank "Pistol Pete" Eaton stated in an audio interview made with him and Rollo Goodnight with the Oklahoma Historical Society in 1938 after observing this virtual elimination of the buffalo in the 1880s, "The white man is the worst waster in the world anyway."[6] This unplanned shortage of wild game would lead to many problems with the Indians as the amount of rations allowed the Indians in the Medicine Lodge Treaty were based on the plentifulness of wild game to augment the food derived from their soon-to-be-taught skills of farming and stock raising. It was really no surprise that many of these Indian hunting parties turned into raiding parties. Montford himself would lose a great number of his stock in the years to come because of depredations involving his cattle and horses.

True to his promise, when the Indians came into the store to trade, Jesse discussed the proposed ranch with them. They all agreed that they would not bother Montford as long as he did not work white men. Especially, they opposed the use of Texans, whom they had sworn to kill on sight. They did not object to Chickasaws or to Negroes; the latter they called buffalo men because their woolly heads resembled the forelock of the buffalo.

During the winter Jesse came to visit the Johnsons down on Caddo Creek, south of Fort Arbuckle. He told Montford he had made all of the arrangements for him to start his ranch in the wild country. Working together, they were able to persuade Montford's wife, Mary, who was the business head of the family, that the move would be a good one. They decided, too, that the place they had camped during the buffalo hunt would make an excellent location for Montford's headquarters. Because of the great number of walnut trees along the creek, they decided to call it the Walnut Creek ranch.

Death as usual was no stranger to these families out on the edge of the world. Montford and Mary E.'s second-born child, William, died in infancy, along with Adelaide's second child, Katherine ("Kate"), during this period too. The two were buried by Michael Campbell's grave near Montford's house by Caddo Creek.

The next spring, Jesse Chisholm, Black Beaver, and a hunting party were camped on the North Canadian River about fifty miles northwest of Council Grove. Jesse, who had recently been ill with cholera, became sick and died after eating bear meat cooked in a brass pot. In spite of the fact that his friend and sponsor had died, Montford Johnson decided to go ahead with the ranch that he had planned with Jesse's help.

Notes

1. Gibson, Arrell M. 1971. *The Chickasaws.* Norman: University of Oklahoma Press, p. 279.
2. Ibid., p. 285.
3. Ibid., p. 279.
4. Cooke, Mary V. Chisholm, 1939. "Memoirs of Mary V. Chisholm Cooke– 6 September 1939," transcribed and annotated by Kerry M. Armstrong, 1995. Chickasaw Historical Page (http://home.flash.net/~kma/index.htm).
5. Dale, Edward Evertt. 1930. *The Range Cattle Industry.* Norman: University of Oklahoma Press, pp. 44–46.
6. Eaton, F. Cassette no. cLL 94, April 23, 1938. Oral History Collection, Oklahoma Historical Society.

Friends: Jesse Chisholm and Black Beaver

Jesse Chisholm and Black Beaver were two of the most interesting men in the Oklahoma Territories during this early period. Jesse was born around 1805 to Ignatius Chisholm and a Cherokee woman known only as "Corn Tassel's sister," or perhaps "Corn Tassel's granddaughter." Corn Tassel was a minor chief among the western Cherokees in Tennessee.[1] Jesse spent most of his childhood in Arkansas where the western Cherokees lived until 1828. In 1826 Jesse joined up with some twenty frontiersmen at Cantonment Gibson on an unsuccessful venture hunting for gold up the Arkansas River into present-day Kansas. In 1834 Jesse joined his friend, Dutch (Bill Greiffenstein), a noted Cherokee warrior, who was guiding an expedition for General Leavenworth to the Wichita Mountains, in order for the U.S. government to make contact with the Comanche and Wichita tribes. For over three decades Jesse was one of the best-known guides for the territory west of the Crosstimbers area. In 1836, Jesse married Eliza Edwards, the half-Creek daughter of the Indian trader James Edward, who had a trading post located at the mouth of the Little River north of the South Canadian River. Their son William "Bill" Edward Chisholm was born during this marriage. During the late 1830s and 1840s, Jesse was constantly traveling, guiding and trading with the Indians from Texas to the Mexican California territory. He assisted Sam Houston in making treaties with the Comanches at Techuacana Creek in 1844.[2] After contributing his skills with another treaty in 1846, Jesse traveled to Washington, D.C., to interpret for President James K. Polk. In July 1846 Jesse returned to his home near Little River.

Eliza died sometime during 1846, and shortly thereafter Jesse married a half-blood Creek woman by the name of Sah-kah-kee. Jesse continued his travels and in 1849 and 1850 he was joined by Black Beaver to act as guide for Captain Randolph Marcy as they mapped out water and camping sights on the California "Gold Road."

In the 1850s, Jesse continued to help in the peacemaking process as he helped avert conflicts between Texas settlers and the Comanches. He was often helped in these negotiations by a Delaware Indian by the name of John Conner. On one of these ventures Jesse helped effect the rescue of eighteen captive children from the Indians. He was still much involved with the Cherokees, Creeks, and Wichitas in the Oklahoma Territories, trying to work out peaceful arrangements between the Plains Indians and the emigrating tribes that were being forced in from their eastern homelands. Jesse's trading enterprises were also prospering in the 1850s as he now opened up a trading post at the western edge of Council Grove. He kept this trading post open until his death, except for a few years during the Civil War when he led a large group of Plains Indians north into Kansas. He set up a ranch in Kansas near the present-day site of Wichita. These exiled Indians were receiving very little help from the government, so Jesse, in October 1864, assisted the various chiefs in drafting a letter to send to President Lincoln, hoping he could do something to relieve their situation.

By the time the war had ended, Jesse was already back operating out of his Council Grove trading post. He also did some scouting for Jesse Leavenworth, a Comanche-Kiowa agent in Kansas. Chisholm attended a council with the Confederates and the Plains Indians at Camp Napoleon near present-day Verden, Oklahoma. In August 1865, he worked on what turned out to be the Treaty of the Little Arkansas. This peace council included Kit Carson; U.S. generals Sanborn and Harney; Black Kettle, Cheyenne; Satank, Kiowa; Little Raven, Arapahoe; Iron Shirt, Apache; and Ten Bears and Buffalo Hump of the Comanches. Jesse could not attend the Medicine Lodge Council himself in 1867 due to illness. The only known photograph of Jesse Chisholm was taken in 1867 while he was picking up $25,000 worth of trade goods from a Leavenworth trader, E. H. Durfee. Jesse's friend James Mead noted: "The picture conveys a poor idea of the man when in his prime."[3]

Jesse recovered enough from his illness to continue his trading and had even helped rescue some surveyors being threatened by a group of Plains Indians near his salt-mining operation up on Salt Creek in north-central Oklahoma Territory. Shortly afterward he became ill and died while returning to Council Grove. His friends and family buried him near Left Hand's Spring, some nine miles northeast of present-day Geary, Oklahoma. His old friend, Comanche chief Ten Bears, placed his own

Jesse Chisholm, circa 1868. Courtesy, Oklahoma Historical Society, #1757 OHS, Archives and Manuscripts Division.

gold peace medal gently on Jesse's chest as they wrapped him in buffalo skin and buried him on that hill that overlooked the Canadian River valley.

In the May 23, 1890, issue of the *Wichita Eagle*, his longtime friend and fellow traveler, James Mead, was said to have spoken these words as a eulogy: "He was by nature noble, chivalrous, and brave. An arbitrator and peace-maker among the wild tribes of the plains and territory, beloved and respected by all. A few days before his unexpected and sudden death, in course of a conversation he said: 'I know little about the bible and churches, but the good God who sent me here, gave me the knowledge of right and wrong. I have never wronged any one in my life. I have done all the good I could. I have been a peacemaker among my brethren. No man ever went from my camp hungry or naked, and I am ready and willing to go to the home of the Great Spirit, just as I am, whenever he calls for me.'"

Jesse's family and friends continued on to Council Grove where they held a wake in his honor. James Mead, Dutch Greiffenstein, and Judge Greenway, to name a few, toasted Jesse with whiskey and firing salutes to him with their buffalo guns. At least for them it ended an era of western history. The Civil War was over and the western migration was soon to explode, changing radically and quickly the land that Jesse had ranged over. Already, Texas cattle herds were crossing the Indian Territory by way of the soon-to-be famous "Chisholm Trail." This half-Scot, half-Cherokee frontiersmen left an indelible mark on the West, especially here in Oklahoma.[4]

Black Beaver was born near the present-day site of Belleville, Illinois, in 1806. His name first crops up in a letter sent to General William Clark regarding the tribe's desperate condition in February 1824, while the Delawares were living on the White River in Arkansas. The letter, cosigned by Black Beaver, head chief William Anderson, and other tribe members reads: "Last summer a number of our people died just for the want of something to live on . . . We have got in a country where we do not find all as stated to us when we was asked to swap lands with you . . . Father—We did not think that big man would tell us things that was not true . . . Father—You know it is hard to go hungry, if you do not know it we poor Indians know it . . . We are obliged to call on you onst more for assistance in the name of God."[5]

When Black Beaver was twenty-eight he acted as interpreter for Colonel Richard Irving Dodge at his conference with the Comanche, Kiowa, and Wichita in 1834 on upper Red River. Dodge wrote of Black Beaver and his people: "Of all the Indians, the Delawares seem to be most addicted to these solitary wanderings, undertaken, in their case at least, from pure curiosity and love of adventure. Black Beaver, the friend and guide of General (then Captain) Marcy, was almost as equally renowned for his wonderful journeys."[6]

Black Beaver also participated in General Henry Leavenworth's celebrated Dragoon expedition in 1834. From that time on, Black Beaver was always in demand as a guide and interpreter. In 1846, during the war with Mexico, a company of Delaware and thirty-five Shawnee Indians under Captain Black Beaver were mustered into service by General Harney in June, but were released from duty four months early, having completed their assignments. They also were not paid for their services.

In April 1849 Captain Randolph B. Marcy ran across Black Beaver while escorting five hundred emigrants to California in Shawneetown where the road forked. Captain Marcy engaged Black Beaver as guide and interpreter and had this to say about this most useful man: "He has traveled a great deal among the western and northern tribes of Indians, is well acquainted with their character and habits, and converses fluently with the Comanche and most of the other prairie tribes. He has spent five years in Oregon and California, two years among the Crow and Black Feet Indians. Has trapped beaver in the Gila, the Columbia, the Rio Grande, and the Pecos: has crossed the Rocky Mountains at many different points and indeed is one of those men that are seldom met with except in the mountains."[7] Captain Marcy in his book, *Thirty Years of Army Life*, also wrote that Black Beaver had been employed by the American Fur Company for ten years and that during that time he had visited nearly every point of interest within the limits of our unsettled territory.

The grace and rapidity with which Black Beaver carried on conversations with Indians of other tribes astonished Marcy. This was done by pantomime, and the Captain wrote that their facile gestures would compare with the most accomplished performance of opera stars. Marcy recounted that when he had a Comanche as a guide with Black Beaver, the latter was describing the earth as a sphere; the Comanche, incredulous, asked if the Delaware thought him an idiot. Beaver replied that white people knew such to be a fact. The Comanche said that anyone could see that the prairie was flat, and that his grandfather had been to the end of it, where the sun disappeared behind a wall. Beaver then described the steam engine and other strange things he had seen among the whites. But the Comanche thought them all a figment of the Indian's imagination, and he replied in his own language, "Hush, you fool!" Captain Marcy tried to explain to his guide the operation of the telegraph, but Beaver refused to communicate this to the Comanche, saying, "I don't think I tell him that, Captain; for the truth is, I don't believe it myself."[8]

Black Beaver (Delaware). Photo by William Henry Jackson, 1868. Courtesy, National Museum of the American Indian, Smithsonian Institution.

When the army abandoned Camp Arbuckle in the spring of 1851, Black Beaver and a small band of fellow Delawares, with the army's permission, moved into the old camp. They remained there for the better part of the 1850s before they moved to their own tribal land. Black Beaver didn't budge much from Camp Arbuckle, or Beaversville. as it was often called. In 1858 Lieutenant Edward F. Beale, ordered to survey a route from Fort Smith to the Colorado River for a stage line and wagon road, approached Black Beaver to engage his services as guide, but he refused and Jesse Chisholm took the job instead.

By the fall of 1860 Black Beaver, the Delawares, and some Caddo Indians were living on the north side of the Washita on Sugar Tree Creek, near present-day Anadarko. The new Indian agent, Matthew Leeper, reported Black Beaver had by far the nicest home in the area. "He has a pretty good double log house, with two shed rooms in rear, a porch in front and two fireplaces, and a field of forty-one and a half acres inclosed with a good stake-and-rider fence, thirty-six and a half of which have been cultivated."[9]

In May 1861 Black Beaver was called into service again, leading the retreating federal troops north into the Cherokee Outlet and on to Leavenworth, Kansas. Colonel Emory stated that "of all the Indians upon whom the Government had lavished its bounty, Black Beaver was the only one that would consent to guide the column."[10] The command reached Fort Leavenworth in fine condition without the loss of a single man, horse, or wagon. In doing this he abandoned his property, which was confiscated and destroyed by the advancing Confederate troups. The only compensation he ever received from the federal government was less than 25 percent of his actual loss some seven years later.

After the war, in July 1867, Black Beaver acted as guide while preparing for and during the removal of the tribes from Kansas to the Leased District, for which service he was promised one thousand dollars a year. A report filed by F. A. Rector stated that, "had it not been for the presence of Black Beaver, it would have been impossible to have kept the Indians together and affected their removal to the Leased Lands at that time."[11] Black Beaver was left in charge of the Indians for several more months without a government agent, after their arrival in the Leased District.

Black Beaver had moved back to his Sugar Tree Creek farm after the war and continued his farming efforts on a quarter section of land that General Hazen had plowed for the Delawares. Black Beaver was the only tribal member to give it a go. In 1869 he worked for James Wortham as an interpreter and was short-changed, again receiving only one-third of his agreed-upon pay. In 1870 he was a delegate to the International Indian Council in Okmulgee, where he delivered a speech intended to calm down the wild Plains Indians. Every two years he attended these council meetings, encouraging the younger chiefs to "keep the war hatchets buried. . . . We all want peace among ourselves and with the United States. We want our country; we love it all here together. Well, now after we make friends, all of us, no more bad, then we are no more afraid to go any where; go all over the United States; meet white man; he asks what tribe you belong to; we tell him; he say that is mighty good Indian. We like that. I hope we are all united togther, all chiefs that's what we want--peace. That much I talk to my brothers."[12]

Black Beaver was baptized in 1876 and became a Baptist minister. He still attended the council meetings into his seventies. Thirty-four tribes were represented at the "Grand Council," which met in Okmulgee in May 1878 to discuss forming a state government with representatives and a governor.

E. B. Johnson knew Black Beaver and remembered him this way to Grant Foreman: "I knew Black Beaver well. He was typically named as he was an unusually dark Indian, [he] often came to Father's [Montford's] on his journeys & said he was with Jesse Chisholm when he died. [He] lived among the Caddo Indians when they lived in what is now known as Pauls Valley. Most of them lived in grass houses or teepees, and when they were moved out to Sugar Creek he went with them, but often returned for his usual visit."[13]

Black Beaver died on May 8, 1880. Indian agent P. B. Hunt wrote of him in a letter to the commissioner of Indian affairs in Washington: "He was many years ago a noted guide and acted in that capacity for Fremont, Auderbon [sic] and Marcy; had acquired a fair knowledge of English & delighted in speaking it, when occasion offered; was a good friend of the white man, had professed religion, had consented to two of his daughters marrying white men, & set his red brethern [sic] a good example by his untiring industry & earnest desire to follow the white man's road to the end."[14]

His burial took place the day following his death, and more than 150 persons showed the esteem in which he was held by following the remains to their last earthly resting place. Black Beaver's grave, which was a short distance from his farm, was relocated to the Chief's Knoll in the Fort Sill Cemetery, Lawton, Oklahoma, in the 1980s.[15]

Notes

1. Hoig, Stan. 1989. "The Genealogy of Jesse Chisholm." *Chronicles of Oklahoma*, Oklahoma Historical Society. Vol. 67, summer, no 2, p.199.
2. Hoig, Stan. 1988. "Jesse Chisholm: Peace-Maker, Trader, Forgotten Frontiersman." *Chronicles of Oklahoma*, Oklahoma Historical Society. Vol. 66, winter, no. 4, pp. 354–357.
3. Ibid., pp. 365–370.

4. Ibid., p. 351.
5. Office of Indian Affairs, Retired Classified Files, "1824, Delaware on White River"; Foreman, Grant, 1930. *Indians and Pioneers.* New Haven, CT: Yale University Press, 1930, pp. 228–229.
6. Foreman, Carolyn T. 1924. "Black Beaver." *Chronicles of Oklahoma,* Oklahoma Historical Society. Vol. 24, p. 269.
7. Foreman, George. 1925. "Early Trails in Oklahoma." *Chronicles of Oklahoma,* Oklahoma Historical Society. Vol. 3, no 2, pp. 107–108.
8. Foreman, Grant. 1937. "Adventure on the Red River." *Chronicles of Oklahoma,* Oklahoma Historical Society. Vol. 15, pp. 163–164.
9. Foreman, George A. 1942. *A History of Oklahoma.* Norman: University of Oklahoma Press, p. 98.
10. Wright, Muriel H. 1933. *Advancing the Frontier.* Norman: University of Oklahoma Press, p. 278, fn. 12.
11. Foreman, Carolyn T. 1924. "Black Beaver." *Chronicles of Oklahoma,* Oklahoma Historical Society. Vol. 24, p. 281.
12. Ibid.
13. Johnson, E. B. 1934. "Letter to Grant Foreman." September 29, 1934. In Carolyn T. Foreman, 1924, "Black Beaver," *Chronicles of Oklahoma,* Oklahoma Historical Society. Vol. 24, p. 291.
14. Indian Archives Division, Kiowa. Oklahoma Historical Society. Vol. 11, p. 136.
15. Foreman, Carolyn. 1946. "Black Beaver." *Chronicles of Oklahoma,* Oklahoma Historical Society. Vol. 24, pp. 269–292.

Wild Indian Raids

here are many historical records concerning the activities of the Plains Indians in the part of the country where Montford Johnson planned to establish his ranch. Two such books are Colonel W. S. Nye's *Carbine and Lance: The Story of Old Fort Sill,* and Stan Hoig's *Fort Reno and the Indian Territory Frontier.* From accounts similar to this, and from the Johnson family records, can be sketched briefly the condition of the country when Montford first arrived and what happened later.

After the Medicine Lodge Treaty was signed in 1867, the Plains Indians had been placed on reservations west of the ninety-eighth meridian. The government supplied the Indians with annuities in the form of clothing, axes, bedding, and other domestic and farming implements. The government did not, however, keep the buffalo hunters out of the Indian Country. These hunters did not kill the buffalo for food, but for the hides alone; this practice and the violation of the treaty angered the Indians. Since the government had fallen down on what seemed to them the most important part of the treaty, and because they loved the thrill of the chase, the Indians continued their raids in both Kansas and Texas. In May 1868, the Indians even raided their own agency, stealing everything they could find and destroying the buildings. The garrison at Fort Arbuckle, which consisted of ignorant and poorly trained freed slaves, was only a joke to the Indians. To show their disrespect for the soldiers, they passed near the fort and raided the small ranchers to the south, stealing many horses. Among the Chickasaws who suffered losses were Henry Colbert and Adelaide Campbell. Because of the raids south of

Fort Arbuckle, Cyrus Harris, governor of the Chickasaws, organized an Indian militia to protect the border ranches.

During the spring and summer of 1868 the wild Indians ran virtually unchallenged in Texas and Kansas, attacking homesteads, scalping settlers, and taking many of the women and children captive. In the autumn of that year the government finally took action and sent General P. H. Sheridan to put an end to the Indian outrages. In a whirlwind campaign during the fall and winter, the Indians were driven back to the reservation. In November General George A. Custer and the Seventh Cavalry attacked and killed Black Kettle at the so-called Battle of the Washita, where many Cheyenne women and children were slaughtered. The winter months were not good for raids anyway, and the Indians were ready to make some new promises. After the Indians had been somewhat subdued and been moved onto their reservation, the government realized that Fort Arbuckle was too far from the agency, and decided to establish a new post. This post, established in January 1869, was placed where the government felt they could keep in close touch with the Indians and the agency. They built this fort near Medicine Bluffs and called it Fort Sill, just north of present-day Lawton, Oklahoma.

In the spring of 1869, Ulysses S. Grant was inaugurated as president of the United States. He was approached by a group of pacifists, known as Quakers, who convinced him that the Indians were not being properly handled. These Quakers induced the president to put them in charge of the Indian agencies and allow them to attempt to tame and civilize these "wild savages" with kindness. These peace-loving Quakers fitted in admirably with the plans of the Indians. For the more adventurous Indians, the raids became a kind of game. When they grew tired of the chase, they headed for the reservation as a haven of rest and refuge.

One of the first Quaker agents put in charge was a Mr. Tatum. The Indians, after looking him over, decided to try him out. They raided the agency and stole twenty head of horses and mules. This raid was conducted by the Comanches in May 1870. A month later the Kiowas decided to outdo the Comanches and raided the quartermaster's corrals at Fort Sill. They stole seventy-three head of mules. This was accomplished so easily that they planned to stampede all of the horses and set the soldiers afoot. Just for the fun of the thing, they also shot arrows into the cattle that had been brought to the agency to be issued to them, to see them run and bellow.

During the winter of 1870, the weather was extremely cold. The Indians remained quietly on their reservation except for an occasional raid into Texas. On one of these raids they killed four Negroes and scalped them. They did not consider these scalps worth keeping because of the shortness of the hair, but tossed them back and forth to each other as they returned and, at last, threw them away. In May 1871 a group of Kiowas, Kiowa-Apaches, and Comanches, after deciding at a council fire to seek revenge on the Tehannas, attacked the Warren wagon train loaded with arms and ammunition. They captured the wagons and made off with the contents, leaving seven dead in their wake.[1] On the night of October 9, 1871, the Quahada Comanches, who were considered outlaws, made a successful raid on the camp of Colonel Ronald S. Mackenzie at the foot of Mount Blanco. Colonel Mackenzie was the commander at Fort Sill who headed an expedition against the raiding Indians. Yelling and dragging dry buffalo hides, the Indians rushed at full speed into the camp and stampeded his horses, which they later caught for themselves.

Indian raids picked up in the spring of 1872 with the Kiowa, Apache, and Comanches being the most active, as Thomas C. Battey wrote: " Not less than forty whites have been killed, several hundred live stock have been stolen and three children taken captive."[2] In July 1872, representatives of the Five Civilized Tribes met with the chiefs of the wild Indians in a peace council. They urged the Comanches and Kiowas to stop their raiding. During the council they also talked of the rapid disappearance of the buffalo and warned the wild Indian chiefs that they should begin raising their own cattle, so that they would not have to be dependent upon the government for food. Figures showing the extermination of the buffalo are given by the Arapaho and Cheyenne Agency at Darlington. During the buffalo hunts in the fall of 1876, the Arapahoes killed 7,000, and tanned 15,000 hides of buffalo killed by traders. In 1877 they killed 219 buffalo and tanned 640 hides for traders. In 1878 they did not report any killed or any hides tanned; by 1879 the buffalo had disappeared. But in spite of the advice, later proved to be sound, given by the Five Civilized Tribes, the wild Indians replied that they could always get plenty of beef by raids in Texas.

In 1873, the year after the peace council, the government, as a punishment upon the wild tribes for failure to deliver to the authorities certain Indians who had gone on one of these Texas raids, withheld rations from the Indians. Since the buffalo were already decreasing in number, the Indians had to go to the Plains for their food. During the winter of that year, after an unsuccessful series of hunts, the Indians began to grow restless. Their rations were meager; many of them had to butcher their mules and horses to survive. With the coming of spring in 1874, hostilities began anew. In June some of the Indians left their reservation and staged the historic battle of Adobe Walls, located near the South Canadian River in the Texas Panhandle. In July the Cheyennes and Arapahoes attacked a wagon train and shot Pat Hennessey, near the present-day town of Hennessey. By the middle of July they were raiding the herds of the beef contractors who were holding their cattle near the reservations. The Indians stole those cattle for food.

By this time the Quakers had thrown up their hands and admitted that the Indians were out of control. The entire management of the Indians was then turned over to the army, and Colonel Davidson was placed in charge of the troops. He gave the Indians until August 3 to return to the reservation and to enroll as friendly. Many took advantage of this offer, but the rest were so desperate that they went on the warpath. In August, after a hot and dry summer, the first clash between the Indians and the troops occurred at the Anadarko Agency, which included the looting of the Shirley's store. Since the dry summer had brought a plague of grasshoppers that destroyed all the vegetation, the troops did not actually take to the field until the fall rains set in.[3] The Indians were soon chased down and forced to return to the reservation. When the Indians were captured, their horses were taken away from them, and they were set afoot. Many of the horses were shot at once; some were taken west of the fort to be killed. This policy was soon abandoned because the wind brought the smell of the dead horses into the fort. The government then decided to auction off the rest of the horses to the highest bidder; most of them were bought by neighboring cowmen.

The leading rebel chiefs came running back to the reservation like runaways, repentant and hopeful that they would be forgiven as they had been in the past. But they got a bad shock; the army method of handling them was different from that of the Quakers. They were shackled and thrown into the guardhouse. By April 1875, most of the rebel chiefs had surrendered. Lieutenant Richard H. Pratt took them to the prison at Fort Leavenworth, Kansas; they were later moved to Fort Marion, an old run-down Spanish fort left over from the seventeenth century in Saint Augustine, Florida. This is where Montford Johnson and his son E. B. visited the survivors a few years later. In June 1875, Quanah Parker and his wild band of Quahada Comanches surrendered, and the Indian War was finished.

Although Montford's Camp Arbuckle home was on the outskirts of the country used by the wild Indians, the Walnut Creek and other ranches he established later were in the heart of their hunting grounds. Raids were made on all sides of him by Kiowas, Cheyennes, and Arapahoes, but he was never molested. Relying on the word and honor of the chiefs who had given their word to his friend Jesse Chisholm, Montford moved into the midst of the wild Indian country and was accepted by the Indians as their friend and brother.

One Indian did make a test of Montford's bravery, but found him to be made of sterner stuff than the Quaker agents. Late one evening as Montford was returning to his Walnut Creek ranch, a young Kiowa brave burst out of a thicket and charged straight toward him. He was dressed in full war regalia and, leaning low over his horse, drew his arrow to his bow. Seeing him coming, Montford stopped his horse, pulled his pistol, and took deliberate aim. Just as he was ready to pull the trigger, the Kiowa threw up his bow and arrow and stopped his running horse. Recognizing Montford, whom he had almost shot, he came up laughing and complimenting him on his bravery in standing his ground. Montford, in turn, acted as if the affair was a good joke, but told the warrior that he had come very close to going to the happy hunting ground.

Notes

1. Nye, W. S. 1969. *Carbine and Lance: The Story of Old Fort Sill.* Norman: University of Oklahoma Press, pp. 124–131.
2. Steele, Aubrey L. 1939. "Beginning of Quaker Administration of Indian Affairs in Oklahoma." *Chronicles of Oklahoma,* Oklahoma Historical Society. Vol. 17, p. 384.
3. Nye, W. S. 1969. *Carbine and Lance: The Story of Old Fort Sill.* Norman: University of Oklahoma Press, p. 211.

Jack Brown, Montford's First Partner

In the spring of 1868, Montford Johnson collected a crew to help him build an operating headquarters for his ranch on Walnut Creek. They took two yoke of oxen and two wagons loaded with a camping outfit, axes, saws, wedge-irons, and other building equipment. As soon as they arrived, they staked out a site for a cabin at the eastern edge of a small blackjack grove, about a mile north of Walnut Creek and about eight miles above its mouth. This site is about two miles northeast of the present town of Washington, Oklahoma, and about thirty miles from Chisholm's store at Camp Arbuckle. In a month the crew had built a two-room cabin of blackjack logs. It was similar to the house Montford had built for his family, but was not floored. They also built two large corrals of poles in which to hold the cattle at night. These corrals covered several acres and provided the cattle with ample room to bed down. Adjoining the larger corrals was a smaller circular one for the horses. This one was made of pickets, standing upright; the cattle corrals were made of poles tied in horizontally.

Jack Brown, one of the Johnsons' former slaves, married Grandmother Campbell's Negro cook, Aunt Eliza. After they returned from visiting their kinfolks and friends on Wild Horse Creek, Montford made an agreement with Jack, by which he was to have charge of these new headquarters and look after the cattle. As payment, he was to have every fourth calf, making Jack Brown Oklahoma's first sharecropper. Montford had originally asked Ed Cohee to take charge of the new ranch, but his fear of the Comanches had made it impossible for him to take advantage of this proposition. Jack did ask that his brother-in-law, Henry Cole, and his wife, Caroline, come along with them to the Walnut Creek ranch until they felt comfortable in their new location.

Upon returning to his Caddo Creek homestead, the ranch crew started to search out and round up the wild cattle. Montford was collecting so many unbranded cattle that he did not purchase any more of the branded ones on which he had options. As fast as the unbranded cattle were caught, they were branded with what he called the hookety-hook brand. This brand was placed on the left side of all cattle he intended placing on Walnut Creek. The best young bulls were saved and branded. Montford turned over the rest of the bulls and steers to the friends who had helped him in the roundup. Part of these cattle originated from stock that the Chickasaws had brought from Mississippi. They were all colors, but were much superior to the Texas longhorns that, for the last two years, had been seen passing through the mountains.

Although Montford had purchased the Campbell's cattle and their figure-eight brand, he decided to give his sister Adelaide a new start of stock and branded all the calves for her that he found running with the figure-eight brand. The brand he gave her was called the Circle-A. These Circle-A cattle were kept with the home bunch that he planned to have at his new home at Camp Arbuckle, so that they wouldn't be mixed up with the share deal he had made with Jack Brown. These brands, and the others Montford used on his and his family's cattle, were recorded from time to time in Pontotoc County at Stonewall, Indian Territory.

Because the spring and summer were busy times, it was fall before the herd was in shape to move to the new ranch. After all the cattle were branded and the supplies ready, Montford and his crew, along with Jack Brown and his wife, Aunt Eliza, headed up the Shawnee-Arbuckle Trail established by the Texans. After crossing the Washita River, they headed straight north toward the new ranch. They arrived at the new location with something over eight hundred head of cattle, consisting of bulls, cows, calves, and a few hundred yearling steers. Jack Brown, with the aid of two other Negroes, Ed Cohee and Henry Cole, herded the cattle in the daytime and penned them in the corrals at night. Besides herding, these men had to keep the buffalo and wolves frightened away. If the cattle became mixed with a buffalo herd, they would drift out of the country with them. And, as the wolf packs could take down a wild buffalo, it was nothing for them to kill some wandering domestic cow.

Jack Brown had a few horses and mares of his own, and Aunt Eliza had chickens and hogs that they took with them to the new ranch. The hogs were turned loose in the blackjack grove to feed on the small acorns. To keep them partially tamed, Jack made a trough from an old log in which he placed the swill from the house. By the time Jack and his cattle were located, Montford found that it was too late in the fall to begin work on his own home at Camp Arbuckle and decided to wait until the following spring.

In the spring of 1869 Montford hired some Mexicans who had worked with Jesse Chisholm to help him build his new ranch house because his own men were busy looking after the cattle. The Mexicans were un-trained as carpenters, and by the time the house was far enough along to afford the family some shelter, the summer set in. Pressed for time, Montford did not do his spring branding at Walnut Creek, but even then he was not able to finish his new house. He had also purchased some sheep that were at the home place on Caddo Creek. He knew they would be alot of trouble to move. Because of these growing numbers of problems and the onset of the summer heat, Montford agreed with the women in the family and postponed their move until the fall.

Around the first of October 1869, an ox wagon with a small trailer was loaded with all the Johnson family belongings as they prepared to leave the Caddo Creek home behind. After rounding up his livestock, Montford was ready to leave the mountains for his new home on the prairie. One of his farmhands drove the oxen, accompanied by Grand-mother Campbell. The rest of the family was on horseback. Mary Eliza-beth rode a sidesaddle as was her custom, with young Leford on a pillow held in her lap. Ella rode behind her mother, Adelaide; C. B. was on his horse, Bally, and E. B. rode his little white pony. The procession strung out behind the livestock, which were herded along ahead. In the herd were eight mares, ten head of milk cows, forty head of sheep, two nannie goats, one billy goat, ten sows, and one boar.

The whole family was in good spirits and happy, all except Leford. Leford had been born a short time after the death of young William, Montford's second son. After William's death the young mother had trouble with her breasts and had not been able to nurse Leford, who had to be bottle-fed. As the party drove along and Leford became hungry and fretful, Montford would toss a rope on old Betsy, one of the milk cows, dismount, and, taking Leford's bottle, milk enough from Betsy for a feeding. At the end of the first day, camp was made near the spring at Fort Arbuckle.

The next day the party continued on their northerly path and passed through Cherokee Town, near the present town of Pauls Valley, located in a big valley on the Washita. At that time the valley was covered from one end to the other with Caddo Indians, many of whom were living in grass-covered tepees, others in tepees made of hides. Montford followed an old trail that led to a ferry across the Washita. The worst trouble there was with the sheep. The first bunch was taken over on the ferry. Before the remaining ones could be rounded up, they panicked and jumped into the river. After some time and a lot of bleating, they managed to catch up with the rest of the flock. The next time he ferried sheep, Montford took the precaution to build a corral of quilts and wagon sheets, so that the sheep left behind could be penned in where they couldn't see out. After much ado, all the belongings were ferried across the Washita, and the family camped for the night near Dr. John and Mary Shirley's home at Cherokee Town, some two and one-half miles southeast of present-day Pauls Valley. The Shirleys were old friends of Montford's and Mary Elizabeth's. The two Marys had known each other since their childhood school days at Fort Arbuckle. The Shirleys had a mercantile store and erected the first bridge on the Washita.[1]

On the third day the pioneer ranchers headed out to the northeast along Peavine Creek and arrived at their home near old Camp Arbuckle. The house was a good deal like the old one, but more sturdily built. The roof was nailed on with wooden pegs, the chinks between the logs were dressed with lime, and the chimney was made of rock. A cabin used as a kitchen and dining room was joined on behind. The livestock were penned in the stockade that had been built when the camp had been established in 1850. Unfortunately, the house was not yet finished, so the family had to camp out for another two weeks before they could move in. Finally, the women began the chore of moving in and putting their belongings to rights.

North of the stockade the whole flat down by the South Canadian River was covered with the camps of wild Indians who had come to do their fall trading at the Chisholms' store. Montford felt compelled to visit the Indians at their camp and at the store. Since Jesse Chisholm was dead, he had to depend on himself to make friends with these Indians. They were having a happy, carefree time while they were trading. They held horse races, gambled, and danced. One sport they indulged in created a terrible commotion in the camp. A young Indian brave would buy a bolt of cloth, and taking one end of it in his hand, mount his horse, and ride whooping and yelling toward the camp with the cloth flapping in the wind. As the Indian rode his frightened horse into camp, dogs barked and children screamed as they ran for cover. The squaws rushed out and tried to grab the cloth from the charging horseman. If they got a good hold on it, he would let them have it or be jerked from his horse by the tugging women. It was a game with the Indians, the object being to ride through the camp without being unseated. If the squaws won the contest, there would be a scramble to see who got the largest section of cloth.

When the Indians broke camp, the tall tepee poles, about twenty feet long, were first lowered; the tanned hides, which made the covering for the lodges, were folded into a compact bundle. The squaws did this work and, after the horses had been caught, began packing them with their belongings. Some of the Indians had saddles resembling pack-saddles. To these were fastened the butt ends of the poles, an equal number on each side of the horse, the other ends of the poles extending to the rear of the horse and dragging on the ground. To the rear of the horse a small crosspiece was fastened securely between the two groups of poles extending down each side. To this crosspiece the cooking pots and utensils were tied. Then the folded hides for the tepee were thrown across the horse's back and tied on with a lariat. Those who did not have pack-saddles placed the hides on first, and secured the tepee poles to this pack.

The children packed their belongings and placed them on the backs of their dogs in much the same manner that the elders packed their horses. Some had a light leather harness that was placed over the dogs' shoulders and backs. Their small tepee poles were about ten feet long. They fastened these to the harness and tied their playthings to the con-necting crosspiece at the rear of the dogs. All this packing was completed in a short time and without confusion. Probably this was because the women did all the work and were not bothered by the sound advice that the fond husband of the present-day attempts to give at such times. The Indian men and older boys were much smarter than their present-day civilized white brothers. As soon as the horses were caught, they mounted them and rode away, leaving the women in full charge.

With everything packed, the squaws placed the babies in the buffalo-hide pouches that they tied either to their backs or to the sides of their saddles. Many of them had extra horses to ride, but a few scrambled up on top of the pack, which already looked as if it would mash the horse to the ground. The children mounted or were placed on their own ponies. Sitting just as proudly as the braves, and much straighter than the squaws, they joined the slowly moving column, which headed west.

After watching the Indians, Montford's wife decided she needed some extra protection to keep the Indians, panthers, and wolves away from the house. She had her husband build an eight-foot picket fence around the yard. Enclosed in the yard were cabins for the Negroes, a smokehouse, and a small chicken house. Four large greyhounds lounged around out-side the picket fence. They were an added protection because they did not permit any strangers to enter the gate unless someone of the house-hold spoke to them and assured them it was all right for the person to come in. At night the dogs served also as guards for the chickens, which were a choice delicacy for such nocturnal prowlers as opossums, skunks, and weasels.

After using the old stockade for some time, Montford built a small corral for the livestock a shorter distance from his house. Before long he gave up the sheep business entirely. One day at noon, while the young Negro who herded the sheep was eating his lunch, the sheep stampeded and fled. The stampede was supposed to have been caused by wolves. Although some time later a few of his flock were reported seen near Stonewall, Montford let them go; he said they were a good riddance. As a precaution in keeping track of the rest of his livestock, he kept them herded most of the time. He also belled a cow, a sow, and the stallion. When any of the livestock broke away from the rest of the herd, they could be located by the ringing of the bell.

For food during that fall and winter, the new ranchers had mush, corn bread, potatoes, milk, and all kinds of wild game. Occasionally there were biscuits made from wheat flour, and for sweets there was plenty of honey, which was obtained from the bees that hived in the trees. Hunting a bee tree was a hide-and-seek game with the youngsters. When the bees were making honey, they often were found at work getting water from a small spring or hovering around a blooming plum thicket. Sometimes a small piece of honeycomb was tied to a bush, and watch kept for the bees to put in an appearance. It was common knowledge that, as soon as a bee was loaded, it would make a straight flight or "bee line" for home. Watching the bees take off, the direction of their flight could be sighted and followed. Coming to a tree in the line of flight, the boys looked for incoming bees and for a hole that might be the entrance to the hive. Generally, the entrance could be spotted by the color of the bark around the hole; it was brownish in color and worn slick by the entering bees. When a hive was located, it was marked so it could easily be found when the time came to rob the hive. In season there were also wild fruits: grapes, plums, and blackberries.

Coffee was bought green and roasted at home in a Dutch oven, as one would roast peanuts. The roasted coffee was kept in a can or crock and ground as it was needed. Sometimes the coffee supply gave out; when this happened, corn was parched in the Dutch oven, and a small quantity of molasses added. This corn was then ground and used just as one uses coffee. During the food scarcities of the Civil War, other coffee substitutes ranged from parched wheat to roasted sweet potato peelings and even dried okra; these were all referred to as "Lincoln's coffee."[2]

Cornmeal was one of the principal items of food, and it was necessary to keep a supply on hand. Usually it was ground at Governor Hams's mill at Mill Creek, about thirty miles away. Sometimes during a long spell of bad weather, the wagons could not go to the mill, and it was necessary to use the hand mill that was fastened to a forked stump near the house. This was slow and tedious work that none of the children liked. Besides using the meal for food, it was used to make the lights last longer. These lights were made by filling a can with a mixture of cornmeal and lard or tallow. A twisted cotton rag served as a wick. The saturated cornmeal fed the oil to the wick slowly. The cornmeal was also used for cleaning chapped and dirty hands.

All of the soap was homemade. A hopper was built in the yard into which was poured all of the wood ashes. When soap was to be made, water was poured over the ashes, and the lye water that came out the bottom was caught in a bucket. To this was added pure tallow and then boiled, making a hard white soap that was used as a toilet soap. For washing clothes and for kitchen soap, old lard was added to the lye water, together with waste fat and drippings, to make a dark brown soap. The washing was always done in the open. The clothes were placed in a big iron kettle under which a fire was built. The clothes were then boiled, rinsed, and hung on wires to dry.

Occasionally the supply of salt ran out. When this happened, the farmhands went to the smokehouse and scraped up the dirt where salt had been used in curing meat. They poured water over this dirt and caught the water that seeped through. After the dirt had settled to the bottom, they poured off the water and boiled it down; this produced enough salt for table use until they got a new supply.

In those days doctors were few and far between, and home remedies were relied upon. Grandmother Campbell's former slave, Aunt Eliza, was doctor and nurse combined for most of their troubles. Montford's second son lived only a few months. After his death, his mother's breasts hurt so badly that it was necessary to drain off some of the milk. Since there was no baby available to place to her breasts, Aunt Eliza came up with a solution. One of their greyhounds had a litter of puppies. Aunt Eliza took one of the puppies,wrapped up its feet, and held him to the young mother's breasts, relieving the pain. The puppy was used as a breast pump until Mary's breasts become normal again. As the pup grew into a dog, the family teased her by saying that she was partial to him and always gave him the best scraps.

After they had lived at Camp Arbuckle for some time, Leford became very sick with a high fever, and Aunt Eliza, who was living on Walnut Creek at the time, was sent for. As a cure for fever, Aunt Eliza used the old remedy of cupping. She made a shallow incision on Leford's back where she wanted to draw the blood. Over this she placed the wide end of a cow's horn, the point of which had been sawed off to leave a small opening, like the opening of a powder horn. She put a small lump of beeswax into her mouth, and began sucking the air from the horn. As soon as the air was sucked out, she skillfully pressed the lump of beeswax over the opening with her tongue and sealed the horn. The base of the horn was held firmly against the child's back, creating a vacuum that pulled the blood from his body. After waiting a little while, Aunt Eliza unsealed the small end of the horn, and emptied out the blood. She repeated the operation until she had taken all the blood she thought the child dared lose. In Leford's case, the treatment did not prove successful and he died. During this resettlement period, the family lost its eldest member, Grandmother Campbell. Depressed and brokenhearted after the loss of three sons and the departure of her husband, Charles, early in the Civil War, she waited for news from him that apparently never came. She eventually lost hope, got sick, and died. They both were buried under a large oak tree a short distance southeast of the house.

The favorite remedy for a hacking cough was crushed horehound and rock candy mixed with whiskey. For a deep cold in the chest, the patient was given a hot foot bath and then put to bed, wearing over the chest a heated flannel cloth soaked in a mixture of lard, kerosene, and turpentine. Poultices made of tobacco or tobacco and earwax were used for insect bites and stings. Molasses and baking soda were used to soothe burns. For toothache, a small piece of tobacco was placed on the infected tooth, and a bag of hot ashes held against the jaw. Children undergoing this treatment often found their heads swimming as a result of swallowing some of the tobacco juice and became so sick that they claimed the tooth had stopped aching, so that they could quit the treatment. In extreme cases, the tooth was pulled with a small pair of pliers. In the spring everyone took a course of sulphur and molasses as a tonic. In later years, sassafras tea was popular as a means of thinning and purifying the blood.

The near neighbors of Montford's were the storekeeper, Phil Smith, and Dick Cuttle or Tuttle, a teamster. Phil had a small place about three or four miles northeast of Montford's, on the north side of the river, which may have served as Jesse's trading post before his death, although other reports say that Jesse used the former building of Chouteau's Trading Post, which was a few miles further east, north of present-day Lexington. Phil and Dick had worked for Jesse Chisholm, but with his death, Jesse's son, William ("Bill"), took over the store there by Camp Arbuckle (William was an intermarried Chickasaw). Jesse always kept his trading posts on the north side of the Canadian, out of the Chickasaw Nation.[3] This description would also fit with E. F. Beale's wagon road map of 1853, in the *Chronicles of Oklahoma*.[4] This store consisted of two cabins with a hall between them and was near the small cabins where the Indians traded their hides. In these cabins were stored the hides of buffalo, beaver, otter, deer, panther, and bear. The Indians traded these hides for the merchandise that the traders brought from Fort Smith, Arkansas.

The wagon trains of the traders were kept constantly on the road in order to keep the trading post stocked. Some of the trains were drawn by oxen, others by mules or horses. Extra animals, driven by a Mexican horse wrangler, were taken along for replacements. At noon and at night, the work animals were hobbled and allowed to graze. At least one saddle pony was staked close by the camp so that the stock could be rounded up. This rounding up was sometimes quite a job, for in a short time the horses and mules learned how to use the hobbles and could run short distances in them as well as they could without them. It would usually take Dick, accompanied by two or three men to help, between one and two months to make the round trip. There were established trails, but with no bridges yet built, so every stream, creek, and ravine had to be crossed carefully. Losing your flour, sugar, or other perishables in the river you were crossing was wholly unacceptable.

There was a Negro settlement west of the store about ten miles. Beyond this settlement a few miles lived a Cherokee Indian, Sampson Harom (Harmon). He was almost blind and was cared for by his good Chickasaw wife, known to all as Granny Vicey. To the east of Montford, down the South Canadian River, lived Jesse Chisholm's son, Bill, and his family. About twenty miles southeast lived Alec (Elick) Cochran, a Cherokee and his Chickasaw wife, Arnaca, on Spring Creek. Both Bill Chisholm and Alec Cochran had large families. They visited with Montford's family occasionally, staying two or three days at a time.

The Johnson homestead was on the western edge of this so-called civilized world, so most travelers called upon them before moving on. In October 1875 Father Isadore Robot and Brother Dominic Lambert arrived at the Johnsons' front door on their way to the Pottowatomie reservation. Montford's wife, Mary, who was herself a Catholic, was delighted to share their humble home with these two Benedictine Monks. They had recently arrived in Indian Territory after a long journey from France, via New Orleans, to Atoka. After staying the night with the Johnsons, the two monks traveled northeast across the South Canadian to the Bourbonnais's cabin, where they held the first Mass in the region. There they stayed a few days baptizing Indian children. It was during this first visit that many of the prominent men of the Pottawatomies expressed their strong support concerning the establishment of a permanent mission among them. Before 1876 had passed, the Sacred Heart Mission was established in this, the Pottawatomie district.[5]

As soon as Montford and his family were settled in their new home at Camp Arbuckle, and before the winter set in, he began his ranching operations. Since the cattle had not been branded in the spring, the first job was to round up and brand the cattle at Walnut Creek.

Notes

1. Cassal, Reverend Hilary. 1956. "Missionary Tour in the Chickasaw Nation." *Oklahoma Chronicles*, Oklahoma Historical Society. Vol. 34, p. 399.

2. Warde, Mary Jane. "Now the Wolf Has Come." *Chronicles of Oklahoma*, Oklahoma Historical Society. Vol. 71, no. 1, p. 79.
3. Strickland, Pat (Chisholm). Conversation in 1998.
4. Foreman, Grant. 1934. "Survey of a Wagon Road from Fort Smith to the Colorado River." *Chronicles of Oklahoma*, Oklahoma Historical Society. Vol. 12, p. 76.
5. Michalicka, Br. John. 1970. "First Catholic Church." *Chronicles of Oklahoma*, Oklahoma Historical Society. Vol. 50, p. 482.

Walnut Creek Ranch Trip

ontford's wife decided she would go along with him to Walnut Creek so that she could see the new ranch country. Since all of the family was eager to go and to visit their old nurse, Aunt Eliza, Montford made it a family party. There was no road and barely a trail, so all of the family rode horseback. Montford rode his big sorrel, Sambo; his wife rode a gentle horse called Rex. E. B. rode his little pony, and cousin C. B. rode his. Montford led an extra roan horse carrying a light pack of clothes and bedding. Nute Burney, Aunt Criss, and the other Negro farmhands were left at home with Grandmother Campbell and Aunt Adelaide to look after the household.

In the frosty morning twilight they started out, with the excited dogs jumping and barking at the horses' heads. By the middle of the morning they had passed through the Negro settlement, where they picked up some men to help brand the cattle. About noon they reached Granny Vicey's cabin. She insisted that they come in and have some of her "Tom Fulla" or "Tom Fuller," a dish for which she was famous. This Tom Fulla was much like soured hominy that had been mashed into a thick paste, then water was added for a more souplike texture. Another favorite was Pashofa, which was basically cracked corn cooked with pork and water. Since Granny insisted, they stayed for lunch, although there was food in the saddlebags. After lunch they rested and visited for about an hour.

Granny Vicey was very upset over the death of Jesse Chisholm, who had been a good friend to her and her late husband, Sampson. She told Montford that Jesse's death had upset their plans for her to take charge of his store on the west side of Council Grove, on the North Canadian River. Jesse had originally opened it in 1858, abandoned it during the Civil War, and reopened it after the war and had planned to built a larger one. She said that the logs for the store were already cut, ready and waiting out at Council Grove, about six miles west of what is now downtown Oklahoma City. (A historical marker now commemorates the spot just west of Tenth Street and Council Road, south of the Lake Overholser dam in Oklahoma City.) She had talked to Jesse's son, Bill, but he had refused to go on with the Council Grove store after his father's death. Granny wanted Montford to finance her so that she could build the store, but at that time he did not feel able to give her a definite answer.

As they went on across the prairie in the afternoon, the dogs loped on in the lead, flushing quail, prairie chickens, and wild turkeys. They sighted several bands of antelope, which started running so that they could pass in front of them. As they disappeared from sight, the last thing seen was a big white patch at their rear; sometimes an old buck would turn, give the travelers a final looking over, and then lope on off behind his band. Near the South Canadian River, as they were riding along a rocky hill, the four dogs began barking as they circled a small clump of rocks. They had cornered a rattlesnake, and by circling and barking they tried to get the snake to start moving so that they could kill it. They were careful not to get within a striking distance as long as the snake was coiled. Montford dismounted his horse and threw a rock; immediately there was an angry hissing sound, and the snake began crawling for his hole. That was the end of the snake. In a flash, the dogs grabbed, shook, and threw it into the air. As it hit the ground, another dog grabbed it and repeated the treatment until the snake was torn to shreds. Rattlesnakes were very common in that country, and because they were so poisonous, Montford kept a bottle of whiskey on hand, even though alcohol was not permitted in the Indian Nations. If a person were bitten, he tied the arm or leg tightly to keep the poison localized, while the victim drank whiskey until he became drunk. Enough whiskey in the system was believed to counteract the poison. The injured arm or leg was cut and allowed to bleed freely; if it could be had, indigo was mixed with water to form a poultice that was placed on the wound. This drew out the poison, which turned the indigo poultice white. New poultices were placed on the wound until the poultice ceased to change color.

Following along the river, there were some buffalo bulls in the riverbed pawing the sand and throwing it up over their heads, then casually strolling after the rest of the herd. They passed several prairie dog towns, some of which looked as if they covered about forty acres. The luxuriant buffalo grass was short, and small paths were worn between the mounds.

As they approached, the little reddish-brown prairie dogs, not much bigger than squirrels, ran for their holes. Standing on the heaped-up mounds around their holes, they held their bodies erect and let out little sharp yaps at passersby. Before being approached too closely, and before the greyhounds could catch them, they gave a final bark, twitched their tails, and disappeared into their holes. A few small burrowing owls, who lived in their holes near the prairie dogs, flew around, settled on top of the mounds, and twisted their heads around to look at Montford and his family. These holes were also quarters for rattlesnakes, making it a very democratic community.

Riding past a small blackjack grove, they startled a flock of blue jays whose sharp, harsh cries seemed to challenge the right to trespass on their territory. On the open stretches of prairie yellow-breasted meadowlarks sailed lazily out of the path. They also saw an awkward, loping grey badger slide into the safety of its burrow. Overhead, a long flight of glistening black crows extended for miles. A few broke from their course and chased a large hawk that had been floating majestically over them. The honking of geese and the swift flight of a few early ducks warned that winter was on its way. The leaves of the cottonwood trees were beginning to turn a bright yellow that, with the yellow flowers of the goldenrod, gave a splash of color to the landscape. Persimmons, a little larger than a plum, were turning light brown, but were still puckery to the taste and would not be sweet enough to eat until there was more frost.

Just before sundown Montford sighted Jack Brown's cabin, standing on a hill north of Walnut Creek; soon after, they rode into camp. For some time they were kept busy with a gang fight among the two sets of dogs, but they finally got them separated and tied up. Jack and Eliza had been expecting them for some time and were overjoyed. Eliza had reared Montford's wife and E. B. and had cared for all of the other children before she moved to Walnut Creek ranch. Everything was spotlessly clean, and after a delicious supper everyone went to bed. Jack and Eliza having given up their bed, slept on the floor in the other room. The extra hands, whom Montford had brought in from the settlement, unrolled their beds in the yard. For a while before going to bed, Montford and Jack planned the next day's branding.

After breakfast next morning, they went out to the corrals where the cattle had been penned the night before. Looking over the size of the job, Montford decided to turn out the cattle from one corral and let one man herd them. In the other corral, the upper bars of the section that served as a gate were removed, so that the older cattle could jump out. Since they were accustomed to being let out each morning, it was easy to let the cows and bulls jump over the lower bars and to keep the calves frightened back into the pen. As soon as the calves were all separated from their mothers, a fire was built in the corral with dead blackjack wood. This made an excellent bed of coals and kept the branding irons hot. Now they were ready to begin branding, starting with the smaller calves that the farmhands could flank. Once a calf was lassoed with a rope, one of the Negroes would work his way down the length of the taught rope, grabbing the calf by the left flank and foreleg, and flop it down on its right side. While one man held the calf's left foreleg and head, another sat on the ground at the calf's rear, caught the calf's left hind leg in his hands, placed his left foot against the hock of the calf's right leg, and shoved it forward as far as possible. The calf was then ready to be branded and marked. Montford branded them with the hookety-hook on the left side and hip, castrated the bull calves, and marked both ears by cutting a small curve out of the top of each ear. This was called a finger over slope of each ear.

E. B. carried the bucket with the dope in it to mop the calf's sack after he was cut. The dope, which was a mixture of tar, creosote, and grease, was applied with a swab and served as a sanitizing fly repellent. Every precaution had to be taken to keep flies away so as to avoid screw-worms getting into any fresh cut. The operation finished, the calf was turned loose and another one caught. Every fourth calf was branded LI on the left hip for Jack Brown. Jack always called his wife Lize instead of Eliza. The brand he decided on was the first two letters of her name according to his pronunciation and spelling. Jack's brand was put on every fourth calf, bull, or heifer branded, whichever it happened to be. His calves' ears were also earmarked with an underbit in the left ear and a swallow-fork on the right.

Some of the calves were too large to flank by hand, so Montford brought his horse, Sambo, into the corral, mounted him, and roped the calves. A large forked post had been placed solidly in the ground in the corral, the fork about as high from the ground as the back of the horse. He roped one of the big calves, rode to the post, threw the rope between the forks, and then dragged the calf up to the post and off the ground. The extra hands grabbed the calf, and flopped him on his side; then the same branding process was followed as on the smaller calves.

Usually four flankers worked at one time. They were relieved by others or changed places from time to time with someone who was performing a less strenuous task. Dust swirled in blinding clouds; the pungent smell of burned hair and seared flesh filled the noses of the flankers; there was a continuous clamor of lowing or mooing cattle and bawling calves. Piercing this din were the high-pitched voices of the flankers as they held the struggling calves, yelling for the "hot iron" or "dope boy." When the calves were turned loose, they were usually "on the prod,"

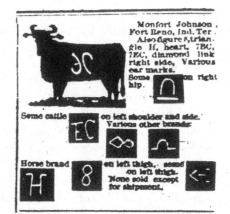

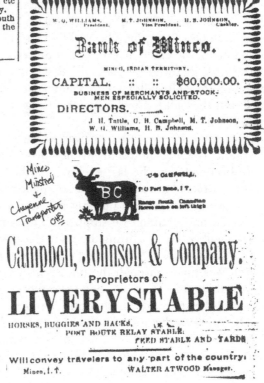

Cattle and horse brands and other newspaper ads. Left side and top right from the Cheyenne Transporter, *circa 1883–1885. Center right and lower right from the* Minco Minstrel, *circa 1891–1893. Courtesy, Oklahoma Historical Society, Newspaper Archives.*

and the flankers on the ground, engaged in holding another calf, were easy victims to attack. As the mad calf charged, someone usually kicked a spurt of dust in his face, and as he swerved irresolutely, he took one final angry kick with his two rear hooves at the straining cowboy on the ground. If this was followed by a resounding thump, grunt, groan, or a choice bit of profanity sounding through the dust cloud, you knew that the calf had hit its mark.

By the middle of the afternoon, Montford saw that they could not finish with this bunch in one day, and decided to turn them out to water and graze them until time came to pen them up for the night. All the cowhands caught their horses and rode outside the bunch of cows bawling around the fence. One of the men took the bars down, and the calves came rushing out. They had a few hard races with the calves, sometimes with a frantic cow in hot pursuit. But after they had held them a while, they began to mother up and were eased down to the creek to water. After watering them, they herded them while they grazed. When it was time to pen, the cattle that had been turned out early that morning were put in first, followed by the cattle that had been worked that day. After penning, they all rode back to Walnut Creek for a swim; the water was cold, but they all felt much better after getting rid of the dust that covered them.

For several days this plan was followed, turning out the cows and bulls and keeping the calves in the corral, until finally all of the calves were branded. On the last evening, as they were driving the cattle to water, an old blue roan became so angry and upset by the continuous bawling and the smell of burning hair and blood that he took off down the creek and couldn't be stopped. "Let him go," said Montford, "the wolves will get him." During the night there was the howling of a pack of wolves, and he said, "That is old roan's swan song." The next morning a search was made through the thicket in which the bull had hidden; all that could be found was his head and pieces of his hide. The wolves had eaten all the meat and carried off his bones.

Before they departed for the homeplace, Montford and Jack decided that something should be done to exterminate the wolves. Once back home at Camp Arbuckle, he purchased and prepared a large supply of ammunition to be taken back to Walnut. He intended to have one of the Negroes shoot wolves while the others herded cattle. He also purchased several bottles of strychnine to try poisoning them. Loaded with what he called "wolf bait," he returned to Walnut Creek ranch.

Next morning, after Montford's arrival, he held up a calf of inferior quality to butcher. He and his men roped and dragged it some distance from the corral and then killed it. Before they started out, they tied up all of Jack's dogs, so that they couldn't get any of the poisoned bait. After skinning the calf and rolling the paunch out on the ground, they cut off small pieces of the liver. Making a shallow incision in each piece, they shook in a small dose of strychnine and placed all of the pieces under the paunch. Three-quarters of the beef they hung in a tree. Jack carried on his horse the remaining quarter, and Montford dragged the fresh green hide, wet side down, along the grass. This trail was to make a lure leading to the paunch.

Arriving at a long valley northwest of the cabin, they tied ropes to the quarter of beef Jack had been carrying. Starting on one hillside and dragging the beef along the grass between them, they rode across the valley to the other hillside. Here they took up the beef and carried it about a quarter of a mile up the valley where they made another lateral across the valley. After making several of these laterals, which were to lead the wolves to the bait line, they cut a large number of small slices of beef, placed strychnine in the slices, folded them over, and ran little stakes through them. While Montford dragged what was left of the beef quarter down the center of the valley, Jack followed with the baits. At frequent intervals Jack dismounted and stuck one of the baited stakes in the ground. They extended the line all the way back to Walnut Creek, establishing a bait line several miles long. Carrying what was left of the beef, they went on home to await results. Sitting around the cabin after dark that evening, they heard the long, dismal, and hoarse howl of a lobo from the direction of the valley, and they felt sure that a wolf had picked up the scent of fresh blood. This howl was soon answered by others. Far off, they heard answering yelps, which indicated that other packs were out hunting. Anxiously they listened, waiting for the wolves to hit their bait lines. From the yelping, snarling, and fighting, they could almost tell when the first wolf fell over in convulsions as the poison took effect. This turmoil was caused by the other wolves jumping on and consuming their unfortunate companion. When the yelps came closer, Montford felt sure that they were getting results and turned in for the night.

Early next morning Montford and Jack hurried out to the paunch, which was the nearest bait, to see what had happened. At the paunch were five dead black wolves, and an enormous lobo staggering around almost blind. Montford shot him, and Jack held up the carcass so that he could measure him. He was about three feet tall. Going up the valley, they found many dead wolves strung along its length, some of them partly consumed by the rest of the pack. They picked up all the unconsumed baits so that the dogs wouldn't get them and returned to the cabin well satisfied with their venture. Similar bait lines were afterwards run in different directions from the camp. The later results were not so good as the first, but many wolves were killed. The others, not understanding exactly what was going on, but realizing, somehow, that it was a very unhealthy district for wolves, began to thin out and leave. They also shot wolves whenever they could get within range. Even if they did not hit them, the wolves were so badly frightened that they left the neighborhood.

When Montford returned to Camp Arbuckle, he ran bait lines there too, but with only mediocre success. There were too many people moving around through the country, or the wolves were too suspicious. In any event, the wolf population decreased so that it was no longer necessary to pen the livestock. At Walnut Creek, Jack rode line on them to hold them on their range and to keep the buffalo frightened to the north and west. After this first campaign, they still made it a point whenever a beef was killed to drag the paunch some distance from the point of skinning and to dope the liver, which was placed under the paunch. Also, if one of the riders found a dead animal a long distance from camp where the dogs would not be poisoned, he made small slits in the hide and placed poison in the openings.

Many years later the cowboys became so accustomed to using strychnine that they became careless and caused the death of at least one cowboy. In the April 30, 1885, issue of the *Cheyenne Transporter*, twenty-five-year-old William Stockwell, who worked for J. P. Baird on a ranch west of Fort Reno, suffered an attack of malaria. He was having chills and fever. Searching for some quinine, the boys found a bottle of medicine on the windowsill. The bottle was unmarked. Several of them, including Bill, tasted it; they all agreed from the bitter taste that it was quinine. They gave Bill a dose of it, and he soon began having strychnine convulsions. Although they did everything they could for him, he died some two hours later. In between convulsions he would ask the other cowboys to shoot him.

During the winter of this year, 1870, Montford laid out a field of fifty acres southeast of the house at Camp Arbuckle. When the ground was not frozen, one of the men plowed and broke out this field. Nute Burney and the other farmhands spent most of their working time during the winter cutting rails. Once the rails were cut and spring was on its way, the fence building began in earnest and took most of the summer to complete. When the ground became warm enough, a garden was planted, consisting of the usual varieties of greens, squash, beans, pumpkins, and other vegetables. When spring was farther advanced and the blackjacks began budding, they planted corn; a little later some watermelons and maize were put out. These fields were tended by workers under the direct supervision of Nute Burney.

When the green heads of grass started pushing up through the ground, Montford burned off several square miles of old dry grass around Camp

Arbuckle. While this burned country was growing fresh grass, the live-stock were taken across the creek to the west to graze on the yet un-burned grass. When the new grass became tall enough to pasture, the cattle were brought back to the new range, which they preferred, and the rest of the country was burned. After the country around Camp Arbuckle was burned, Montford went to Walnut Creek and set afire his range north of Walnut. The cattle were shoved south of the creek to feed on old grass. Since the ground was damp and the weather warm, it took only a few days for the grass to grow out, and then the cattle drifted back onto their own range again.

Every spring, as long as he lived, Montford continued this practice of burning his range. The old grass was needed to winter on because the cattle had to rustle for themselves. But there was so much country, and the grass grew so coarse and rank that it had to be burned to get rid of the old growth in order to make room for the new. The grass was so tall that oftentimes during the entire winter the cattle grazing in the bottoms could find green grass growing under the cover of the old grass. In a mild winter the cattle came through in fine shape and remained fat all winter. Besides helping the new grass, this burning of the old grass burned most of the old carcasses on the range and prevented the spreading of dis-eases. It also kept down the spread of ticks, which caused trouble to the ranchers whose ranges lay near the trails of the Texas herds. These Texas cattle scattered ticks wherever they passed.

In those hopeful days, each spring was a new year and a new start for everyone. This year Bill Chisholm decided to move the remnants of Jesse's store down the river to his home. He closed down his holdings at Camp Arbuckle and transferred Phil Smith and Dick Cuttle to his new location to run the store for him. These two men, who had worked for Jesse for so many years, did not care for Bill Chisholm and his manner of doing business. They came to Montford and suggested that he buy out Bill's interest in these buildings, set up his own store, and let them run it for him. Since Montford knew that they understood the intricacies of bargaining with the Indians and how to trade with them, he bought the cabins from Bill and hired Phil and Dick to run the store. After Montford purchased the cabins, he moved them about a mile south to get away from the dust of the stockade and trail.

This stockade had been built by Captain Marcy, who established Camp Arbuckle and wintered there in 1850. It was made of oak posts fourteen feet long, set four feet in the ground. The entrance had two taller posts rising about fourteen feet above the ground and tied together at the top by a log. Cattle drivers moving their stock north used this stockade as a corral for their cattle when they stopped at this point on the trail. After relocating his newly acquired cabins, Montford sent Dick Cuttle to Fort Smith, Arkansas, for a stock of merchandise, and, in addition now to his other cares, he had become a merchant.

A few years earlier, in 1866, the first herd of Texas cattle came along what was called the Shawnee Trail. They came from the south and bedded down near Henry Colbert's home on Hickory Creek. Henry and his son Joe worked the herd and cut out the cattle of their own that had drifted in with them. Leaving Colbert's, the herd grazed up the divide between Hickory and Henry House Creeks. They passed about eight miles west of Fort Arbuckle, crossed Wild Horse Creek, angled slightly northeast to the Washita, and crossed it about where Maysville is now located. They continued in the same direction to Camp Arbuckle. From there they headed north across the South Canadian River, near what is now Lexington, Oklahoma, thence up Chouteau Creek, which at that time ran north and south, then angled northeast to their shipping point at Chetopa, Kansas.

When the herds first used this trail, they were usually worked by Mexicans, who carried their bedding and chuck on packhorses. In May 1871 a party with chuck wagons and, for the most part, white men as herders came into the camp near the stockade. The herds ran about fifteen hundred to two thousand longhorn steers; there were no cattle that could be classed as Durhams or Herefords.

In the evening, Montford often rode over and visited with the men as they lounged around their campfires. He had some steers that were old enough to be sold and arranged with these men to buy them. He usually sold his steers when they were two years old and then delivered them to the buyers coming through the country the next spring as coming three-year-olds. Since the big steers rode down the stock cattle during the breeding season, Montford always got rid of them before they were old enough to give him any kind of trouble.

The Shawnee Trail was seldom used after 1870 because the herders dreaded crossing the eastern part of the Indian Territory. Even in this year, the last few herds headed north, angled a little west after crossing the South Canadian River, and crossed the North Canadian about ten miles east of Council Grove. This route was called the West Shawnee Trail and was a short distance east of the trail started in 1871, later known as the Chisholm Trail. Since this trail led for the most part through open country, the herders were able to protect themselves against the depredations of the Creeks, Seminoles, and Negro freedmen who levied tribute upon the herds as they passed through their country. The worst losses to the cattlemen came from the habit these Indians and Negroes had of providing for their own futures. Their favorite trick was to ambush and stampede the herds into the timber. The cowmen would be delayed several days trying to round up their cattle, but the Indians and Negroes shoved what cattle they could into another part of the country, where they kept them to eat at their leisure. It was no wonder that the cattlemen enjoyed the western movement of the cattle trails, but it also moved herds away from Montford and his store at what was becoming known as Johnsonville.

After selling his steers, Montford decided to round up his pigs and mark them before the fly season was too far advanced. Calling the four big yellow greyhounds, he headed for the timber where the hogs fed. These hogs were almost wild, of inferior quality, and most of them mule-footed. When they jumped them, the old sows and their pigs scattered like quail, but the dogs knew how to handle them. If an old sow bristled up in a thicket and tried to put up a fight, two big dogs would rush in and, each one grabbing her by an ear, would lead her out squealing like a spoiled child. The squealing of a caught hog rallied all the others in hearing distance to her defense. When the frothing-mad hogs appeared, the dogs, to save their own hides, turned loose and slipped to one side. They surrounded the bunch and kept them together until they cooled off, then drove them to the corrals. The pigs were cut away from the sows and run into a small pen where they could catch them; the sows were driven into the main corral. When they began marking the pigs, they squealed. And the old sows, frothing at the mouth and rearing upon their hind legs, looked as if they might climb over the top of the corral. After the pigs were marked and doped, they were turned loose to return to the timber. From the number of pigs gathered, they knew that they were going to have plenty of hog meat and lard the next winter.

At the end of May Montford rounded up his home bunch of cattle at Camp Arbuckle and Aunt Adelaide's cows and their calves. They cut out the Circle-A cows and branded their calves with the Circle-A for Aunt Adelaide. The rest of the herd were branded with a figure-eight brand and earmarked by cropping both ears and splitting the right. This was the brand and stock of cattle Montford had purchased from the Campbells.

After branding the home stock, Montford got ready to go to Walnut Creek. As she often did, his wife accompanied him and his crew, this time carrying with her the new baby born during the winter and named Henry Belton. She rode Old Henry, one of the workhorses, with a pillow placed across her lap and young H. B. on it. Nute Burney was left behind to watch and check the trail herds as they passed through their ranch.

The course taken to Walnut Creek was much the same as the one followed before. When they arrived at Granny Vicey's, they found that her blind husband had died and that she had buried him near her cabin. She claimed that there were evil spirits around the place and said she was afraid they would kill her as they had killed her husband. Again she urged Montford to put her in charge of a store at Council Grove. He put her off after assuring her that he would do something to help her.

At the Walnut Creek ranch, which they reached that night, they had a warm welcome. Aunt Eliza at once took charge of H. B., whom she had not seen since she assisted at his delivery. This year it was necessary to round up as well as brand the cattle. Dividing the range into sections of fifty or sixty square miles each, they moved everything in one section to the corrals. After branding the calves in that bunch, they were taken where they had been located and turned loose; the next day another section was rounded up. This process was continued until the whole range had been worked. Montford was pleased with the calf crop and found that the cattle were thriving in this new location. After all the cattle had been turned loose, one of the Negroes was sent out to ride line on the divide south of Walnut Creek and to keep the cattle on their home range by shoving them back when they attempted to drift south toward the Washita.

Adelaide Marries Jim Bond

Upon returning home, Aunt Adelaide told Montford that she had met and fallen in love with a trader and stockman named Jim Bond who had been stopping by to call on her rather often. He traded for horses and for anything else on which he could make a few dollars. Jim and Aunt Adelaide said they wanted to get married but did not know where to find a preacher. Montford didn't think too much of these hasty marriage plans, but told them there was an old Seminole Indian, John Jumper, living about twenty miles north of him who claimed to be some kind of an Indian preacher. Horses were saddled and Aunt Adelaide and Jim rode off to be married. After the ceremony they stayed overnight with one of Aunt Adelaide's friends, a Delaware Indian couple, John Deer and his wife, who lived a few miles south of present-day Asher on the north side of the river. Next day they returned home and began making plans for a house of their own.

The site for the new house was about two miles south and a little east of Montford's. With extra help from the Negro settlement, a small house was hastily thrown together, and as soon as it was completed the newlyweds moved in. Shortly after, Ella, Aunt Adelaide's daughter by her first marriage, went to live with her mother, but her son, C. B., refused to go. He bawled around several days, making a fool of himself, and swore he would kill Jim Bond when he got a little bigger. Needless to say, C. B. was still a very young man and was more jealous of this new man in his mother's life than anything else. In later years the two men became good friends and business partners as well. Aunt Adelaide's judgment was sound, for Uncle Jim Bond became one of the best citizens in the nation.

After Aunt Adelaide married, Montford settled up his business connections with her. He gave her fifteen head of cows and calves and some two-year-old beef steers, worth all told about eleven hundred dollars. Since she had lost most of her horses during foraging raids in the war, he gave her and the two children each three mares with their colts, and promised her that when C. B. and Ella were a little older he would start them a brand. C. B.'s brand was to be BC and Ella's EC with earmarks under the back of each ear.

Not long after Montford returned from the roundup at Walnut Creek, Alec Cochran came by for a visit, accompanied by a very dark-skinned Indian who addressed Montford as Cousin Montford. His name was Chub Moore, and he said he wanted to stay and work. This Chub Moore had some education, but he seemed to be showing off, and in a short time told everything he knew. Seeing that Montford had very little help, Moore suggested that he bring some of his orphan relatives to the ranch. These orphans, he said, were poorly clad, half-starved boys and girls who were being handed around from one relative to another. Montford told Chub he might bring a few of those orphans to help his wife with the children and lent him a pony to ride back to his settlement, where he could borrow a team and wagon. About two weeks later Chub returned with a wagonload. Two of the orphans, Frank Dwyer and Josephine Harris, seventeen, were almost grown; the younger ones were Lon, sixteen, and Lucinda Gray eleven; Sally (Thomas) Thompson, ten; and Henry, four or five, and Muggs McLish, about three. Montford's wife, who was usually equal to any emergency, was stunned. She did not know how or where she would bed them down for the night, let alone have them live with her. Finally, she decided to call on Aunt Adelaide to take some of them. Aunt Adelaide took Josephine Harris and Henry McLish, who were half brother and sister. Josephine had a sweetheart, William (Tode) Blevins, who came a short time later and persuaded her to marry him. They had two children before Tode was killed around 1874, allegedly by night riders. Josephine, a half sister of Robert M. Harris, governor of the Chickasaw Nation from 1896 to 1898, then married Charles Stewart in 1878. Somehow, all these children were thought to be related to Montford. All of these children were, arguably, offspring of Julia Tontubby, who had originally grown up in the Blue River bottomland just as Montford had. There is no way to prove the speculation that ties Julia to Montford's grandmother, Sallie Tarntubby (Tahnetubby or Tontubby). Julia had been married to Joseph D. Harris, John Thompson, and George Frazier McLish.[1] As a sidenote, polygamy was legal in Indian Territory until 1875.[2]

James Bond, circa 1890–1891. Photo by William J. Lenny and William L. Sawyers, Purcell, Indian Territory. Courtesy, Oklahoma Historical Society, #1623 OHS, Archives and Manuscripts Division.

Adelaide (Johnson) Bond, with sons, from left, Ed and Reford. Reford was a lawyer for the Chickasaw Nation in the early 1900s. Courtesy, Norma Jean Gambill.

Granny Vicey was also sent for. She was anxious to get away from her old homeplace and agreed to go into the ranching business with Montford. She took with her Lon and Lucinda Gray and Frank Dwyer. That left Sally Thompson, Muggs McLish, and Chub Moore to make their home with Montford and Mary.

The ranch for Granny Vicey was to be located at Council Grove. It was also referred to as Johnson's Grove by some of the old-timers.[3] Montford rode down to see Bill Chisholm and trade for the logs that had been cut at Council Grove. These logs were to be used in building a cabin for Granny Vicey and her late husband, but when Montford arrived at Council Grove he found that the logs had been burned. Granny, however, was so eager to get away from the evil spirits that she and the children moved to the new ranch site and lived in dugouts in the river bank until new logs were cut and the cabin built. The location of the house was a little over two miles east of Jesse Chisholm's old store, on the northwest corner of present-day Tenth Street and MacArthur (see map, Figure 8.4). This ranch crew of Vicey Herman (Harmon), Lon and Lucinda Gray, and Frank Dwyer, has been called the first permanent inhabitants of the Oklahoma City metropolitan district.[4] After building a cabin and corrals, Montford went back to Walnut to get livestock for the Council Grove ranch. He cut out fifty head of the oldest and best heifers, two milk cows, two of the best young bulls from his hookety-hook brand of cattle, and five ponies. These he branded with the flying H on the left side. Since he had caught several bands of wild horses and tamed them, he gave Granny a few mares and a stallion branded with the flying H on the left shoulder. The contract with Granny was the same as that made with Jack Brown at Walnut Creek; Granny was to take care of the stock and to receive every fourth calf and colt.

Since there was a fine grove of oak trees around Granny's new ranch, Montford agreed to build a hog corral in the grove and stock the place. One of the first thrilling adventures was the trip made when the hogs were taken to Granny Vicey's ranch. Montford had hired two men, Bill Barnett and Gus Leslie, white men who had wandered out to the Territory. Barnett went along to help with the hogs, and he was very entertaining. The wagon carried a small camping outfit and also some roasting ears to feed the herd of eight hogs and a boar. Since the weather was hot and dry, they went along the South Canadian River, to be closer to water much of the time. Just as they were crossing the river to head north toward Council Grove, a large Comanche hunting party came charging down from the south bank. As soon as Montford's crew sighted the Comanches, Barnett, who had flaming red hair, slipped under the bedding and wagon sheet, out of sight. A scalp of red hair was coveted by all Indians, and Bill had a dandy. E. B. took the lines and drove along

Granny Vicey Herman (Harmon), widowed by Sampson. Neil Kingsley Collection.

Map of Council Grove, by Ray Asplin, ©*1967. Reprinted from the* Chronicles of Oklahoma, *Oklahoma Historical Society, Oklahoma City, 1967.*

trying to look unconcerned until they caught up. Rushing up, the Comanches made a circle around the hogs and wagon. The frightened hogs had run under the wagon and stood facing the surrounding Indians. These hogs were the first the Indians had seen, and the mule-footed ones were peculiar-looking even as hogs. Most of them had wattles under their jowls. These wattles are small, teatlike growths hanging from either side of the throat. They are very small where they are attached, but spread out until they they are almost as large as a finger, and covered with long hair. A mule-footed hog with wattles looks like a narrow-faced old lady with long earbobs dangling to her shoulder.

Most of the Indians dismounted, made signs, laughed, and pointed at the wattles under the hogs' throats; some tried to imitate the grunting and squealing of the frightened hogs. After a short time that seemed like ages to E. B., Gus, and especially Bill, they remounted and, still laughing and pointing at the hogs, rode off in a high lope. Montford was really frightened because the Indians usually rummaged in the wagon for something to eat, and in working a white man, Montford had broken his word with the Plains Indians. When the Indians were out of sight, Bill crawled out dripping with sweat and pale as a ghost. "My heart was beating so loud, I was afraid it would knock a hole in the bottom of the wagon," he said. After that incident, Montford nicknamed him Comanche Bill, a name that stuck with him for the rest of his days. They reached Granny Vicey's without further adventure and penned the hogs in her corral. The ground, covered with acorns, was a hog's paradise. Granny had to keep the hogs penned and herded most of that year until the panthers and bears were cleaned out. After that, the hogs were turned loose in the grove, about three miles square, and kept themselves on the mast. When they moved to Silver City in 1878, this herd had grown so that Montford was able to get all his meat by slaughtering his share of these hogs at Council Grove.

During that summer, E. B.'s chief job was to protect the stock from fly bites, especially watching the horses and dogs and doctoring immediately any little scratch or sore to be found. The green-headed flies, which were the worst, were very fond of the dogs' tender ears. When these green-headed flies bit through the skin or found a sore, they laid their eggs in the wound and, in a short time a case of screwworms developed. The cattle, when they could reach the sores, often licked the worms out, but on most of the cattle and on the less expert horses, tar and cresylic ointment was used to protect the sores and keep the flies away.

The corn this autumn produced a bumper crop. After it was gathered, Montford and his men, not having much pressing work, spent part of their time catching wild horses. There were many wild-horse bands covering his range, and as he planned to raise and improve his own horses, he did not want the blood of the wild Spanish mustangs to be mixed with the band; but he often shot the old stallions running with the band, keeping the young ones and the mares. After castrating the young stallions, he put these young geldings and the mares with his tame horses. Very soon they could be driven and handled.

The most important job of the early winter was the butchering. Taking dogs and men, they rounded up the hogs as had been done in the spring. After they were penned, the hogs and pigs that had not been marked were worked on, then turned loose; the hogs to be butchered were put into another pen. Iron kettles full of water were set up and fires built under them. When the water was scalding hot, a hog was killed and immediately rolled into a vat full of scalding water. The scalding loosened the bristles, which were then scraped off, and the hog was then hung by the hind legs from a pole between two forked posts. They were washed off with cold water, split open, the entrails removed, and the carcasses allowed to hang overnight to cool out. Next morning the work of cutting up the hogs began. Everyone was busy. The hams, shoulders, and side meat were cut out and salted down in the smokehouse, where they remained until the meat was cured. The smaller and less choice pieces were ground up and made into sausage; seasoning was added and the sausage stuffed into small sacks which were hung in the smoke house. The fat was cut into small pieces to be cooked in the big iron kettles and rendered into lard. During the cooking the fat was stirred with large wooden paddles to keep it from sticking and burning. When the lard was rendered out, the crackling was strained off and the lard poured into ten-gallon cans that were stored in the dugout. When the hams, shoulders, and side meat were cured, they were removed from the salt, washed off with hot water, and hung in the smokehouse. A small smudge fire of oak and blackjack was built on the dirt floor and left to smolder for days. Since they always put up a supply to last a year, this hog killing, butchering, and curing lasted some time. By the time they were finished with the work, they were sick of the whole procedure. E. B.'s stomach was usually upset from eating too much of the crackling.

In the winter days that followed, Montford's wife, when she could find a little time, often got out a book and tried to teach C. B. and E. B. how to read and write. E. B. was a very apt pupil, but was more interested in the life that he was living in this wild Indian country. One adventure he had this winter is typical. Montford and E. B. went over to the Walnut Creek ranch to see how Jack Brown and Aunt Eliza were getting along. The night was very cold. After banking the fire in the large fireplace, they retired for the night. Shortly before midnight, Montford was awakened by the pounding noise of running horses. By the time he slipped on his clothes, ten cold Comanche Indians, returning from a raid, stamped into the room. They were taken aback at finding Montford there, but said that they were cold and hungry and would like to spend the rest of the night. Montford lighted a candle, raked the ashes off the coals, and rebuilt a blazing fire. Eliza and Jack were also awakened by all the commotion. Feeling better with Montford and E. B. there, Eliza got up and cooked some meat and brewed some coffee for the intruders. After they had finished eating and been warmed by the coffee and fire, the Comanches stretched out on the floor to spend the night.

Hog Harvest. Courtesy, Phyllis and Ron Murray.

When the first rooster crowed, the Indians were roused from their sleep. A few slipped out to investigate the strange noise, but returned in a short time. When it was light enough for them to see, they discovered that the source of the strange sound was one of Aunt Eliza's roosters, perched on the rail fence, crowing and flapping his wings. The Indians laughed, flapped their arms, and tried to imitate his crowing. When he stopped, they jumped at him, hoping to make him crow some more. The frightened rooster flew down off the fence. When the Indians saw his beautiful plumage, they took after him, and after a wild chase, caught him. They plucked all his best feathers for hair decorations. When they finally dropped him to the ground, he was, indeed, a sad-looking creature.

About this time, Jack Brown's hogs sauntered up for their morning swill. The Indians circled around them and tried to catch them, but the hogs broke through and made for the brush. As they disappeared, the Indians laughed again and entertained each other with their attempts to imitate the oink-oink of the frightened hogs. Aunt Eliza called them into the house and fed them again, whereupon they mounted their ponies and headed toward their reservation. Their hosts sighed with relief at their departure.

The following year, 1871, there was another group of Indians that rode up to the Walnut Creek ranch. This was a small band of Kiowas, including squaws and children as well as the braves. They had been hunting, but had come too far south and had very little luck. The buffalo hides that they had were rolled up on the dragging poles, which were tied to the sides of the saddles. Their household equipment and utensils hung from the saddles and on the crosspiece that held the dragging poles together. They complained about their unsuccessful hunt and said that they were hungry and that they would like to have a beef. Near the corral was an old blue cow that had a small lump on her jaw and Montford told them that they could butcher her. Several of them mounted their ponies and took after the cow. Riding up to her side, they placed arrows to their bows and shot her. The cow stumbled and fell to the ground. The squaws, who usually did the skinning, ran to her, and one of them, with her long knife, cut the cow's jugular vein, making a very small incision. The whole band, braves, squaws and children swarmed around and caught, in their cupped hands, the blood as it spurted out. As soon as one filled their cupped hands, they backed away and sucked the warm blood, while another took their place.

When the bleeding stopped, the squaws jerked out their knives and began skinning. While cutting the hide loose, they kept it spread out on the ground under the beef. After skinning her, one of the squaws opened the cow down the middle, then cut from the breastbone downward along the rib to the backbone. Then several of them, working together, rolled the paunch and entrails out on the hide. The intestines and ribbons came out last. The squaws cut off small pieces of these guts and handed them to the Indians who were crowded around the beef. Holding a piece of the gut in one hand, an Indian would grasp it close to the top with the fingers of their other hand. Pressing firmly with their fingers, they pulled the gut through them, thus cleaning the gut of any refuse on the inside. After cleaning the gut in this fashion, the Indians stood around and chewed on this raw gut while it was still warm.

Montford began laughing at a young squaw who stood nearby, chewing hungrily. She looked up angrily and her eyes flashed. Seeing her draw back her arm to throw the gut, Montford turned to run. He had just attracted the attention of the band when the squaw, chasing him, swung the gut twice around her head and threw it like a lariat. Her aim was good. The gut rapped around Montford's neck like a tie. All the Indians whooped and yelled with delight. Montford stopped, grinned rather sheepishly, unwound the slick thing from his neck, waved at them, and took off for the house. Arriving there, he found Aunt Eliza busy hiding everything eatable, because she had become accustomed to these hungry Indians dropping by and begging for everything in sight. After quartering the beef, the Indians loaded the pieces on their horses and rode off to a camping ground along Walnut Creek. Their flickering fires could be seen as darkness settled down in the valley.

The eating of the entrails was not unusual. E. B. learned many years later that the Indians, who lived mostly on meat, required the vitamins that are found in the lining of the digestive tract and are destroyed by cooking. Although Montford was amused at the manner in which the Indians ate the raw guts, he usually had a stew made from the "ribbons," pieces of liver, heart, and vegetables when they butchered a beef. The cooks in charge of the chuck wagon always cooked such a stew. In polite circles this stew was known as "Son of a Gun."

As E. B. grew older, he said he never saw his father turn down a request from an Indian who was hungry. Montford would just turn to E. B. and say, " Edward, go get them a beef." E. B. felt that this was a primary reason behind Montford's good standing and long term friendship with all the other Indians.

Several other stories and incidents that made a lasting impression on E. B. happened that year. One was the adventure of Lon Gray, the orphan who went to live with Granny Vicey at her new ranch on the North Canadian River. Lon was a very fine hunter and spent much of his time cleaning out the bears and panthers in the big oak grove and along the river. One day, on his way home from a hunting trip, he saw a small, young black bear on the trail ahead of him. Hoping to catch the cub alive, Lon took after him and ran him up a tree. In his excitement he thought nothing of the cub's mother, but dismounted and started climbing the tree. The cub screamed and squealed like a baby and, before Lon had reached the first limb, the cub's mother came running, growling and gnashing her teeth. Lon jumped down, and as she charged him, he jumped around to the other side of the tree. Round and round the tree they went, the cub screaming, the bear roaring, and Lon running for his life. Lon's horse was grazing a short distance away and looked up as an interested spectator of this race that would shortly come to an end. Although tall and a good athlete, Lon was becoming winded. He decided to make a break for his horse. As he came around to that side of the tree, he sprinted away and was going so fast that he ran past his horse, but seeing that he was not followed, he turned back, mounted, and rode away. The old bear had made no move to follow him, but was going after the screaming cub. Lon was so frightened that he never thought about his rifle resting in his scabbard on his saddle until he was almost home.

Bulldogging is a favorite attraction of the modern rodeos. The earliest account of bulldogging was told by Bob Curtis, one of Montford's neighbors, who lived in the Caddo country. As he told it, he thought that he had done a very foolish stunt. He was riding one of his race fillies on the prairies when he jumped a single buck antelope. Taking after it with the filly running at full speed, he reached down and, grabbing the antelope by the head and neck, slid from the filly, and landed on the back of the running antelope. First he and then the antelope was on top as the antelope pitched, hooked, and stamped, but Bob hung on. When they were both about winded, Bob managed to pull his dirk and cut the antelope's throat. Although he had successfully bulldogged the antelope, he found it to be expensive fun because, after the tussle was over, he found his filly standing nearby with a broken leg.

From this year also comes the story of the adventure with a cookstove. A peddler came by the store and traded Montford a cookstove. The peddler said that cooking on fireplaces was out-of-date and that most white people were cooking on stoves. Montford told the peddler to take the stove over to his house and set it up. When the peddler arrived with the stove, Mary, Montford's wife, was so angry at Montford for squandering money on what she thought was a foolish contraption that she did not listen to the peddler and would not let him install it in the kitchen. When Montford returned home, his wife said, "I have always cooked on good hot coals in an open fireplace, and if you do not like my cooking, Montford Johnson, you can eat somewhere else." He closed the incident by having the farmhands carry the stove to the smokehouse for storage. Some days later, while Montford was gone for the day, Mary became conscience-stricken and told the Negroes to get the stove and set it up. One of them claimed that he knew how to install the machine and how to work it. With the children standing around watching, he managed to get it put up, then shoveled some hot coals from the fireplace and carefully placed them in the oven. He put on some sticks of wood and, fanning the coals with his hat, got the wood burning. Then he closed the oven door. Smoke began to puff out from everywhere, and the stove looked as if it was going to explode. As the cabin filled with smoke everyone rushed outside, with smoke pouring out after them. Mary ordered the farmhand to go back and put out the fire, but he said, "No suh! Mrs. Johnson, this nigger ain't ready to die yet. I's afraid it will explode and kill a good nigger." Not wanting to lose her house, she threatened him with a club, and at last he went in with a bucket of water, opened the oven door, and threw the water on the smoldering fire, which had, by this time, almost smothered itself out.

When Montford rode in that evening the children rushed out to tell him of their narrow escape. He roared with laughter, which was unusual with him, because he seldom showed much emotion. The peddler had explained to him how the stove worked; so, leaving the rest of the family outside, he went into the kitchen and built the fire in the firebox, where it belonged. Soon the fire was roaring away. Mary was still very prejudiced against the stove and seldom cooked on it. Sometimes she used it for heating water, but for preparing the meals, she continued to use the fireplace.

Notes

1. Blair, Naldia. 1997. *Pioneers of Chickasaw Nation, Indian Territory*, vol. II, edited by Nova A. Lemons. Miami, OK: Timberceek Ltd., p. 395.
2. Grady County Genealogical Society. Vol. 5, summer 1989.
3. Asplin, Ray. 1967. "A History of Council Grove." *Chronicles of Oklahoma*, Oklahoma Historical Society. Vol. 45, pp. 433–451.
4. Van Zandt, Howard F. 1935. "History of Camp Holmes and Chouteau's Trading Post." *Chronicles of Oklahoma*, Oklahoma Historical Society. Vol. 13, p. 329.

Chickasaw Renter

9

The year 1872 marks the beginning of a number of changes in the way of life of the family. In the spring of that year, a Texan, O. T. White, and his two sons came up the Shawnee Trail with a herd of one hundred cows and six bulls. Most of the Texas herds by this time were taking the Chisholm Trail, farther west, to Kansas, but the Whites were not headed to market; they were grazing their cattle through the country and looking for a place to locate. White, during one of his visits to the store, worked up a trade with Montford. He sold him all his cattle except five cows and one bull. In addition, White made an arrangement with Montford and leased five hundred acres of land. White was to fence this tract, build a cabin on it, and break the land for cultivation. In return for his labor, he had the use of this land free for ten years; at the end of that time, this tract and improvements reverted to the use and benefit of Montford. The Chickasaw tribe owned the fee simple title to all the land granted to them by the government. This land was held in common by the tribe, and any Chickasaw Indian could use as much of it as he wanted so long as he did not encroach on the holdings used by some other member of the tribe. About the only restriction was that the land could not be sold, mortgaged, or the title passed in any way. Montford established the boundaries for his ranges, and the land included in the ranges was under his control. Although he could not sell the land, he could lease it and vouch for the lessee. This area of Montford's range later became known as the Cushman Farm; it was located south and east of the mouth of Walnut Creek, where it emptied into the South Canadian

River. It was about three miles northeast of the present town of Wayne, Oklahoma.

Nute Burney, another former slave, had long been envious of Jack Brown's position as Montford's partner in the ranching business. When Granny Vicey was started on her ranching position at Council Grove, Nute became all the more insistent on getting his own place. Now that Montford had bought the White cattle and brand, Nute persuaded him to let him start a ranch. He selected a range on Pond Creek, a little southeast of present-day Newcastle, which was about halfway between the ranges of Jack Brown and Granny Vicey. This creek got its name from the large pond that was formed by a big beaver dam. The water was backed up the creek about a mile. In the middle of the pond was an island that was made by the beavers for their home. Sometimes in the evening they could see the beavers swimming around in the lake. The water was very clear because of the heavy moss that, in many places, grew to the top of the water. This moss caught and held all the silt that flowed into the lake. Old trees and bushes, deadened by the water, stood in the lake, which resembled a forest that had been swept by fire.

During the early summer Nute got together a crew of Negroes to help him build a cabin and corrals. The cabin was made of blackjack logs, and the corrals of long poles. Both were located just north of the beaver pond. Later in the fall when Nute returned after completing his construction, Montford arranged for a crew, rigged up a chuck wagon, and headed up the Shawnee Trail toward Nute's range. They turned west from the Shawnee Trail at a point near the present site of Norman. In the middle of the afternoon, Montford sighted an Indian lookout stationed on a hill overlooking the South Canadian River bottom. Pushing the herd to this hill [most likely where West Robinson Street peaks in elevation in between Thirty-Sixth Street and Forty-Eighth Street in Norman– *C.N.K.*] where they could see the river bottom, there was an enormous Comanche Indian camp. Montford estimated there to be over five thousand Indians camped down in what he referred to as the Ten Mile Flats. The tepees, made of buffalo skins, were scattered along the banks of a small creek. Montford stopped the herd, and they just sat there on their horses and took in the scene. They could see little puffs of smoke floating out of these cone-shaped lodges. Several large bands of horses were grazing on the nearby flats. The horses were herded by Indian boys. One very large group of Indians was assembled on the flat several hundred yards from the creek. A few appeared to be mounted, but most of them were just milling around on foot.

Montford waved to his son, E. B., to join him. The two of them rode over to the crowd to see what this group of Indians was doing. When Montford rode up he held up his hands and grunted "Chokma" and began talking to some of the Indians by sign language. He turned to his son and explained to him that the Indians were on a buffalo hunt and were just resting and running horse races. They rode over toward the finish line, and Montford greeted many of his Indian friends. They were betting piles of buffalo hides for the next race. The backers of the different horses continued piling on hide after hide until the betting was finished. The horses to be raced were brought out and mounted by young Indian boys, who appeared to be about ten years old. They were the jockeys. They all rode bareback. Many did not even have bridles, but merely used a strip of rawhide that was looped over the lower jaw of the horse. After mounting, the boys rode along with the starter up the flat about half a mile, along a track that had been made by trampling down the grass with the horse herd. The horses lined up at the starting point, then they heard the faint echo of the starting drum, and they were off. A few of the horses flew the track with their young riders and ran full speed into the horse herds, which were grazing to one side. Most of them, however, stayed in the race and pounded down to the finish line, with the Indians yelling for their favorites. The backer of the winning horse took possession of the pile of hides and began looking for betters for the next race. These Indians loved fast horses and, with the races and with the excitement of betting, were having a grand time.

After watching the races for some time and visiting with the Indians, Montford and E. B. headed back to join their cow herd, which was watering along the creek. Before they left, the Indians urged them to return that evening for some big dances. As they passed near the Indian lodges, they were challenged by the loud barking of a horde of mongrel dogs. At the camp the squaws were busy preparing and curing the buffalo meat. The older squaws were in charge of cutting the meat into long strips, which they handed to young girls to hang over some small poles. They were not following the usual method of curing the jerked meat in the sun, but instead were hurrying the process by fire. A frame was made of forked sticks that were stuck in the ground at four corners, and connected by light, green willow poles. On these were placed a crisscross pattern of small green sticks, forming a network to hold the meat. The meat was placed on these sticks, where it dried in the sun or cooked over a smouldering bed of coals in a shallow pit under the frame. The method was somewhat like the modern one of barbecuing.

Other squaws were scraping the meat and tallow from the buffalo hides, which were stretched out and pegged to the ground. One squaw was marking off lariats on a freshly cleaned hide. With a stick of charcoal she began a line on the outside of the hide and continued it, around and around, and worked toward the middle. After the pattern was marked, she took a sharp knife and cut a strip about an inch wide until she had a

length sufficient for a lariat. Montford told his son, E. B., that after the
strips were cut, they would be stretched between two trees to dry. After
the drying they would be boiled in tallow until the strip became saturated with fat; this kept them soft and pliable. Montford followed a similar
method at home in making rawhide ropes, except that they cut narrower
strips, removed the hair, and then plaited the strips to make a round
strong rope.

At the camp that evening, Nute Burney declined Montford's invitation to go with him to see the dances. In declining Nute said, "No, Suh!
I don't want to see them. They look wild enough as it is from here,
without seeing them with scalps tied to their belts." Montford and E. B.
hurried through supper, and after giving some instructions on guarding
the camp and herd that night, they rushed back to the Indian camp,
where they had been promised by some of the chiefs that they would
see, all in one evening, war, medicine, and scalp dances. They expected
some warriors in with some fresh scalps that evening. When they arrived
at the Indian camp and big bonfire, the tom-toms were already beating
and many of the squaws and children were dancing. As the rhythm got
faster, they began to whoop and yell. As the young Indian youths began
to join in the dancing, the squaws and children dropped out. The stamp-
ing of their moccasined feet was so fast that the dancers seemed to be
floating on air. Suddenly the cadence of the chanters and the tom-toms
changed, and the dancers swung into the medicine dance. After some
time an old chief arose, called out something in Comanche that Montford
could not understand, but the youths faded away, and the returned warriors, decked out in their war bonnets and finery, came into the ring.
Their faces were painted in many colors, making their features grotesque.
A mighty whoop went up from the Indians that seemed to shake the
whole valley. Scalp locks, some fresh and some dried, hung from their
belts. E. B. could feel his own hair stand on end at the sight. When the
warriors danced close to him, a nauseating smell or stench hit him in the
face. He could not tell from whence it came, the scalps or the warriors
themselves. It was a spectacle that he was never to forget. While the
dances were still going on at a rapid pace, Montford and his son mounted
their horses and rode back to their own camp. They could still hear the
drums and went to sleep with the weird rumble of the tom-toms still
pounding their ears.

The next morning the Indians departed, leaving behind only their
refuse and the circling buzzards to clean it up. That same morning
Montford, E. B., and their cowboys crossed the South Canadian River
and by midmorning arrived at Nute's cabin and corrals. They permitted
the cattle to graze that afternoon and then penned them in Nute's corrals
for the night. Next morning they began branding. All the cows and calves

were branded with a diamond link. The cows to be branded were roped by the heels and dragged down on their haunches, then one of the men would grab the cow by the tail and jerk her over on her side. The small calves were branded in the customary manner. The agreement with Nute was that in the future he was to have every fourth calf, which was to be branded a seventy-four bar.

On their return journey, besides the Comanches, they met some more of their Indian neighbors, who had been moved from Kansas in 1867 in accordance with the Treaty of 1866. The Sacs and Foxes, Shawnees, Pottawatomies, and Iowas were placed on a reservation extending westward from the Seminole Nation to the Indian meridian and bounded on the north and south by the two Canadian Rivers. This placed the Pottawatomies just north and a little east of their homeplace at Camp Arbuckle. One of the Pottawatomies they met was riding a large gray Norman stallion. After a lot of bickering and sign language, Montford traded several of his cow horses for this stallion. The Indian agreed to deliver him at Camp Arbuckle headquarters after their return home from the ranch on Pond Creek. This horse proved to be an excellent breeder and improved the quality of his stock.

In June 1872 Montford certified that Mary, Don, and Henry B. Courtney were hired to work for him.[1] In those Pickens County records, Montford was referred to as "Mumford Johnston"; he would not know how to spell his name until his father reappeared in 1877. It is not known whether or not these were kinfolks of his late mother's family.

The next spring, 1873, they had three ranches to work, and with the increase in their cattle, Montford had to employ a much larger crew to help round up and brand them. Regular camping equipment and a chuck wagon were assembled at the homeplace, which they worked first. The crew then worked the Walnut Creek ranch and later moved up to the Pond Creek ranch. At the Pond Creek encampment by the corrals near the beaver pond, they found that the water moccasins were about to overrun the place. There seemed to be millions of these green slimy snakes crawling over the sticks in the beaver dam, and later in the day when the sun got hot, they moved from the water to the poles that made up the corrals. There they stretched out and took their sunbaths. All during the branding there, the cowhands had these snakes for an audience, which kept everyone on edge and away from the fences. Fortunately no one was bitten, but Montford instructed Nute to change his headquarters as soon as possible. That fall, after building new corrals, Nute moved his cabins northwest about a mile further up Pond Creek. The snakes could have that area to themselves.

This same year Montford started improving his cattle by importing some bulls from Kansas. Ted Bond, who was also in the cattle business in

Kansas and a brother of Uncle Jim Bond, came down for a visit. Ted was much impressed with the grazing lands, but thought that their local cattle were cold-blooded and inbred. He promised when he returned to Kansas that he would purchase some improved bulls and that he would deliver them in the early winter after the fever-tick season was over. As promised, Ted delivered to Montford three wagonloads of livestock: two red roans, three dark red Durham bulls, and a Berkshire boar. Montford kept the boar penned at the homeplace and bred him to a few sows that stayed close to home. This way he kept the boar safe from the wild boars that ran and lived in the woods. Since the roan bulls came from fine milk stock, Montford kept one of them at the homeplace, and after the others became acclimated, he scattered the others at the different ranches and began the process of improving the quality of cattle he produced.

Ted and Uncle Jim Bond accompanied Montford while he delivered these bulls to the different ranches. The night that they arrived at the Council Grove ranch they heard the bloodcurdling scream of a panther. It sounded as if some woman was screaming in deadly terror. Ted was frightened at first, but when they explained the situation to him, he replied that he would like to kill a panther. To please Ted and to repay him for bringing the bulls, Montford decided to celebrate and take him on a hunt.

The orphan boy, Lon Gray, who lived with Granny Vicey, had become an excellent hunter and had already cleaned out most of the panther and bear in the grove, but there were still plenty of both along the North Canadian River. Next morning they saddled their horses and, led by Lon and his dogs, headed for the river. Shortly after the party reached the river bottom, the dogs jumped a panther. After a brief run, the dogs ran the panther up a large cottonwood tree that stood in a dense briar thicket. The leaves, bright yellow from the frost, were still on the tree and made excellent cover for the animal. Ted was very excited, and they yielded to him the privilege of making the kill. Lon took Ted in charge and led him around the thicket to a spot where he could point out the panther to him and help him get a clear shot. Ted sighted the panther all right, and Lon told him to shoot. Ted aimed and fired, but he was so nervous that he just wounded the panther, which let out a scream as it was hit and began stumbling and jumping out of the tree. They got glimpses of him in the briar thicket, but were unable to get a clear shot. When the panther hit the ground, the dogs rushed into the thicket after him. As they closed in, the panther lashed out with his sharp claws and cut deep gashes in their bodies. Lon had raised and trained these dogs and, like any good hunter, waded into the briar thicket to help them. There was so much confusion and noise, with the animals partially obscured by the thicket, that Lon could not shoot his rifle without running the risk of shooting a dog. Finally he grabbed the panther by the tail with one hand, and with dogs helping, hanging on each side of the beast, he drew his pistol and shot the panther through the back of the head. The rest of them moved in and helped drag the panther out. When they stretched him out, he measured ten feet from the tip of his nose to the end of his tail.

The dogs were cut up, but not badly enough to stop the hunt. So, after hanging the panther up in a tree, they continued with the hunt. Before the day was over, they got another panther and two bears, all of which they carried back to Granny's camp. At supper that evening, Ted told them how he was going to brag about killing his panther when he returned home. He did not realize he had made a very poor shot that had made Lon take such a chance in protecting his dogs. No one said anything to dampen his enthusiasm, but they all knew that they had had enough panther hunting with a greenhorn.

Note

1. Permits to Non-Citizens, Chickasaws (Pickens County). Microfilm, CKN 18, vol. 3, 14, 5. Oklahoma Historical Society, Archives and Manuscripts Division, Section X.

Charley Campbell Becomes Partner

fter returning from the Council Grove ranch in the fall of 1873, they had another visitor, Uncle Charley Campbell, who had been run ning a hotel in Tishomingo. While visiting, he accompanied Montford on a trip to the Walnut Creek ranch. When they arrived there Aunt Eliza was in tears, because her husband, Jack Brown, had been gone several days. Montford waited until he returned and when he came in, he looked as if he had been on a big drunken spree. By questioning Jack and Aunt Eliza, Montford found out that he had been running with some of his old Negro friends down south on Wild Horse Creek. Aunt Eliza said that Jack often went down there and stayed drunk for a week. The trouble seemed that Jack did not have enough to do. He did not have to pen his cattle any longer, and he had boys to ride line for him. His portion of their cattle business was beginning to get rather large and, like many others unequipped for success, Jack did not seem able to stand his new found prosperity. Montford told Jack that he had been partner with him long enough and that Jack had so many cattle of his own, he had better locate him a new ranch and be independent.

Uncle Charley had listened in on all the talking and when he learned the number of cattle Jack was going to receive, he got ranch fever and urged Montford to let him take over the Walnut Creek ranch. Montford finally promised him the place, provided he got rid of his hotel and brought in help that would not be objectionable to the wild Indians. Although Uncle Charley was related to Montford by marriage and was an intermarried Chickasaw, Montford hesitated for him to take charge of the ranch because he was a white man and did not have much ranching experience. At this particular time there was considerable unrest among the Plains Indians and trouble could easily break out at any moment.

In spite of this, Uncle Charley returned to Tishomingo and four weeks later came back to Camp Arbuckle with a train of wagons loaded with all his belongings. Since Montford did not have room for him, they built a new cabin about two miles southwest, where Uncle Charley spent the winter.

That winter Frank Dwyer, one of the orphan children that Granny Vicey had taken at Council Grove, took pneumonia and died. Granny was so afraid of evil spirits of the dead that she would not permit Frank to be buried at Council Grove and made Lon haul his body some fifty miles back to Montford's house at Camp Arbuckle. They buried him in a small plot where Montford's son, Leford, lay and enlarged the picket fence to include both graves. As the years passed, Montford moved away, the picket fence rotted down, and the large oak tree that was a marker died and was cut down. Now, with their locations unknown, these two dear boys rest deep in the ground while above them teams of horses and tractors have worked these fertile fields through a rotation of crops for more than a century.

Although the unrest among the Indians was increasing, Uncle Charley moved in and took charge of the Walnut Creek ranch in the spring of 1874. The cattle were rounded up, and all those bearing the Lize brand were cut out for Jack Brown. Jack moved his herd of about six hundred head southeast to a new place near the present town of Wayne, Oklahoma. This later was known as the Stovall place. After Uncle Charley took charge, he built a new cabin on the west side of the blackjack grove. He decided to do some farming and hired the Suttons, a father and two sons, to split cedar rails to fence his fields. They set up a camp near the present town of Noble and cut about ten thousand rails for the fence. [Jack Brown later bought back his old place from Charley, apparently living out his life there. He died November 21, 1895, at the age of seventy; his tombstone still remains on the property.–C.N.K.]

For help, Uncle Charley hired a few Negroes and white men. A young Arkansas boy, Mark L. Brittain, was placed in a dugout camp near a spring on the east bank of the South Canadian River. His job was to keep the cattle that drifted across the river from the Walnut Creek ranch thrown back west so that they would not wander into the Pottawatomie country. He also checked any trail herds that came up the Shawnee Trail.

Near the spring where Brittain had his camp was a large elm tree. The bark had been cut from it on one side and the name "Norman's Camp" had been burned in it with a hot iron. This name had been given to the spot by a government surveyor named Abner Norman, who had been sent out to survey land west of the Indian meridian back in November 1872. Montford had met and befriended Norman's crew when they were camped at a spring southwest of his Camp Arbuckle or Johnsonville ranch as they worked their way north from the initial point a short distance south of Fort Arbuckle. A few years later, in 1880, when the Santa Fe Railroad surveying party came through the country working out the right-of-way, E. B. met them camped on Little River to the east. This was off of their route, and they asked E. B. if he knew where they could find a suitable spring for a camp. He told the party about this spring and they moved their camp to the new site. After the railroad was built, a section house was built near the spring, where E. B. and his cowhands often stopped for delicious, homemade fifty-cent meals. It sure beat heating up a can of beans at the dugout. Sometime later, a boxcar with "Norman" printed on the sides was placed nearby to serve as a temporary station. When E. B. asked the Santa Fe agent where they got the name for the station, he was told that it was taken from the elm tree marking the spring. As the years passed and a town grew up around the station, it took the same name. E. B. would move his family to this town, Norman, in 1898 and live there the rest of his life.

Since E. B. and his cousin, C. B., had dogged Montford's footsteps ever since they were able to ride, they were both very good cowhands, but had very little book learning. In 1874 E. B. was eleven years old and knew little more than the alphabet and his numbers, which his mother had taught him and C. B. Several times Montford had tried to enroll the two boys in the Manual Training School at Tishomingo, where he had gone to school, but this school was reserved for full-blooded Chickasaw boys. By 1874, Fort Sill had become a large frontier fort, and many of the soldiers had moved their families to the post. For the children of these families, the government established its own school.

The summer of 1874 was very hot and dry. There was little to be done but watch the pastures and fields burn up, so Montford, hearing about this government school, rode over to Fort Sill to try and make arrangements for the boys to go to school. While he was gone, the boys kept up the chores around the homeplace and struggled to keep cool. Each morning the run rose in a light blue, cloudless sky, and by midmorning the constant wind was scorching hot. Often in the afternoon a few white clouds appeared, but soon disappeared below the horizon without bringing any shade or rain. The grass was dry as cut hay and covered with dust. The baked ground opened in large cracks. The grasshoppers ate many of the leaves off the trees, the blades from the corn, and even much of the grass. One of E. B. and C. B.'s chores was to roll the wagon wheels into holes of water in the creek to soak up the spokes and rims so that they would hold together. They washed saddle blankets to remove the sweat and salt that, if allowed to harden, rubbed galls on the backs of the horses. Even the hair on the horses was sunburned and lost its gloss. Chinch bugs migrated from the dry grass into the fields and assisted in the destruction of the crops. More and more buzzards floated lazily in the sky and occasionally swooped down to feast on the dead animals that they helped devour before the screwworms took charge. Everyone slept on the ground out in the open where the air became fresh and cool sooner than anywhere else at night.

After about a week Montford returned and told the family that E. B. and C. B. were to enter the school at Fort Sill at once. That night, fortunately, there came a good rain that broke the drought. Next morning, feeling much better after the rain, they hurriedly bundled up their few clothes and climbed into the wagon to make the trip to Fort Sill. When they arrived at Fort Sill in the middle of September, it was an exciting place. The wild Indians had gone on the warpath and the Plains war was in full blast. Most of the troops stationed at the fort were in the field chasing down the Indians, who had left the reservations and gone on the warpath on the Plains. E. B. and C. B. kept their ears open for all the rumors that ran through the post and tried to keep track of what was going on. They boarded with an army widow who was a great gossip and who helped keep them informed. She was lovely to the boys, but was very bitter toward the wild Indians, whom the boys considered their friends.

Colonel John W. Davidson, who was in charge of the campaign, had taken the field about September 7, 1874. As the Indians were overtaken and captured, they were placed under guard and returned to the fort. As they were herded in, the Indian chiefs who had taken an active part in the rebellion were thrown into the guardhouse. The others were placed in patrolled camps. The boys watched these straggling columns of Indians as they were brought in; they were worn out by the constant effort of trying to dodge the pursuing troops. They did not resemble the proud, carefree Indians that the boys had seen around Camp Arbuckle. Especially hard on these Indians was the fact that, as soon as they were captured, their horses were taken away from them and turned over to the army quartermaster.

By the latter part of October the column from Fort Sill reported that "during the month the command has killed three Kiowas, captured one hundred and thirteen, Cheyenne, Kiowa and Comanche warriors, three hundred and fifty women and children, two thousand ponies, ninety-two mules and destroyed all their arms. It also captured and destroyed a Cheyenne camp of about eighty lodges on the headwaters of the north fork of [the] Red River and pursued the fleeing Indians 70 miles up on the staked plains."[1] On November 2, Satanta, one of the outlaw Kiowa chiefs who had been paroled from the Texas prison, was led from the guardhouse. His arms and legs heavily shackled and closely guarded by a detachment of soldiers, he began his return journey to the prison at Huntsville, Texas.

All of the captured Indians had a subdued and hangdog expression, not at all resembling the happy people that the boys had often seen passing through Montford's ranches. The boys also felt hemmed in because they were not accustomed to any kind of confinement. The small schoolhouse they attended was, like most of the soldiers' quarters, made of pickets and adobe mud. The floor was dirt and the puncheon seats were made of rough narrow boards that were very hard and uncomfortable. Like the Indians, the boys were without their horses, or they probably would have slipped away and returned home.

On November 6, they heard that Colonel Davidson, who had established headquarters at Rio Negro, Texas, was splitting his forces, and the two groups were going to patrol the country for fleeing Indians as the troops returned toward the fort. The first column was ordered down south along the North Fork to the Red River and Elk Creek. The second column was to proceed north toward the Cimarron River, then to scout the country between the Cimarron and the North and South Canadian Rivers to the Darlington Indian Agency. Then another group was sent out to cover the country between the Washita and South Canadian Rivers. On November 17, the main body of troops left their camp on Sweetwater Creek and headed toward the fort. The night before there was a heavy rain and severe storm. In crossing the swollen stream, several horses and mules were drowned. About the first of December, Colonel Davidson and most of his troops returned to Fort Sill. All of the Indians had been captured except Quanah Parker and his small outlaw band of Comanches.

Often when the Indians and their horses were captured, the horses were killed on the spot, but so many were brought into the fort that it was impossible to feed and care for them. Some of them were stolen by horse thieves who fled with them to Texas. A few were taken out west of the fort and killed, but in a few days such a nauseous odor was carried back to the fort by the prevailing westerly winds that this plan was discontinued. A different solution was needed. With so many horses around the fort there was the danger that the Indians might escape from the patrolled camps, steal the horses, and go back on the warpath. In desperation, the officers decided to auction off the captured horses to the highest bidders. Notices were sent out to all the ranchers, and they were urged to attend the sale.

The day before the first sale, E. B. and C. B. were overjoyed to see Montford, Bill McClure, Jim Bond, Uncle Charley Campbell, Sam

Garvin, and Henry Ingram ride into the fort. The boys joined their camp and were delighted to be with their own kind of people again. After supper the older men sat around the campfire and mapped out their plan for bidding on the horses. They agreed that three dollars should be the highest bid for a single horse. After they had bought all the horses they wanted, they were to pool their purchases and trade and divide with each other.

The next morning they went to the corrals and pens where several thousand horses were penned. The horses were divided among four pens, each of which was connected to a smaller crowding pen. These were connected to a long chute. C. B. and E. B. crawled up on the fence to watch the excitement. School was out and perhaps over as far as they were concerned. The soldiers cut about fifteen horses into the crowding pens at a time. The auctioneer began his ballyhoo and as fast as the horses were sold, they were moved down the chute, where a small tally brand was burned on each horse, as agreed to by Montford's group beforehand. Then the horses were herded into their separate groups by their purchasers. In the main corrals the soldiers were busy shaping up the various groups of horses, the auctioneer kept up his auction chant, and the milling horses squealed, fought, and kicked. Outside the corrals there was further clamor and confusion. Many of the old squaws waddled up and soon figured out that it was their horses that were being disposed of. As they recognized some of their favorite mounts being sold, they screamed, tore their hair, and beat their breasts because they were so upset. Some of them grabbed clubs, charged the fences, and began to threaten the soldiers. It was not only a sad sight, but a frightening one as well. As the horses came out of the chute, the Indians kept closing in until the soldiers, with drawn guns, had to make a lane so the horses could pass by them. When Montford rode out of the corral, a big Kiowa woman rushed up and struck at him with a club. He saw her in time to dodge, but the club swished past his head and glanced off of his shoulder.

Montford's party bought so many horses that he rigged up a number of hackamores that he placed on each pair of ponies. He instructed E. B. and C. B. to help the soldiers herd their purchases and see that none were stolen. All the ranchers were disgusted with the whole proceedings. They had purchased more horses than they really needed, so they drove their herd away from the fort and the Indians to make a camp for the night. After supper the men discussed the conditions around the fort. The boys urged Montford to let them go home. Many of the men agreed with the boys, so Montford accompanied E. B. and C. B. back to the fort to pay off their landlady, gather up their belongings, and returned to the camp. Their school days at Fort Sill were over.

The next morning their party began the homeward journey, driving ahead of them about three thousand head of horses—mares, stallions, and geldings. As they grazed along, the ranchers discussed the merits of the horses, caught a number of them to try them out, riding them about the herd to test their wind, speed, and general usefulness. As good as many of these Indian ponies performed, they were most likely fine-bred Texas and Mexican horses that had been stolen by raiding parties. Bill McClure traded for about a thousand head of the paint or spotted horses. Montford took about five hundred head, including a coal black stallion of the Kentucky whipstock breed. This stallion proved to be an excellent breeder: three of his colts were Stroner, a red roan bald-faced horse; Mack, a chestnut sorrel; and Caddo, a coal black racehorse. He broke all three horses and kept them for his private mounts. Caddo lived long after Montford passed away.

Uncle Jim Bond went over the limit of three dollars and bid seven dollars for a deep bay stallion, which he called Belt. This proved to be one of the greatest horses in the Territory. At one time Uncle Jim rode him to Fort Smith, Arkansas, where he had been summoned to court as a witness. When he left home, his wife, Aunt Adelaide, was very ill. As soon as he testified he asked to be excused, saddled Belt, and headed for home. He rode the three hundred miles in three days, and when he unsaddled Belt, he rolled over a couple of times, kicked up his heels, and ran to join the other horses. Uncle Jim claimed that he could have ridden him seven hundred miles in seven days and found him at the end in the same frolicsome condition. A number of years later, Uncle Jim sold Belt to Joe Colbert, a nephew of Uncle Charley Campbell. He bred him to a gray Comanche mare that had been purchased by Henry Ingram at the same horse sale. The gray colt produced from this union was named Rabbit. Rabbit broke all records for the half mile on racetracks throughout the South. He was finally sold for ten thousand dollars, which was a considerable sum of money in those days.

By the time they reached home, the ownership of most of the horses had been decided. As you can imagine, Mary, Montford's wife, was surprised to find C. B. and E. B. trailing along with the other riders of the herd. Bill McClure, who had traded for the paint horses, had a ranch on the North Canadian River and east of Montford's Council Grove ranch along with one east of Johnsonville in the Pottawatomie lands. McClure used the 7C brand. He decided to drive his horses to this ranch and then take some of them on up to southeastern Nebraska, to his home in Table Rock. To do this he needed help and proposed that C. B. and E. B. should go with him on this trip to Nebraska, where they could live with his family and go to school. The boys were anxious to go and their parents gave their consent. After Bill had separated his paint horses, the boys said goodbye to E. B.'s new baby brother, Robert. They left with the herd of paints and herded them north and east through the Pottawatomie country. When they arrived at Bill's ranch, he kept about one hundred head of the best cow horses, a few mares, and a stallion. The boys herded the horses while Bill and his cowboys rounded up the steers Bill was delivering to Muskogee, Oklahoma.

When the herd of steers was shaped up, they headed east with their cattle and horses, cowboys, and chuck wagon. Bill had told the boys that the M.K.&T. railroad ran through Muskogee. The boys were very anxious to get there to see their first train and were impatient with the slow-moving herds. Each time they topped a hill, they were excited by the hope that they might see the smoke from the engine. After what seemed like years to them, they drove their colorful herds into the Muskogee stockyards. The townspeople turned out in a body and sat around on the fence like blackbirds to admire the beautiful paint horses. Their large herd was just as exciting to the townspeople as the railroad and this "metropolis" was to the young boys.

After the steers were loaded, the chuck wagon and part of the crew returned to Bill's ranch. The ones going to Nebraska packed up their bedding materials, put together a camping outfit on their horses, and headed off for Nebraska. The horse herd moved much faster than the steers; they traveled across the territory and Kansas without any trouble or adventure. By the time they reached Table Rock, the country was covered with snow and the boys were covered with lice. Mrs. McClure, Bill's wife, made them stay in camp the first night and the next day boiled all their clothes and bedding and doped them to get rid of their lice.

Nebraska looked bare and ordinary to the two boys. Most of the houses were built of sod, and there were very few trees to break up the landscape. They tramped through the snow to a sod schoolhouse the rest of that winter and the next. By the spring of 1876 they were tired of school and, like cooped-up wild Indians, longed for home. They had spent many long evenings around the fire talking to Mrs. McClure about the wonderful country from which they came and finally made it sound so attractive that Mrs. McClure consented to join her husband in the Territory. Bill McClure built a home for his wife in the new town of Johnsonville. Their house was just a short distance from Aunt Adelaide and Uncle Jim Bond's house. Bill's wife returned to Kansas for the birth of their first son, Guy. She then returned to the Indian Territory and moved to Atoka in 1878, about the time Montford moved to Silver City. In 1877 Bill McClure built one of the first loading corrals near the site of the Santa Fe Station at the future site of Oklahoma City.[2]

When the boys arrived home, they discovered that many changes had taken place during their two-year absence. The fields had been enlarged and fenced with rails, many new people had moved in, and it looked more like a farming community. There was a big improvement in the quality of the young livestock. Although Montford had lost two of his imported bulls from Kansas, their presence in the herds was showing up in the quality of his calves. Montford saved the best bull calves from his Durham bulls, and many of them were old enough for service. The old range bulls of scrub stock were castrated or shot down on the range to make way for the young ones.

There were changes in the family as well. Another brother, Tilford, had been born, and Sallie Thompson, one of the orphan children living with Montford's family, had married a widowed merchant named Walker. Since Sallie had worked faithfully for the family for years, Montford gave her as a wedding present his interest in the Camp Arbuckle store, five head of cows, and ten head of mares. Sallie branded her little herd with H (2 and 4 connected), and placed it on the left side. When Sallie's husband, Walker, took charge of the store, Phil Smith, Montford's old manager, quit. He could not understand the new class of trade, which had changed from wild Indians to Arkansas settlers and civilized Indians. The buffalo were fast disappearing, and the wild Indians, confined to the reservations, no longer brought in skins and hides to trade. Most of the wild Indians were supported by annuities and rations, which were issued to them by the federal government. The Johnsonville Post Office was activated on October 5, 1876, with Bill Walker as postmaster.[3] Supposedly, the government stamp could only accommodate nine letters, so they had to shorten the town's name to Johnson in order for it to fit on the official post office stamp.

During this spring and summer, two friends of Montford's named Jones and Cruckshank talked him into establishing a purebred herd separate from the rest of his cattle, so that he could continue to improve all of his cattle. They agreed to be partners with him and were to receive for their share one-third of the increase, and Montford could move his young bulls to his other ranches. After the plan was agreed upon, Jones and Cruckshank fitted up a chuck wagon, rounded up a few horses, and headed for Kansas to buy their bulls. They returned about two months later with six purebred Durham bulls. Montford topped one hundred and fifty of his choicest red and roan heifers to put with them. They picked a new ranch site for this herd between two creeks, near the present town of Tabler, which is about five miles east of the town of Chickasha, Oklahoma. There was plenty of cold, clear running water, but with so much gypsum in it that the water was very bitter. Because of this, the creeks were named East and West Bitter Creeks. These cattle were branded heart on the left hip and an X, or cross, on the jaw. They were moved to this range early in the fall. This venture did not prove very successful because it was located almost on the Chisholm Trail that went up the divide between the two Bitter Creeks. Although the range was burned clean the next spring, fever ticks began to appear on all the cattle. None of the bulls were immune and three of them died, as well as a number of heifers. Two years later Jones and Cruckshank, who could not keep the Texas cattle passing through their range from contaminating their herd, sold out to Uncle Charley Campbell. He placed a man in charge, and since it was not very far from his Walnut Creek ranch, he ran them both for some time. Later, after the Chisholm Trail gave way to the railroads, this became Uncle Charley's principal range. As the surviving cattle became accustomed to the ticks, the herd regained its strength and multiplied.

During the summer of 1876 E. B. accompanied his father on a tour of their ranches. When they approached Granny Vicey's headquarters, it looked as if a cyclone had passed through the grove. The destruction was not caused by a cyclone, but by a buzz saw. The government had decided, after the end of the Indian war in 1874, to establish Fort Reno. It was a short distance east of the Darlington Agency and south of the North Canadian River. This was known as Cheyenne and Arapaho country. The first quarters at the fort had been made of pickets or small logs. These pickets were placed upright in rows in a trench, then the loose dirt was packed around the base to hold them in place. The space between the pickets was filled with clay. After throwing up these temporary barracks, the government set about constructing more substantial quarters. In 1870 Edwin F. Williams, an experienced engineer and mechanic, accompanied the saw to the Darlington Agency where it was used for a number of years. He was replaced by William Darlington, an engineer and son of Brinton Darlington, the original agent at he Darlington Agency. William was placed in charge of reconditioning the old sawmill at the Darlington Agency and moving it to Council Grove. This mill was located on a site close to where Jesse Chishom's old trading post stood. The timber around the agency had been mostly cottonwood. It was very soft wood and warped easily. The timber at Council Grove was mostly post and western white oak. This grove was about three and a half miles square.[4] At the time E. B. saw the grove, most of the heavy lumber, such as sleepers, sills, joists, studding, and rafters had been cut, and most of the slabs and loose lumber had been hauled to the fort for fuel. Later, this grove was set aside as a wood reserve for Fort Reno, which was located on the bald and open prairie. When Oklahoma was opened for settlement in 1889, this grove was still a reserve, but it too was thrown open and sold off in 1899.[5]

When September and school time rolled around, E. B. and C. B. were about to be sent to a school at Cane Hill Academy in Boonsboro,

Arkansas. It had been recommended to Montford by Clem McCullough, a clerk in Walker's store at Camp Arbuckle. The boys were about ready to leave when Montford was informed that there was a place for them in the Harley Male Academy at Tishomingo. The name had been changed from the Chickasaw Manual Training School. Aunt Adelaide's daughter, Ella, and Uncle Charley's daughter, Addie, were also old enough to go to school, so a wagon was prepared and the four children piled in. One of the Negro ranch hands drove the wagon and Montford rode horseback. When they reached Tishomingo, the boys got out and the girls were taken on to Denison, Texas, where they were placed in a Catholic convent.

The boys enjoyed their school at Tishomingo much more than the ones that they had previously attended. The students were about their own age and had been reared in the same kind of environment. Many of them acted like wild Indians when they were first brought in. Their hair was long and oftentimes matted with lice. E. B. became the official barber for these students. Some of the older boys would hold them in the chair while E. B. sheared them. The hair was so full of lice that it would almost crawl when it hit the floor. They swept it up carefully and burned it. After the haircut a fine-tooth comb was used to comb out the nits, and the boy's head was smeared with a red ointment, which was an exterminator for any remaining nits. Itch was also another prevalent malady and was treated with a homemade remedy of grease and sulphur. The older students often recommended to the new gullible ones that a sure cure for the itch was a plunge into the icy waters of Pennington Creek.

Between classes they played games. One that attracted crowds of Indians was an Indian ball game that was something like the modern game of lacrosse. The ball field was on the open prairie. At each end of the field, which was about one hundred yards long, were two posts about fifteen feet high. Each pair of posts was the goal or target for the opposing team. The object of the game was to hit these posts with a small ball as many times as possible. Each player had two small sticks that, when held scissors-fashion, formed a cup at the ends, where the head had been hollowed out and laced across with buckskin. The ball could not be touched with the hands, but was scooped up with these sticks and hurled toward the goal. When the ball hit the ground, the players of each side rushed after the ball to get it in their loop to throw it again. These melees after the ball produced many cracked heads and shins. It was a wild, thrilling game that required courage, stamina, and speed.

In their leisure time they explored caves and with their bows and arrows hunted in the woods and along the streams. In the woods they shot squirrels and rabbits and, slipping along the creeks, they shot frogs and fish that could be seen in the clear water. The game they brought in had to be cleaned and delivered to the school cook, who prepared it for their next meal. When it was warm enough, they swam in Pennington Creek. A large flat granite boulder, surrounded by cedars, made a convenient place to undress. The smaller boys had another hole in which to swim that was shallow and not as dangerous as the one by the granite boulder. This rock was also a favorite rendezvous for a feast after a raid on some neighbor's chickens.

When school was out for the summer, Montford came back down, picked them up in a wagon, and they returned home to help with the work on the ranches.

Notes

1. Microfilm 617, Roll 1173. Western History Collection, University of Oklahoma.
2. Lester, Patricia. 1980. "William McClure and the McClure Ranch." *Chronicles of Oklahoma*, Oklahoma Historical Society. Vol. 58, no. 3, pp. 296–307.
3. Shirk, George H. 1948. "First Post Offices Within the Boundaries of Oklahoma." *Chronicles of Oklahoma*, Oklahoma Historical Society. Vol. 26. p. 210.
4. Collins, Hubert E. 1932. "Edwin Williams, Engineer." *Chronicles of Oklahoma*, Oklahoma Historical Society. Vol. 10, p. 341.
5. Asplin, Ray. 1967. "Council Grove." *Chronicles of Oklahoma*, Oklahoma Historical Society. Vol. 45, p. 451.

Boggy Johnson Returns

I n the summer of 1877 Montford was much surprised to receive a letter from his father, Charles "Boggy" Johnson. Thirty-two years before, Boggy had abandoned his two Chickasaw children a short time after their mother's death. Boggy was well enough educated that he could have kept in touch with his children if he had tried. He had been in the Indian Service for many years and knew exactly the steps to be taken to locate a particular Indian. Montford's name had appeared in the report of the commissioner of Indian affairs in 1858; it was recorded as "Monford," but the similarity to Montford was enough to merit an investigation. Montford's marriage certificate, his brands, and his stolen horses were recorded in the Chickasaw records. So the fact that Boggy did not communicate with his children before 1877 is good evidence that he never tried.

In his letter to Montford, Boggy gave his address as 17 Dey Street [a short little street on the Lower East Side of Manhattan Island–*C.N.K.*], New York City, and asked Montford to answer so that they could arrange a meeting. Montford took the letter to Aunt Adelaide, his sister, who insisted that a meeting be arranged as soon as possible. After an exchange of letters, it was agreed that the family was to meet Boggy in Denison, Texas. As the eventful day approached, Montford's wife, the younger children, Uncle Jim, and Aunt Adelaide prepared to go overland by wagon for the meeting. When they left, Montford rode alongside on horseback. Arriving at Denison, they registered at the hotel and asked the clerk if they had a Boggy Johnson registered there. The clerk said that he had checked in, but that he had just stepped out and that he would return shortly. A few minutes later he returned and, guided by fatherly intuition or by Montford's western clothes, Boggy rushed over to greet his lost family. Aunt Adelaide, always the big-hearted peacemaker in the family, shed a few tears and said that she was so proud that they were finally reunited.

The next two days were spent visiting and talking through the years of their father's absence. Boggy told Montford that he located him during a recent visit to Fort Smith, Arkansas. He was in town when court was in session and met several Chickasaw Indians on the street. Going up to them and talking in Chickasaw, he introduced himself, "Chukma. Sah hotchi foh ut Charles Johnson." He then asked if they knew his son Montford: "Hohmi, un chepoto nukni Montford?" Yes, they said that they knew of a Monford Johnson: "Ehn, ishto ituksolli hattak Monford Johnson." They went on to say that they thought Montford had a big ranch on the South Canadian River: "Hattak ayyasha milinka ah bokoshe South Canadian."

While he was visiting with these Chickasaws, one of the Indians pointed to an old Negro farmer who was walking along the street. The Indian said that he recognized this Negro man as someone who lived near Johnsonville and possibly knew Montford. Boggy, after hailing the man, questioned him about knowing Montford. The old farmer replied, "Yes, Suh, I knows Monford well. I has worked for him at Johnsonville." Taking the address given by the old man, Boggy had written the letter that Montford had received. Boggy claimed that he had written several letters to Montford via Tishomingo, Indian Territory, but had never received a reply. This story sounded a little fishy to Montford, because he was well known to a great many people in Tishomingo.

In the exchange of personal histories Montford told about his boyhood and the development of his ranching business. Boggy inquired about many of his old friends who lived around Boggy Depot, but most of them were dead. Boggy told them that after he left the Chickasaw Nation, he went to Philadelphia where he met and married Rose Bachman, a beautiful woman of German descent. It is probably while he lived in Philadelphia that Boggy became a naturalized citizen. They had a daughter named Belle, who was Montford's and Adelaide's half sister. Belle had married a man named Edward Simpson, who was in the wholesale liquor business with Boggy. He painted a glowing and enticing picture of the money to be made in the liquor trade.

Boggy claimed that he had many influential friends in Washington, and Montford saw an opportunity to do something for his Indian chief friends who had been taken from Fort Sill in late April 1875 to be imprisoned in the three-hundred-year-old Spanish Fort of San Marcos, renamed Fort Marion, in Saint Augustine, Florida.[1] Through the recently promoted Captain R. H. Pratt, who had been placed on special duty to care for them, these chiefs had written Montford a number of pathetic letters explaining their plight. These Indians, in the wake of the short-lived Red River War, which lasted from July to December 1874, were to be made examples of by the U.S. government. The federal government wanted these "bad" Indians banished, without trials, to a remote eastern fort, where they were to be held indefinitely as prisoners. The government had promised to release these Indians, but had done nothing about it as far as Montford knew. There were some seventy Indians at the fort from the Cheyenne, Kiowa, Arapaho, Comanche, and Caddo tribes. Montford suggested that they go to Saint Augustine, look the conditions over, and see what could be done for them. Boggy agreed to go and said that he would notify Montford when and where to meet him to make the trip.

There was much to be done on the ranches at this season of the year, and as they were pretty well talked out, Montford brought the reunion to an end. The women made a few purchases, and Montford bought a new hack that he thought he would trail home behind the wagon. Uncle Jim drove the wagon, but the women wanted to try out the riding qualities of their new hack and convinced Montford to let them ride home in it. Montford left separately, returning by way of Sherman, Texas, so that he might visit with the managers of the M&P Bank where he deposited his money. Banking in those days was on rare occasions and oftentimes done through an agent. For example, when Montford sold his steers, he arranged for the purchaser to deposit the money in the bank when the steers were marketed. The year before, Montford had sold his steers to Bill McClure, who took them to his ranch on the North Canadian and fattened them for market. It was almost a year from the time of delivery until Bill had sold the steers, collected the money for them, and paid Montford. Montford cached money received at home in a leather pouch that he kept in a box built into the foot of his bed. He kept it there until he had an opportunity to get it to the bank.

In the December 3, 1931, issue of the *Tuttle Times*, Meta Chestnut Sager recalled in her speech at the dedication of the Silver City Marker, a fourteen-ton stone, sponsored by the Daughters of the American Revolution in November of that year: "There Montford Johnson lived his quiet, reserved life. He was a great banker, but his bank was a receptacle in a heavy walnut bedstead. Could you see at one time the money that bank has held you would think a U.S. Reserve bank had poured out its contents before you. I have in my possession now the old leather folder that contained the money, the history of which parallels much of the history of the old (Chisholm) trail."

As soon as they returned home, Montford rested up a little from his trip and then made a tour of the ranches where he made arrangements with his foremen to run everything in the event that he should be called away to make the trip to Florida. Late in the summer Montford received a letter from Boggy arranging a meeting in Jacksonville, Florida. Uncle Charley Campbell decided to go with Montford, and at the last minute Montford decided to take his son, E. B., with him. Chub Moore drove them in the new hack to Atoka, where they boarded the train for Houston, Texas. This was the first train ride for E. B., and he followed his father into the train with a faint heart and heavy feet. When they reached Houston without having a wreck, his confidence in the iron horse grew. Houston looked like an old town. The streets were lined with moss-covered oak trees, and parked along the streets were large-wheeled log wagons, pulled by a string of oxen. Whenever a load stopped near the trees, the oxen turned aside and tried to graze on the moss. The party took the eastbound train out of Houston and headed for the Mississippi River. When they reached it, they did not jump in and swim across as Montford's mother had done some forty years before, but they crossed in a boat. They stayed overnight in the fancy St. Charles Hotel in New Orleans. This was another first for E. B. and quite a step up from his own home or even the boardinghouse at Fort Sill. Although the time was early fall, mosquitoes were everywhere, and everyone was talking about the yellow fever that was spread by them. Uncle Charley was so frightened that he wanted to turn back to Hot Springs, Arkansas, to boil out the malaria, but Montford insisted that they all stay together and compromised by promising that when they were on their return trip home, they would go by way of Hot Springs.

Two days and a night on a slow-moving train brought them to Jacksonville. The roadbed wound through the northern Florida swamps, which swarmed with alligators. The alligators found the tracks an excellent place to sun themselves. Usually they glided into the slimy water at the approach of the train, but sometimes they piled on the track so thick that the train had to stop. Then the train crew grabbed their alligator guns, walked ahead of the train and shot at them. The air was full of flies and mosquitoes, and from the swamp there arose a nauseating stench caused for the most part by the dead and swollen alligators carcasses that had been killed on previous trips. They saw a few cattle in the canebrakes. They were brown in color, with big heads and small, dwarfed bodies. Many of the cattle were bobtailed because the alligators had snapped off their tails. When they saw or heard an alligator approaching, they hoisted their tails or stumps and headed for higher ground.

The few natives they saw were poor, half-starved Negroes and a scattering of Indians. They were mostly Seminoles, who had preferred staying in the swamps to going to their new home in the Indian Territory. The few souls that they saw looked to be an inferior breed and looked much worse off than those that had moved to the Oklahoma Territories.

When their long and tedious journey ended, Jacksonville was a great disappointment. The buildings were mostly small wooden shacks that were scattered around without much plan. The sand was about six inches deep along the streets. The native trees, like those in Houston, were moss-covered. Lounging under the trees were large groups of half-clad Negroes. Everywhere they went, they seemed to run into a foul-smelling fish market. At last they arrived at the hotel, and E. B. met his grandfather for the first time. He looked like a very important person to him. His grandfather was dressed in a dark suit, white shirt, and a stiff collar. E. B. was especially impressed by his high-top beaver hat and the beautifully carved cane that he carried.

Next morning the four of them took a boat up the Saint Johns River to Saint Augustine. They still saw many alligators along the route, and lining the banks of the stream were groves of wild lemon and orange trees. E. B. enjoyed this trip, which was much more enjoyable than chugging along behind a puffing, snorting, cinder-belching engine. Arriving at Saint Augustine, they took a mule-drawn bus to the prison. After crossing a small moat, they entered through heavy iron gates. Montford introduced himself to the commander and asked to see the chiefs. Permission was granted, and they were taken down a long corridor that opened out onto a courtyard. As they entered it, Montford called out to several of the chiefs, whom he recognized. They rushed to him, threw their arms around him, and danced up and down like happy children. Others came up and, learning who it was, beat him on the back, whooped and yelled and carried on so much that E. B. was afraid that they were going to injure his father. Montford introduced the chiefs to the rest of the party and told them that Boggy knew the Great White Father in Washington and that he was going there to intercede for them. Upon hearing this, they rushed at Boggy and clapped their hands. One of them grabbed Boggy's beaver hat, sat down over it, and pretended that he was sitting over a latrine. The Indians all roared and whooped at this pantomime. The Indians were all anxious to tell their pathetic story. They said while they were being transported to Saint Augustine, they were all heavily shackled. Wherever they stopped, curious people flocked to gaze at them as if they were wild beasts. Some of them committed suicide on their trip or soon after they reached this damp, dark, depressing prison. The Indian prisoners told Montford about the many who had died and if they did not get out soon that they would all die or go crazy. They were a sad-looking lot. Their hair was dirty and matted, and their eyes sore and red, with matter running from them.

When the Indian prisoners arrived at Saint Augustine, Captain Pratt had removed the shackles and showed them every possible kindness,

Group of Indian Prisoners at Fort Marion, Saint Augustine, Florida, circa 1875–1877. Captain Richard H. Pratt standing at left. Courtesy, U.S. Army Military Institute, #RG 998-CIIS, Box 1.1.

but had been unable to parole them. Pratt had doggedly pursued better conditions for his prisoners. He constantly wrote to his superiors and prominent East Coast individuals, such as Harriet Beecher Stowe, to improve the Indians' plight.[2] The locals, originally frightened by the presence of these Indians, became themselves a lot more sympathetic to these incarcerated souls after the prisoners themselves were let out late one night to quell a raging fire in the town of Saint Augustine.

In what became a regular outing for the prisoners, they were recruited to help fish for sharks in the bay. A large group of Indians would drive a large post into the beach, tie a rope to it, and send the rest of the rope out in a boat to the spot where the sharks usually frequented. The hooks were then baited and cast into the bay from a small boat. Once the shark took the hook, it became a great tug of war between the shark and the Indians on the beach. The prisoners took great delight in these battles and referred to their noble adversary as a "water buffalo."[3] A number of these prisoners also became very well-known artists. They painted mostly scenes from their memories of life on the Plains before

James Bear's Heart (Kiowa), "Catching a Shark, July 1875," from a series of drawings, circa 1875. Fort Marion, Saint Augustine, Florida. The drawings are titled in pencil by Lieutenant Richard Henry Pratt, U.S. Army., later the founder of the Carlisle Indian School, Carlisle, Pennsylvania. Presented by Miss Eleanor Sherman Fitch. Courtesy, National Museum of the American Indian, #20/6231, Smithsonian Institution.

their imprisonment. Some of their names were Zotom and Tsentainte (or White Horse), who were Kiowa; and Buffalo, Making Medicine, and Bear's Heart, who were Cheyenne.

Montford had asked Captain Pratt's permission to bring the Indians a butchered cow for a barbecue, and after getting his consent, detailed his son, E. B., to locate a butcher. The butcher and E. B. had difficulty in finding anything suitable to kill since most of the cattle were thin and of a very inferior quality. Mosquitoes and flies bothered them most of the time, and the coarse dry grass had no fattening qualities. They finally located a four-year-old dry cow, which the butcher dressed and delivered to the prison for twenty dollars. He also brought some pine logs, which burned too rapidly for good barbecuing. When E. B. and the butcher arrived inside the prison with their beef and wood, the Indians began to whoop and dance. In a short time they dug a trench and had a fire started. Many of them crowded around E. B. and patted him on the back for this favor. Montford and his party had to leave before the meat was cooked so that they could catch the afternoon boat. When Montford informed the Indians that they had to leave, they filed by with tears in their eyes to shake hands and bid him and his party good-bye.

During the boat trip back to Jacksonville, Montford's father, Boggy, urged him to send his son back to New York to finish his education so that he could learn the white man's ways. Montford left it up to E. B., who had seen so many things on this trip that be began to realize just how ignorant he was. E. B. decided that he should have some more schooling in the Territory before he ventured so far from home. The next day they parted ways. Montford's party headed for Hot Springs, Arkansas, and after taking a course of baths to get the suspected malaria out of their systems, they returned home.

Boggy went straight to Washington and called on his friend, Senator Garland, with whom he talked about the condition of the imprisoned chiefs, the Chickasaw country, and the conditions on the reservations. The senator seemed very much impressed with the information that Boggy brought him and promised to discuss their plight with President Hayes. No one knew how much, if any, Boggy's visit to Washington had to do with the release of the chiefs from Saint Augustine, but by April 1878 the War Department had returned all of these Indians to the Indian agencies in the Territory, except a few of the younger ones who were sent to schools in the East, like the Carlisle Indian School in Pennsylvania, which Captain Pratt was instrumental in starting and running.[4]

A few years later Captain Pratt placed a letter in the July 25, 1881, *Cheyenne Transporter*, hoping to find summer jobs for some of his Carlisle students. He had approximately seventy-five boys and twenty-five girls to place each summer. His wish was for the young men and women "to learn the industries of common life, agriculture, mechanics, etc. We ask only room and board and when worthy a small remuneration to them so they might feel they are appreciated."

Notes

1. Nye, W. S. [1937] 1969. *Carbine and Lance: The Story of Old Fort Sill.* Norman: University of Oklahoma Press, p. 231.
2. Pratt, H. Richard. 1964. *Battlefields and Classrooms.* New Haven, CT: Yale University Press, 1964, pp. 155–157.
3. Ibid., p. 127.
4. Ibid., p. 191.

Law and Order

In the autumn of 1877, after their return from Florida, C. B. and E. B. reentered Harley Institute in Tishomingo. There, life was uneventful. They studied their books and played their games. They made many friends among their fellow students, who later became the leaders in the Chickasaw Nation. A sampling of their classmates included: Burris, Chase, Cheadle, Colbert, Goldsby, Harris, Kingsberry, LeFlore, Love, Maytubby, McLish, Perry, Pickens, Walton, Wilson, and Alfred Murray.[1]

More interesting than their school life were some of the happenings at home, which illustrates the kind of society in which they lived. Although law and order was officially enforced by the U.S. marshals, the Chickasaw officers, and the soldiers at Fort Sill, each rancher was a good deal a law unto himself in the section of the country in which he lived. One such case is an incident that happened in Montford's range. Between Johnsonville and the Walnut Creek ranch was a settlement of Carolina Negroes who were noted for being tough characters. One of these Negroes attacked and raped the wife of Jimmie White, who was one of Montford's renters on the Cushman farm northeast of present-day Wayne, Oklahoma. At any time, rape is a ghastly crime, but especially so in a pioneer community, where the few women present are looked upon with so much respect that it amounts almost to worship. When Montford heard the details of the gruesome attack on Mrs. White, he set off at once with some of his most trusted cowboys for the Negro settlement. He did not wait for officers or soldiers to appear many days after the crime had been committed. After inquiry and investigation,

Montford took the most likely suspect to the scene of the assault. Mrs. White positively identified the attacker.

Although feeling was running high and many of the hotheaded neighbors wanted to lynch him, Montford protected him from the mob and turned him over to Chub Moore and Gus Leslie, to be delivered to the law at Stonewall. Chub and Gus left with the Negro, but the next day they returned and reported that the Negro had attempted to escape and that Chub shot him. This *ley fuga,* or law of flight, was practiced for many years in the South. When a culprit's guilt has been fully established, he is turned over to officers. These officers see to it that the accused has an opportunity to escape. Then the report shows that the accused was killed while attempting to escape or resisting an officer. In this case, the rumor circulated that Chub, knowing the Negro was guilty and disliking the long ride to the county seat at Stonewall, had merely taken a philosophical attitude about the whole case and shot the Negro. This rumor reached the ears of the U.S. marshals, who did not approve of this form of justice and who swore out a warrant for Chub's arrest. A short time later Chub was caught off guard and was captured by about thirty of these Carolina Negroes. They bound him and headed for Fort Smith, where they intended to deliver him to the federal authorities.

The news of Chub's capture reached Montford. He hurriedly assembled some of his men and took after the Negroes. Montford overtook them where they were spending the night in an old abandoned cabin. He surrounded it with his men and instructed them not to start any shooting until he gave the order. He walked to the door and called out to the leader of the Negroes to come out and talk to him. The frightened leader came out and was informed that if they did not turn Chub over that they would riddle the cabin with bullets. Knowing that he would carry out his threat, the man rushed back in the cabin and, with the help of another Negro, carried Chub out and dumped him at Montford's feet. He cut the ropes binding Chub and turned him loose. Chub was so angry that he began to cry and begged for a gun so that he might shoot the whole bunch of Negroes. Montford refused his request, held him back, and as the party rode back home, tried to calm Chub down.

Although there was a warrant out for Chub, he roamed over the Chickasaw Nation for years working for Montford. He was one of the best bronc riders in the Nation. Most of the local law officers knew about the case and never tried to capture him. The rumor spread that twenty-nine of the thirty Negroes who had captured Chub met mysterious deaths; the only survivor fled to California.

Some seven years after the murder warrant had been sworn out for Chub, one of the best deputy marshals in the territories, the Negro Bass

Reeves, discovered the old writ and set out to arrest Chub Moore. Frank Pierce, acting as posse for Reeves, shot Chub in the right thigh, inflicting a severe wound. Chub was placed in a covered hack on a mattress and survived the 265-mile drive to Fort Smith, but died in jail awaiting trial in September 1884.[2] Frank Pierce turned out to be a notorious horse thief and bootlegger. He was later shot in a gun battle with Texas lawmen. Bass Reeves spent over thirty years as a lawman. He rode for Judge Isaac Parker, the "Hanging Judge" in Fort Smith, for many years.

A few cattle were stolen from time to time by some Negro outlaws from Wild Horse Creek. To avoid capture when overtaken, these rustlers sometimes jumped off their horses and took to the brush. Montford's men generally looked over these horses carefully for brands and special marks that might identify these animals in the future. It was just a little unhealthy for anyone to be found riding one of these recognizable horses on Montford's range.

The officers from Fort Sill came sometimes into the Walnut Creek country to hunt horse thieves and whiskey peddlers. The news of their coming generally preceded them, and by the time they arrived, the thieves and peddlers had moved elsewhere. The ranchers dealt with horse thieves themselves and right on the spot. On one occasion five horse thieves passing through the country stole sixty head of Montford's best horses. Some of Montford's men, including Lon Gray, Ben Goode, Gus Leslie, and Owen Hennesy, followed the trail of the stolen horses and overtook the outlaws in the Cherokee outlet. The outlaws were camped for the night in a narrow gulch, and the horses were grazing nearby in a box canyon. When the shooting was over, five dead outlaws were left for buzzard food. They rounded up the stolen horses and headed for home. It became well established not to tamper with Montford's property.

Some of the young men who drifted out to the Chickasaw Nation had committed some offense against society in the older communities to the east. Many of these men, after working for Montford for a while, had enough confidence in him to tell their troubles to him. He always did everything possible to straighten out the man's past life so that he could live in peace. A typical case was that of Tom Wasson, who cared for two of his fine racehorse stallions, did the chores, and kept the homeplace supplied with game. He had shot a Negro in self-defense, and Tom thought that he had killed him. Fearing the penalty of hanging, which was usually the penalty imposed by Judge Parker for such crimes, he skipped the country and fled to the Nation. After Tom confided in him, Montford wrote to Tom's old home and found out that the injured man had recovered. He advised Tom to go back and clear up the case. Montford wrote a long letter to Judge Parker, gave it to Tom, and admonished him to deliver it to the judge in person. Tom presented himself before the judge with the letter. Judge Parker instructed Tom to appear before the U.S. commissioner, who, upon the judge's instructions, dismissed the charge against him. Tom returned to the ranch and worked for Montford for many more years. He later lived in Blanchard, Oklahoma, and said that Montford was the best man that he ever worked for.

In the summer of 1878 William Garrard Williams, better known as "Caddo Bill," came to visit Montford and to ask his advice. Caddo Bill was born in Kentucky in 1839, but had moved to Texas with his family in 1859. When he started out on his own, he only had two dollars to his name, but within twenty years Bill was running over three thousand head of cattle on some sixteen thousand acres. In his early days he occasionally worked for trader John Shirley in Texas and later in Oklahoma. Bill married Annie Eastman, a daughter of Montford's old friend Charley Eastman. They lived around the Pauls Valley area until 1872, when they moved to what later became known as Silver City. Bill and Annie ended up producing eleven children, one of whom, Maggie, would marry C. B. Campbell. Caddo Bill also became one of the most renowned horse breeders in the Oklahoma Territories.

Williams had built a house and small store a few miles east of Beaver Creek (now known as Snake Creek) on the south side of the South Canadian River and near the Chisholm Trail. The house was rather large, a story and a half, with glass windows and a long porch extending the length of the east side. Since the Territory had been surveyed recently, Williams discovered that his improvements were not on the Caddo reservation, but were in the Chickasaw Nation. He said that there was a wonderful range near his home, well watered with running creeks. Montford and Caddo Bill talked it over and worked up a trade. There were so many people moving into the Johnsonville area that Montford had begun to feel crowded. Partly to get off by himself again and partly to accommodate an old friend, he decided to take over Williams's property east of Beaver Creek. Montford traded him eight head of unbroken geldings and his old black stallion, Ben, for the improvements. These horses were delivered to Caddo Bill at the Pond Creek ranch, and he moved them along with his other livestock and personal property to a new location on Stinking Creek in the Caddo country.

Montford soon sold his old Johnsonville home to Judge Tom Johnston. Montford and Phil Smith, the former manager of his Camp Arbuckle store, went to look over their new property. They decided that the store was too small and too close to the house, so they sent Dick Cuttle, their teamster, to Atoka to haul back lumber for a new store building. This was built in the shape of an L, with a lean-to in the rear, and was located about a half mile south of the house. Several names were suggested for the new store. Finally three names were written on pieces of paper and placed in a hat. The first name drawn was Silver City. The name was suggested because most of the money received from the passing cow outfits was silver dollars. The other two suggestions were Boggy Creek and Antelope. It was some five years before the U.S. Post Office opened an office there at the Silver City store.

After moving his household goods, Montford rounded up his cattle and horses and a few hogs to move to the new range at Silver City. Most of the hogs were left to fatten on the nuts and acorns. When he rounded up his horses, he discovered that many of his best horses had joined bands of wild mustangs that still roamed on his range. Charley Whorley, one of his cowboys, claimed to be an expert in catching and breaking wild horses, so Montford made a fifty-fifty deal with him. On the north side of a big bend in a creek that flowed into Walnut Creek, a large corral was built. Long wings were run out from the gate and camouflaged with green branches. From the gate entrance there was no sign of a corral. When this was finished, Whorley and a Negro cowhand, both well mounted and carrying four days' rations of jerked beef, flour, and coffee, started off for the wild-horse range that was used mostly between Bitter, Salt, and Walnut Creeks.

When they approached the first band of wild horses, the wild horses took off with mane and tail flying as they ran ahead of the riders. The two men just jogged along, following the wild ones until they neared and flushed them again. They did this again and again and kept after them for two days, until the wild horses became so accustomed to the two riders that they only moved a short distance to keep ahead and away from them. Whorley now began to try and drive them. He discovered that if he wanted to turn them to the left he should ride up on the left side, because the horses attempted to turn just opposite the direction that he wanted them to go. Keeping after them and turning them first one way and the other, the horses became so confused that they had no idea which way he wanted them to go.

On the evening of the third day the assisting cowhand reported back and informed Montford that they were ready to pen the horses the next day. Early the next morning riders were stationed along the route that Whorley expected to follow. Sure enough, shortly after sunrise the wild bunch appeared on the move, with Whorley fooling along behind them. As they came closer to the corrals, the horses seemed to sense that they were being driven in one direction and started to turn off, but a rider appeared on their flank. When they turned the other way, the same thing happened. They took off down the valley with the riders on fresh horses riding in hot pursuit. As they turned the bend in the creek, they ran into the wing of the corral that directed them inside and the gate was closed before they knew what was going on.

A few of the mustangs attempted to break back past the riders, who were swinging their ropes in readiness for such a move. The ropers attempted to slow the mustangs down gradually when they roped so they would not break their necks. As the mustang stopped, he fought the rope with his forefeet. As he reared back against and fought the rope, the noose got tighter and tighter. With his legs braced, his nostrils flared red, and his eyes bulged out until the whites showed, the mustang collapsed on the ground. The roper then rode forward and flipped the rope to loosen the noose and give it some slack. After several gasping breaths, the mustang began to recover, struggled to his feet, and stood trembling and sweating. The roper would take up the slack again, and this was done a few times before the mustang gave up and followed the horse ahead of him. After the horses were all inside the corral, the men crawled up on the corral fence to look over their catch. There were four broken saddle horses in the bunch, a mediocre mustang stallion, and several good mares that were carrying Montford's brand. The stallion was roped by the forefeet, thrown, hogtied, and castrated. Before letting him up, a short piece of rawhide was tied from his tail to one forefoot. This hobble permitted him to walk, but if he tried to throw out his forefeet and run, the rawhide would trip and throw him. The other wild horses that were not accustomed to being driven were hobbled in the same way.

The horses were left in the pen overnight and let out in the morning. As soon as some of them reached the end of the gate wings, they attempted to run past the riders in the lead and head for the wild open spaces. Many of the horses were thrown immediately, while others ran some distance before being thrown by the trip hobbles. After being thrown a few times, they all gave up and walked along sensibly with the tame horses. They watered and grazed them toward the Walnut Creek ranch, where they were herded until Whorley finished up his job. He made several such drives and caught over one hundred head.

To clean them up, Whorley snared some of them that were too smart to be driven into the trap. The snare was made by setting a loop along a trail to water. The end of the rope was tied to the top of a young sapling. When a horse walked into one of these loops and ran against the rope, he was caught like a fish on a fly rod. The sapling held the horse, but being flexible would not choke him or break his neck. A few old outlaw horses were hunted down and shot. Montford and Whorley divided the horses equally. Montford moved his to Silver City and turned them loose with his other horses. Whorley moved his to the Pond Creek ranch, which he was taking over from Nute Burney.

When Montford moved Nute Burney to his own ranch on Walnut Creek, he went into partnership and started another Negro in the livestock business. His name was Goldsmith and he had been in the cavalry at Fort Sill. Goldsmith was a fast talker, with a roaring belly laugh that caught Montford's fancy. Montford let him have a young gray stallion and some of the larger mares that he had raised from the big Pottawatomie stallion. Goldsmith expected to raise artillery and cavalry horses for the army. His ranch was near Nute Burney's on Walnut Creek. His brand was 2Z, two up and two down on the left hip.

When Montford's relatives heard that he was moving, it was just like playing the game "Pussy in the Corner" when the basket turns over. They all wanted to move too. Uncle Charley Campbell sold his Johnsonville home to Isaac Johnston, the bachelor brother of Tom Johnston. He decided to move to his purebred ranch on Bitter Creek. His two nephews, Joe and Dixie Colbert, were placed in charge of the Walnut Creek ranch. After Montford moved to Silver City, Aunt Adelaide, who had lived with or near him all her life, became very homesick for his family. She stood her homesickness for a while, then insisted that Uncle Jim Bond take her to Silver City. The outcome of the visit was that Uncle Jim and Aunt Adelaide decided to move nearby. They chose a site for their new home about a mile and a half west of Silver City and about a mile east of the junction of Beaver (Snake) and Boggy Creeks.

Johnsonville continued to thrive for many years, but Nathan A. Byars, who had a ranch a mile south of Johnsonville, convinced the incoming railroads to put in their depot at this new town of Byars. The Byars Post Office was opened on April 9, 1903. Two railroads came through Byars—the Atchinson, Topeka and Santa Fe and the Oklahoma City, Ada, and Atoka. The AT&SF passed Johnsonville to the east, crossing the South Canadian on its way between Pauls Valley and Shawnee. The OCA&A passed to the west of Johnsonville and Montford's old place, running between Ada and Purcell.

This created a lot of bad feelings between the two towns. Many of the Johnsonville residents rode fifteen to twenty miles out of their way to McGee or old Sacred Heart for supplies just to avoid shopping in Byars.[3] Johnsonville's post office was deactivated in March 1910. Johnsonville was pretty much a ghost town by World War II. Byars fared a little better, but once the railroads abandoned those routes, the business district all but disappeared.

As soon as the lumber could be transported from Atoka in the spring of 1879, their new home was constructed and the Bond family moved in. Mary and Adelaide were so happy to be near each other again that they called the new home "Happy Hollow." Adelaide and Jim Bond were also famous for their generosity. If the South Canadian River was up, cattlemen usually preferred to cross their cattle at the Bond crossing rather than the Chisholm Trail crossing. The Bond crossing, although a couple of miles west of the Chisholm Trail crossing, was shallower and easier to negotiate in high water. Old-timers sang the praises of Adelaide's never-empty kitchen table and marveled at the amount of food she and her help could put out when the trail crews came by. Mollie described Adelaide's front fence as "looking like a swarm of buzzards" when the cowhands lined the fence waiting for the supper bell to ring. Meta Chestnut remembered Adelaide's usual greeting to strangers riding up as, "Get down and come in," or "You must eat something before you go." She would nurse men, usually total strangers, who were wounded or had become sick on the trail.

Her husband, Jim Bond, was also revered for his helpful ways. He often helped a neighbor in distress with a loan or a helping hand, or spot a young cowboy a few dollars to get him through the end of the drive. As Meta Chestnut said, "There was never a man along the trail who did more for his fellow man than did J. H. Bond. Money, cows, mules, horses, hogs, feed—when a man needed them, he headed for Mr. Bond, and none came away empty handed." The Bond home was appropriately named, Happy Hollow.

Montford soon made a new partnership with Uncle Jim Bond for a ranch on Salt Creek. This was west of the Bitter Creeks. While Uncle Jim Bond was getting settled, Montford was busy closing out his partnership with Jack Brown on the Walnut Creek ranch and moving his share of the cattle to this new range on Salt Creek. These cattle were the hookety-hook brand. Uncle Charley moved his fleur-de-lis–branded cattle on Bitter Creek. They just gathered about twelve hundred cows, which were only about half of the cows they should have found, according to the tally of the spring branding. With winter coming on, he moved what he found to Salt Creek and decided to look for the rest of the herd again in the spring.

When Montford visited Granny Vicey at the Council Grove ranch and told her about moving to Silver City and all of the ranch changes, she got the moving fever too. To satisfy her, Montford moved Granny and Lucinda Gray, one of the orphan children who had lived with Granny when she was not off at school, to the Bond ranch. After Lucinda moved to Happy Hollow, she worked for Aunt Adelaide and lived in a small house in the corner of the yard with Granny Vicey. Lucinda enjoyed the work and company at Aunt Adelaide's. Almost every day some hungry cowboys would stop by to be fed. One of these was Mark L. Brittian, who, after a short courtship, married her. Since Lucinda was a Chickasaw, Mark, by paying fifty dollars for a Chickasaw marriage license, became an intermarried citizen with the right to hold land. After the marriage, Mark left Uncle Charley Campbell and started a small ranch and farm of his own on the south bank of the South Canadian River. This was south of the present town of Norman, in between the C.D. Adkins place and the Graham farm, but still in the Chickasaw Territory. Two of his children are buried there, along with a few of the Adkins family.[4]

Two tragic events distressed the family this year. When Montford moved Granny Vicey from the Council Grove ranch, he placed Gus Leslie and his family in charge. One morning in the early part of the winter, Gus's wife took sick. It seemed like a slight cold, so Gus left her and two small children in the house while he went out to look after some cattle. When he returned at noon, he found his baby son nursing the cold breast of his dead mother and the other child crying beside the bed and trying to warm his mother by putting more blankets over her. Gus did not have lumber with which to make a coffin. In desperation, he tore up an old wagon box and made a coffin out of it. He dug a shallow grave in the frozen ground and buried his wife near the cabin. This done, he bundled up the two children, drove to Johnsonville, and turned the children over to some relatives of his wife.

The second tragedy happened while Montford was gathering, branding, and moving the remnant of his Walnut Creek cattle. He received word that a terrible accident had happened at Silver City. He caught a fresh horse and started out in a long lope for home and, arriving there, found a grief-stricken family. Henry McLish, one of the orphan children, had come down from Salt Creek to spend the day with his brother, Muggs, who lived with Montford's family. The children were playing bank robber, and Henry was the acting marshal. He carried an old carbine to make his official position look more realistic. Muggs, as a fleeing bandit, was ordered to halt and when he refused, Henry raised his rifle to his shoulder and squeezed the trigger. The old gun fired and Muggs fell dead, his head completely blown away by the flat-nosed bullet. Montford's wife, Mary, picked up the body of the dead child, carried him to the house, and sent word to the store and to Aunt Adelaide's. There was nothing to be done to bring back the child. A wooden coffin was built and lined with black cloth. Muggs was placed in it and carried to the sandy hill west of the house where he was buried on this high knoll overlooking the river. Montford later designated this as the burying ground for Silver City, where he and many members of the Johnson, Bond, Campbell, and Tuttle families would be buried.

After locating his family at Silver City in the fall of 1878, Montford decided to take the advice of Clem McCullough and send the children to Cane Hill Academy at Boonsboro, Arkansas. E. B. and C. B. rode their ponies; Ella and Addie, their cousins, George Morris, Mary and Bill Walker, and neighboring children were loaded into a wagon to make the trip. Clem drove the wagon and helped with the cooking. This trip lasted about a week, and all the children enjoyed the outing.

Cane Hill Academy was a much better school and more modern than any that the children had attended. There were three teachers, J. P. Carnahan and his two brothers, Earl and Welch. The children lived together with Clem's family, walked about three miles to school, and ate a packed lunch at noon. E. B. remarked that the food was excellent and was very impressed with their vegetable cache in the cellar. The McCulloughs also had plenty of good cold milk that was kept cool in a small house built over a large, cool, freshwater spring near their house. The children also discovered pawpaws or papaws. These pawpaws ripened in the fall, resembled bananas, tasted like persimmons, and made excellent ammunition, squashing like a yellow custard when they hit their mark. After the first frost they had many pawpaw fights on their way to and from school.

C. B. did not last very long at this school. One afternoon, while chewing tobacco in school, he attempted to spit out the window. Much to C. B.'s surprise, this glass window was down, and the tobacco juice splattered all over it. Mr. Carnahan, the teacher, flew into a rage and bumped C. B.'s head on the desk and then made him get a rag and wash the window. C. B. told his Chickasaw chums that he was through with such a crazy teacher and was going home. He had about five dollars, and E. B. loaned him another five. He saddled his blue gray pony and left for home. When C. B. arrived at Silver City, Montford, totally surprised, was more disappointed than angry with him. Montford felt very strongly that a good education was necessary for his children. He was very aware of the shortcomings of his own education, and he didn't want that fate to be passed on to his children and relatives. Since C. B. thought that he was in love with a girl in Table Rock, Nebraska, he agreed to return there to school. He rode horseback by himself and remained the rest of the winter. When he returned in the spring, that was the end of his romance and his school days.

While the children were in school at Cane Hill, Montford continued to improve his new home at Silver City. He broke out about one hundred acres to farm. Since there was no timber suitable for a rail fence, he dug a ditch with scrapers, and the dirt taken from it was piled on the inside bank to make an earthen wall. This fence was very unsatisfactory, but Montford was too fond of his fine horses to risk the use of the new Glidden or barbed-wire fencing, which he had first seen a few years before during a trip to Texas.

In the spring of 1879 Nute Burney turned over his interest in the Pond Creek ranch to John Whorley. Nute moved his seventy-four-bar–branded cattle to his new ranch on Walnut Creek. Since Whorley had a start in horses from the wild ones that he had caught, he did not share in the Diamond Link–branded horses of Montford. Montford moved his crew to the Washita River and started gathering the hookety-hook cows that he had missed the fall before when he moved part of them to Salt Creek. He had learned that about the time he was moving to Silver City, Bob Love and Buck Sparks had brought in from Texas about two thousand steers and turned them loose on the Washita. They had drifted north and had taken up with the Walnut Creek cattle. When winter hit them, they drifted south, and many of Montford's cows had drifted south with them. Love and Sparks had their crew out there too and helped gather the cattle. They later sold their steers to the Indian agencies, and they in turn issued them to the Indians as rations.

Notes

1. Johnson, E. B. E. B. Johnson Collection, Phillips Western History Collection, University of Oklahoma at Norman.
2. Burton, Art. 1991. *Black, Red and Deadly: Black and Indian Gunfighters of the Indian Territories.* Austin, TX: Eakin Press, p. 192.
3. Fisher, J. B. "Indian-Pioneer Interviews." *Chronicles of Oklahoma,* Oklahoma Historical Society. Vol. 24, p. 290.
4. Rex, Joyce A., ed. 1984. McClain County, Oklahoma, Death Records, 1882–1984, Purcell, Oklahoma.

Texas Trail Herds

To understand some of the changes in their way of life after Montford's clan moved to Silver City, it is necessary to know something of the nature and history of cattle driving and the making of cattle trails. As early as 1850, a few Texas cattle had been driven to Missouri and from there were shipped to the New York or East Coast markets. This meat was thought to be rather tough, but fine-grained and possessing a wild or gamelike flavor. In 1858 George Loving took a herd through Oklahoma Territory to Quincy, Illinois, and sold them to farmers. At the outbreak of the Civil War, this cattle driving came to an abrupt stop. During the war, all the self-respecting Texans were in the Confederate Army. This just left the women, children, feeble-bodied, and a few shirkers at home to look after the wild cattle. They actually ran wild with no one to look after them, and their population increased at a rapid rate. By the end of the war, Texas was bulging with these accumulated cattle, but the owners faced gaunt poverty or bankruptcy because there was no market for them. Thousands of the cattle were butchered for their tallow and hides. In the north there had been no such increase of cattle. The Union Army had offered a steady market for anything that could be slaughtered, so it left a real scarcity in the northern pastures. The price for a matured steer was almost ten times as much in the north as it was in Texas. The Texans began to look to the north for their market and began to explore the hundreds of unknown and untamed miles separating them.

These Texas cattle ranged in color from black, brindle, dun, spotted, buckskin, roan, and white to various combinations of these colors.

Coarse hairs on the forehead and in the ears, with a fish-shaped prominence just back of a line across their hipbones, were special characteristics. In Texas they had grazed on or in the brush, so they were almost as wild as deer and wary as wolves, which did not make them very gentle traveling companions. They sniffed approaching danger from afar, and when frightened broke and ran like bullets from a rifle. One disgusted cowman called them "horned jackrabbits" and the name was so apt that it stuck.

The trail drivers or Texans soon realized that what they needed was a common meeting place for the trail herds and the railroads, a place where the northern buyer could meet and deal with the owners. Joseph G. McCoy, an Illinois dealer in cattle, built shipping pens at Abilene, Kansas. Other towns, and railroads, too, joined the movement. The rival railroads began extending their lines to get a shorter route for these oncoming herds.

The first trail from Texas was the Old Shawnee Trail, which had passed Camp Arbuckle and went northeast from there. As soon as the Santa Fe Railroad reached Abilene, the Texas trail drivers, who had been harassed by the Indians demanding tribute for passing through their country and threatened by the Kansas farmers, chose a route farther to the west where it traversed open country. This new route was established in 1871 and was called the Chisholm Trail. There has been a great amount of discussion about the name of this trail. In the early days of the Chickasaws, it was referred to as the Chisum Trail, named for a Texas cowman who sold thousands of cattle to trail drivers to take north. Sometimes as many as ten thousand head in the same tally brand came up the trail at one time. That many cattle were divided into four separate herds, each with its own separate crew. John Chisum, the Texas cowman, never came up the trail himself. When line riders met these herds, they often asked, "Whose brand?" and the herders replied, "Chisum's." So many cattle went up the trail wearing this Chisum tally brand that the cowboys began to refer to it as the Chisum Trail. The other version of the origin of the name of the trail was that it was named for Jesse Chisholm, Montford's friend, who had the store at Camp Arbuckle. It has been said that Jesse used this trail going for supplies for his store and from that beginning became known as the Chisholm Trail, which is the name that it bears today.

When the first trailblazing herd came in 1871, they had a large crew and more extra cowboys than were needed. They came to protect the herd from the wild Indians, to frighten away buffalo herds, and to establish markers by piling rocks or earth mounds indicating the general direction of the route. They also picked out safe fords and watering places for the cattle and men.

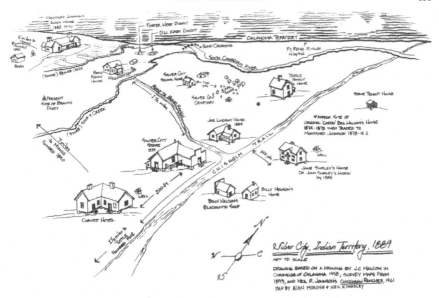

Map of Silver City, Indian Territory, 1889. Adapted from J. C. Malcom's map from the Chronicles of Oklahoma, Oklahoma Historical Society, *Vol. 36, 1958. New drawing by Alan Moring.*

This Chisholm Trail entered Montford's range at a rock-bottomed crossing on the Washita River, east of the present town of Chickasha and west of the little village of Tabler, Oklahoma. The trail then traversed the divide between Bitter and Salt Creeks, west of the present towns of Amber and Tuttle, and crossed the South Canadian River at Silver City. Thence it continued north, near the present town of Yukon, which was west of the Council Grove ranch.

In 1871 about six hundred thousand cattle passed over this trail. So many cattle reached the railroad terminal that the market was glutted. The market broke to such a low point that many of the cowmen held their cattle over in Kansas until the next year. This break in the market slowed down the movement to some extent, but at that time there were so many cattle passing through the Chickasaw Nation that the Chickasaw ranchers as well as the Kansas farmers protested these shipments.

Many of the Kansas farmers lost cattle on account of the Texas fever, which was later discovered to be spread by the cattle ticks. The Chickasaws appealed to the federal government to keep out these infested Texas cattle, but their appeal was ignored. Then the Chickasaws attempted to restrict the movement of cattle to designated trails, with a charge for passing along these trails. Upon the payment of fifteen cents a head, the

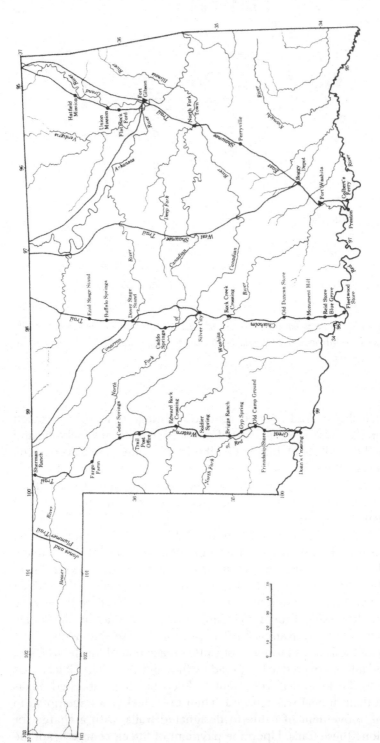

Cattle Trail Map. Map no. 46, Historical Atlas of Oklahoma, John W. Morris, University of Oklahoma Press, 1972.

cattle were to pass through the Chickasaw Nation at the rate of eight miles a day. The cattle were permitted to graze a strip a mile wide on each side of the trail. In the event any of the terms were violated, the herd became liable for one dollar a head penalty, which was prescribed by the federal government for trespassing on Indian reservations.

The Chickasaw Nation passed a further regulation to the effect that the dollar penalty just covered a period of thirty days. If at the end of that time the driver of the herd had not passed on, a sufficient number of cattle were seized to pay the penalty and an additional dollar was charged for each additional thirty-day trespass. The result was that if a herd trespassed long enough, the entire herd could be seized for the payment of the accumulated fines. After the Chickasaw trails were designated, Chickasaw inspectors were appointed to enforce the law and to collect the fees and fines. The inspectors who were appointed to enforce these laws were lenient and gave the trail drivers a lot of leeway when their herds were delayed by high water or other unforeseen difficulties.

In 1876 the railroad was extended to Dodge City, Kansas. The wild Indians had been subdued and placed on reservations and the buffalo had almost disappeared from the Plains. With the Chickasaws levying fees and fines and the Kansas farmers objecting to the herds passing through their country, the trail drivers blazed a new trail west of the ninety-eighth meridian and angling northwest to Dodge City, Kansas. This became known as the Western Trail, and was used extensively from 1876 to 1890.

In 1880 the railroad was extended to Caldwell, Kansas, and soon after minor shipping points were established at Hunnewell, Kiowa, and Englewood, Kansas. In the meantime, the Texas Panhandle ranchers had formed associations that levied grazing fees and fines upon the trail drivers for passing through their country. Since the terminal at Caldwell was so much closer than Dodge City, and since the owners of the herds had to pay fees anyway, many turned back to the Chisholm Trail. Once again Montford found these Texas steers pouring through his range to market, now augmented by the young cattle that had been coming up the Chisholm Trail each spring to stock the ranges in the Cherokee Strip.

Montford kept line riders stationed along the trail to keep his cattle thrown back from it and to check the herds for any of his cattle that may have been picked up. He had Lon Gray, one of his most dependable and competent men, to make the final check on these moving herds and to assist in their crossing of the South Canadian River at Silver City. If the river was up, the herds were moved west and crossed at Uncle Jim Bond's crossing, where the river was much wider and shallower. By keeping these line riders on the job and Lon Gray to pilot the herds across the river, Montford moved each herd out of his range in the shortest possible time.

Bond Ranch, northwest of Silver City, Indian Territory. Alternative crossing point on the South Canadian River for the Chisholm Trail. Adelaide Bond in dark dress, James Bond to her right. Circa early 1880s. Neil Kingsley Collection.

Even with all these precautions, Montford still lost a large number of cattle. Sometimes the river was up so much that they could not even cross at Uncle Jim Bond's crossing. Then the herds piled up around Silver City and ate out his home range.

The Texas cattle were infested with ticks that stuck to their hides until the tick was filled with blood, then dropped off into the high grass where in about fifteen days a new generation was produced. The cattle moved to Salt Creek ranch from Walnut were not immune to this Texas fever and many of them died. "The Department of Agriculture, finding that ticks survived winter only in a warm climate, established a quarantine line in 1889 to restrict the shipment of southern cattle during the hot months except under special sanitary conditions. The federal government experimented with methods of killing ticks and found that dripping livestock in a chemical solution was the most effective solution. Not until 1906 did Congress appropriate money for a national campaign to eradicate the fever tick."[1] Besides causing fever, these ticks pitted the hide of his cattle. At the spot where the tick stuck to the hide, they often left a raw spot. In such places the blow flies got busy, deposited their eggs, and in a short time the animal had a case of screwworms. If these infected spots were located on the animal where they could not reach them with their tongues so as to lick out the worms, and if the cowboys did not find the animal in time to kill the worms, the animal died.

By the time the herd reached Silver City all the thrill and excitement of going up the trail had long since vanished. The job had settled down to a slow, tedious drag that lasted all day and at least one guard shift at night. When the dry weather of summer set in, there was always a heavy cloud of dust raised as the herds drifted down the hill into the riverbed. The cowboys rode hunched over in the saddle, their faces half covered with bandannas to keep out the stifling dust. Their eyes were red and bloodshot from the dust and squinting at the blazing sun. Their clothes were oftentimes torn and travel-worn, almost in shreds. They definitely did not resemble the silk-shirted rodeo performers of today.

Many of them were racked with typhoid and malaria germs. Reckless from thirst, they oftentimes drank from the first water that they found, whether it be muddy, brackish, hot, or cold. When they rode up to a pool, the frogs, snakes, wigglers, and tadpoles moved to the other side. Dismounting, the riders swept away the scum and skimmers with their big hats, then cupped the brims for dippers to drink. The more seasoned riders drank great quantities of coffee with their meals. This was made from water that had been boiled and purified. To help them endure the thirst, some placed small, hard sandstones in their mouths and sucked on them. Many of the riders chewed tobacco, which really increased their desire for water, but the juice coated over their lips and protected them from the wind, dust, and sun. The home riders often found small seeps and springs that were inaccessible to the cattle. They kept these cleaned out and used them for watering places.

When the river was on such a rampage that it could not be forded, a few of the cowboys were left to loose-herd the cattle, and the rest of the riders congregated around the Silver City store. They enjoyed visiting with the men from outfits other than their own and exchanging stories and experiences. They were usually tired of the old shopworn tales of the talkative men within their own crew. To pass away the time around the store, they pitched horseshoes, ran horse races, held jumping contests, and played mumbledepeg, a knife-throwing game. Some repaired their equipment and some had their horses shod. Montford set up a blacksmith shop on the east side of the trail about one hundred yards east of the store. He later built a small hotel to the south of the store to accommodate this growing trade.

As soon as the waters receded, they tackled the river and tried to cross the herds. The cowboys generally removed their chaps, boots, and heavier clothing. These they either piled on the bank to get when they returned or tied them behind their saddles. Lon Gray, who acted as

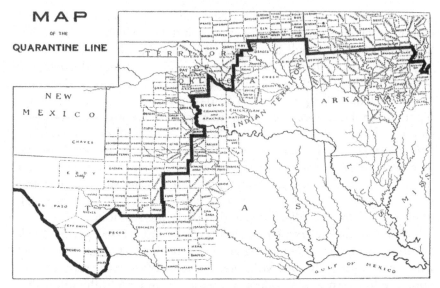

Cattle Quarantine Line Map (from 1912 pamphlet from Cattle Raisers Association of Texas). E. B. Johnson Collection, Western History Collection, University of Oklahoma.

pilot, loosened his saddle cinch, which enabled his horse to swim better, and rode into the stream. Immediately behind him came the remuda of horses, and this was to be followed by the chuck wagon. They placed the bedding and perishable stuff on top of the load. The wagon bed was tied down to the running gear so that it would not wash away. Several cowboys would tie their ropes to the side of the wagon so that they could assist the team and keep the wagon lined up. When the wagon was safely across, the ropes were untied and the remuda was again driven back across to the herd. This back-and-forth trampling of the riverbed by the horses usually helped pack the quicksand and made the footing much safer for the cattle. The horses then preceded the cattle again as the herd began its crossing of the river. As the cattle strung out across the swollen stream, the herd often resembled a long crawling snake slithering its way along.

The river was most dangerous when the floodwaters had about half receded. The quicksand was well mixed with the water, and the steers very often bogged down when they walked into holes or on some of the sandbars. After the herd was crossed, they returned to dig out those that had bogged down. A rope was tossed around the animal's head, the cowboys dismounted and dug the legs loose, sometimes rolling them onto a log or onto their side, then everyone pulled and, with any luck, out they came. If there were several stuck in a hole, the sliding, digging, and trampling around them worked the water from the sand, so that after a few were dug out and pulled free, the remainder could struggle out and walk away as soon as their legs were loosened.

One afternoon they started a herd across and everything was going like they had planned it until the steers hit the swift water where the muddy waves were rolling high. The steers started into this swift water when the waves broke and made a roaring, hissing sound. This noise frightened the lead steers, and they turned back downstream toward the south bank. The current carried them below where they had started out to ford it, and just about the time they reached the bank, they hit an old slough. Twenty-five of them bogged down in a pile. An inexperienced cowboy tossed his rope around the horns of the steer nearest to him and gave a sharp, hard pull. The steer gave a feeble bawl and died. The cowboy had broken its neck. The crew spent the rest of the afternoon digging and pulling the rest of the cattle from this slough. Since the chuck wagon was already across, the men were fed at the Silver City store and hotel, where they spent the night when they were not standing their night guard. The next morning they crossed the now calm river without incident.

Even when the river appeared to be dry, it was still hazardous. Dry sand often blew over bog holes, which made them appear to be dry and solid like the rest of the riverbed. Cattle oftentimes winding their way across would hit one of these places and down they would go. One cowboy, riding a high-headed bronc with his head tied down, chased a wild cow and her calf that were trying to join the herd. The cow and calf hit just such a slough, but managed to struggle out of it. The running horse hit it and, with his head tied down, was unable to catch his balance. He pitched forward and buried his head in the mud. The rider sailed over the horse's head, landed on his stomach, hands, and knees, and crawled out. He jerked out his knife, cut the strap while he held his horse's head down, and managed to pull his head out. After blowing the mud from his nostrils and struggling, the horse stumbled out and stood trembling from the shock.

In the spring of 1879 the government moved many more Cheyenne and Arapaho Indians to the Darlington Agency. Mick or Meek Smith and Jay Forsythe obtained one of the beef contracts to feed them. They moved ten thousand steers from Line Creek on the Washita to what was known as New Castle Flat. This was between the Pond Creek ranch and the South Canadian River. They constructed their headquarters near a large spring that was about a mile south of the river. There were two log cabins and several large corrals, which were made of cedar rails that were cut from trees along the river bluffs. Their big steers ranged on both sides of the Canadian, drifting north to Council Grove and over to Pond Creek. They took up with Montford's cows and became a terrible nuisance, especially during storms when they would drift far away from their pastures.

They called it the Long O Ranch because the brand was an elongated O. Jim Tuttle and Bud Smith, a nephew of Mick Smith, took charge of the camp. They hired W. H. Johnson and his wife, Rachel, to look after their headquarters. Rachel established a great reputation among the cowboys as a cook. In passing through the country, they made it convenient to stop and eat some of Rachel's excellent meals.

Lon Gray worked a lot of people, animals, equipment, and supplies across the Canadian at the Chisholm Trail and Bond crossings. Lon recalled helping pilot a circuit-riding preacher's wagon across one day. Half way across the river, the water ran up into the man's buggy, startling the nervous traveler. Now fearing for his life, the preacher jumped up in fright, not realizing that his Bible and songbooks were now floating off down the river. Lon, seeing this, immediately turned his horse and went splashing off after the books. The preacher, seeing Lon riding away from him and what he thought was his sinking ship, became really frightened and screamed at Lon, "To hell with the Bible, save the Lord's messenger." Needless to say, Lon succeeded in getting both the messenger and his message to dry land.

During these summer months when E. B. was not in school, he worked the range with Lon Gray around Silver City. It was exciting work, but there was little time to relax until the last herd of the day was safely across the South Canadian and disappeared over the hills to the north.

Note

1. Stephens, A. Ray. 1964. *The Taft Ranch: A Texas Principality.* Austin: University of Texas Press, p. 88.

Council Grove Ranch and the Boomers

In the spring of 1880 E. B. returned from school at Boonsboro, Arkansas, and started riding the range as he had done the previous summer. C. B. got home from his Nebraska school sometime later, saying that he had broken up his Nebraska love match, that he was through with the girl and with school, too. Montford had promised to start C. B. in the ranching business when he finished school, so he set out to fulfill his promise. The spring before, a man by the name of Jim Thompson had drifted up the old Shawnee Trail with a herd of two hundred head of large red Durham cows and a few bulls. They were branded with a large hat brand on the left side. During one of Thompson's visits to the Silver City store for supplies, Montford purchased the whole herd at fifteen dollars a head for the cows, with the calves thrown in. Gus Leslie, who was still broken up over the death of his wife and refusing to return to work at Council Grove, was hired to look after this herd during the winter.

Conditions around the Council Grove ranch were deteriorating, and it would not be too long before Montford gave up any attempts to ranch there. Besides that, he knew that the Council Grove area was not in the Chickasaw Nation and he would eventually have to abandon it. However, before Montford completely gave up on his northernmost enterprise, he started C. B. and his sister, Ella, out there the next year, giving each of them one hundred of his cows and heifers. Montford started the two cousins out at the Council Grove ranch initially, with Granny Vicey there part time until they hired a man to cook full time. They remained there until the incursions from the Boomers, with their grass fires and repeated pilfering of livestock, convinced Montford that it was time to give up this northern range. Of course, the relocation of the Cheyenne and Arapaho tribes to the west also influenced his plan to move his stock back south of the North and South Canadian Rivers. Sometime later, when C. B. was set up at his next ranch back in the Chickasaw Nation with a line camp near some springs north of present-day Purcell, Oklahoma, Montford gave him an additional twenty head of young horses to go with the cattle C. B. and Ella already had. Montford also made C. B. a partner in his hat-brand herd.

During the years from 1873 to 1879 a number of bills had been introduced into Congress that organized the Territory of Oklahoma, but Montford had either not heard of them or paid very little attention to the bickering that went on in Washington. These bills and the discussion in Congress about the Territory caught the attention of homeseekers. This was a part of the lands that had been assigned to the Creek and Seminole Indians, but they had never occupied it. Although there were thousands of acres of unoccupied land in the west, none of it looked so good or so attractive to settlers as the lands belonging to the Indians. In the spring of 1879 some Boomers had rushed into this unoccupied district, but had been expelled by the soldiers from Fort Reno. In February 1880, President Benjamin Harrison issued a proclamation that called for homesteaders to keep out of the Oklahoma district because it was reserved for Indian settlement.

In spite of this proclamation, a colony of settlers under the leadership of Captain David Payne, as he called himself, appeared at the Council Grove ranch. These colonists thought that they had found the real promised land. They shot and butchered Montford's hogs and even killed some of his calves. When Montford investigated the colony, Payne informed him that he supposed the hogs belonged to no one, that he was going to colonize Oklahoma, and that this was his first settlement. In May the troops at Fort Reno discovered the squatters and drove them back to Kansas. Payne and William Couch repeatedly led their small groups into the Oklahoma Territory over the next four years. Montford eventually decided to give up this ranch and moved his livestock back south to his home range in the Chickasaw Nation.

Although Payne's first attempt to colonize was broken up by the soldiers, he continued to take advantage of gullible homeseekers and marched them into the district for settlement. Payne has sometimes been pictured as a Moses bringing settlers into the promised land, but the Chickasaws looked upon him in a different light. They found him to be a blowhard who blustered, bragged, and bluffed about what he was going to do. Excluding a few naive families, his followers for the most part were ne'er-do-wells, illiterate and disreputable. They were the kind that you usually found loitering around the early-day saloons. They really did not care about settling down to make a living, but preferred to roam over the country for a change of scenery. Payne charged these colonists two dollars and fifty cents a head for joining his colonist band. He offered to file claims on one hundred and sixty acres for those who did not care to make the trip, upon payment of twenty-five dollars. There was a rumor that Payne was being paid by the railroads to organize these colonists to settle the country, hopefully expediting the railroads' advancement into the Indian lands.

To discourage these wandering adventurers, the *Cheyenne Transporter*, a newspaper published at the Darlington Agency, printed an article describing Oklahoma. It stated that the southwestern part of Oklahoma was a barren and sandy waste, covered sparsely with grass. The valley of the Cimarron River was said to be suitable for cultivation, but the ridges between the Cimarron and the North Canadian Rivers were described as sterile red clay and sand, which were usually barren by midsummer. The southeastern part, from Deep Fork to the North Canadian River, was pictured as a low swamp, scantily timbered country covered with lagoons and bayous. This country was often underwater and impassable. In spite of this publication and in spite of the warning by the president's proclamation, Payne continued to catch suckers, charge them a fee, and send them into the district.

On November 26, 1880, sixty Boomers with their women, children, livestock, and furniture were expelled by the soldiers and Indian scouts. A month later, on December 24, a group of colonists even came into Fort Reno. They had been caught in a blizzard. They and their teams were suffering from exposure and turned to the fort as a haven of refuge. They were surprised to find that they were trespassing and had to move out. One of these colonists had sixty head of cattle, which he had to sell. Cursing Payne as a swindler, they were escorted out of the Territory. In August 1882 Payne and another party were arrested. The settlers were held in a detention camp at Fort Reno and later expelled. Payne was taken to Fort Smith, Arkansas, for trial.

In February 1883 they again showed up quite a bit north and east of Council Grove at North Fork and named their encampment Camp Alice after a young girl named Alice McPherson, whose family was traveling with the party. In April 1884 William Couch established four camps on the North Canadian, the largest of which was set up at the present site of downtown Oklahoma City. One of these camps was set up by William Couch's father, Meshach, just a few miles west of the main camp on the Fort Reno road.

It seemed strange and unfair that Montford Johnson, a half-blood Chickasaw, could claim rights to land that the Chickasaw Nation had never owned. Meshach and the other Boomers considered Johnson and all the other cattlemen-herders in the Oklahoma country trespassers. They could never understand why the soldiers left Johnson undisturbed fattening his great herds of cattle and hogs in the unassigned lands between the two Canadian rivers.[1]

A few days later, on April 22, Lieutenant Charles L. Stevens marched down the Canadian from Fort Reno, arrested all the Boomers, including Meshach and William Couch, and ordered them back to Kansas. Incensed by what they thought was an illegal arrest, the Boomers had to be escorted most of the way back to Kansas. The last paragraph in a front-page column from the August 15, 1884, *Cheyenne Transport* summed up the local disdain for Payne: "Payne is a drunkard and dead-beat of the darkest type, he having succeeded in living off a lot of deluded people now for years and it is high time that his game ended. It is to be hoped that this cleaning out will put a stop to the craze and now that his leaders are to go behind the bars, it is everywhere pronounced a good riddance."

On November 28, 1884, as another expedition was being planned, David Payne died suddenly as he ate breakfast at the hotel he was living at in Wellington, Kansas.

The continued repetition of Payne's invasions and the failure of the government to deal effectively with him and his settlers brought them both into disrepute in the Territory. It seemed to the Chickasaws that the white settlers were so jealous of the inherited rights of the Indian to own land, that they would never be satisfied until the Indians were dispossessed of this right. At first the Indians thought it was a joke that the government was so feeble, but the disgruntled homesteaders, angry at Payne, the troops who threw them out, and the world in general, set the prairie grass on fire, which often swept the entire country. They swore that if they could not settle this land, then no one else could use it either. Fires became so numerous and such a nuisance that ranchers in the district had to move their cattle elsewhere to winter them.[2]

In the summer of 1880, after most of the trail herd had passed, Montford selected eighty young horses that he had sold to the Turkey Track Ranch in the Texas Panhandle. He placed his son, E. B., in charge of the herd. They rigged out a chuck wagon to which were hitched four big horses. Late one evening they camped west of the homeplace. By camping close to home the first night, they had an opportunity to check everything that they needed for the trip. If they had overlooked anything, it was easy to get it before they had gone too far.

They knew the general direction to the Turkey Track Ranch and decided to follow the South Canadian River as far as Mobeetie. Traveling along the river bottoms, they crossed the stream many times. They kept one rider in the lead for the horses to follow and to keep a lookout for bands of wild horses. Occasionally a band was sighted, but they disappeared in a cloud of dust. They took turns at night standing guard on the horses and, for this purpose, used some older and gentler horses that they expected to ride on the return trip.

During the trip they often caught some of these young horses they were delivering and rode them just for the sport of the it. Several of the broncs were almost gentle by the time they delivered them. After eating up the beef that they had started with, they lived off the country for fresh meat by shooting deer, antelope, and wild turkey. At night they hung the meat in a tree to keep cool and early the next morning wrapped it in a slicker and placed it in the bottom of the chuck wagon. In this way they could keep the meat several days.

They stopped at Mobeetie, where there were two rival general stores. One was owned by W. H. Reed and Company, the other by H. Hamburg and Company. There were also two small hotels, which were crowded to capacity because a term of court was in session. There was a very impressive courthouse that was built of limestone and was two stories high. [It is still in use as a historical museum.–*C.N.K.*] They had their workhorses reshod, bought a few supplies, and received directions on how to find the Turkey Track Ranch. They had traveled about one hundred and seventy miles. After leaving Mobeetie, they drove along the north side of the South Canadian River and passed the ruins of the famous small trading town of Adobe Walls. Adobe Walls consisted of four buildings and a corral.

Six years before, in the summer of 1874, Billie Dixon, along with twenty-seven men and one woman, had won renown there in fighting off a band of about seven hundred Comanche, Cheyenne, and Kiowa Indians. As one version of the story goes, on the third day of the siege an Indian patted his rump in derision to show what he thought of the white men as he and his small band watched down from a butte about three-quarters of a mile to the east of the village. At the urging of friends, Buffalo hunter Dixon took careful aim from out in front of Hanrahan's Saloon with his Sharps "Big 50" Buffalo rifle, fired, and waited. A few seconds later the Indian was knocked from his horse, some fifteen hundred yards away, and the other Indians scattered. Being that far away, the Indian survived and was quickly dragged away by his tribe members. This incident, along with the death of their medicine man's (Esa-tais) pony, three days into the battle, helped discourage the Indians from continuing the siege at Adobe Walls, and the battle was soon over.[3] E. B. and his cowboys stopped long enough to speculate on the story as they looked down from the spot on the cap rock where they thought the Indian had been wounded.

After crossing several shallow creeks that emptied into the South Canadian River, they came to a narrow and deeper one that ran like a mountain stream. They turned up this creek and found the Turkey Track Ranch headquarters. It was a new camp and the cowboys were living in dugouts. The manager of the ranch was well pleased with the young horses and paid E. B. forty-eight hundred dollars in cash. E. B. placed the money in a box that he kept hidden in his bedroll.

They returned home by easy stages. They crossed the river and angled southeast back toward Mobeetie. They thought the country was beautiful, but there was a shortage of water between the spring-fed creeks. The temperature during the day became stifling hot, but the nights turned very cool. When each of them went on night guard, they had to put on every piece of clothing they could find to keep warm. Those sleeping had to double up on the blankets.

The following morning, on the south side of the river, they passed through groves of mesquite trees that covered many miles of the flats. The trunks of the trees were from four to eight inches in diameter and not over twenty feet high. The branches were covered with thorns and long pods that were filled with beans. In the fall, these pods dropped to the ground and made excellent feed for cattle and horses. In this part of the country they also saw many mirages. In the middle of the day, when the heat waves were dancing before their eyes, they often imagined that they saw lakes of water, but as they approached them these lakes seemed to skip ahead of them or disappear altogether. Trees and horses, even at a short distance, looked queer and distorted in shape. The rest of the trip home took about a week. They were glad to see their own little town of Silver City after three straight weeks in the saddle.

When they returned home, they found that Caddo Bill Williams and his family were visiting Montford and Mary. When they prepared to leave, Bill reminded Montford that his watermelons were almost ripe and insisted that Montford's family should repay his visit. To make his invitation more attractive, he added that he would put on a barbecue, complete with Indian dances, square dancing, and horse races. The date was set, and in due time Montford loaded Mary and the younger children into the hack. The older children mounted their horses, and they all headed for Bill's ranch on Stinking Creek to the west.

When they arrived at Bill's place, the festivities were in full blast. Bill had a big barbecue ready for them. The Caddo Indians were full of beef, with some of them dancing. That evening, after some stiff toddies had been consumed, Montford and Bill joined in the dance. Some of the younger boys danced for a while, but as they began to slow down, the Indians kicked them out of the circle. They ran several spirited horse races, and after the dances they turned in for the rest of the night.

The next morning Mary complained about a burning pimple on her lip. She said that she had been unable to sleep the night before and that she ought to go home. The drive back to Silver City was hot and uncomfortable. She suffered terribly, and by the time they reached Silver City, she was delirious. Montford summoned Lon Gray and told him that he had to try and cross the South Canadian River, which was on one of its rampages, and go to Fort Reno for Doctor Hodges. Fort Reno was twenty-five miles away and this raging, high rolling river would have to be crossed, not once, but twice to bring help. The sun had just disappeared below the horizon when Lon rode his best horse into the raging river. By zigzagging back and forth, Lon missed some of the worst channels and just as night began to settle in, he rode his horse up on the north bank of the river and waved. E. B. stood alone on the south bank and acknowledged Lon's safe crossing with his own wave. E. B. then hurried back home to report Lon's successful crossing and wait through the night with the others.

Aunt Adelaide had been sent for, and she joined Montford at Mary's bedside. They put cold packs on her burning face. The younger children were put to bed; the rest of them hovered around, speaking in low, frightened voices. They had never seen their mother sick before except when she was having another baby.

At daybreak Lon and Doctor Hodges came riding up from the direction of the Bond crossing, where the river was wider and more shallow. Doctor Hodges hurried to see what he could do for Mary, who by this time was unconscious. He said that she had erysipelas, a streptococcus also know as Saint Anthony's Fire. He had come too late to save her. The infection had already spread throughout her body. All they could do now was to try and make her as comfortable as possible. After much suffering, she died on August 27, 1880.

Phil Smith and the men from the store built a coffin from boxes found there. The women lined it on the inside and covered the outside with black cambric cloth. She was buried on the knoll west of the house and close to where Muggs McLish had been laid to rest.

The death of Mary was a severe shock to Montford. They had married when they were both very young and had grown up together. She had been a great ranchwoman. Leaving the life of a girl at a frontier army post, she had adopted the ways of the civilized Indians and had lived her life with them, on the edge of the wild Indian Country. She had remained cheerful and optimistic. Living so close and knowing all of Montford's peculiarities, she had been able to advise and help him in all his dealings. One of her ambitions was to be economical and save money so that her children could have advantages that their father had missed. Her death came at a time when the future looked most promising.

Mrs. Montford (Mary Elizabeth) Johnson, circa 1880, shortly before her death. Neil Kingsley Collection.

Montford Johnson, a Chickasaw, circa 1891. Courtesy, Oklahoma Historical Society, #1178 OHS, Archives and Manuscripts Division.

Montford was now branding, each spring, about nine thousand calves, six thousand of which were his own. His cattle ranged from the Pottawatomie country on the east, the North Canadian River to the north, the Wichita reservation to the west, and to the Walnut and Washita Rivers on the south. His horses and cattle were generally known to be of the finest breeding stock in the Chickasaw Nation.

Besides the anguish and sorrow of losing his beloved companion, Montford had to assume the responsibility of caring for and rearing seven young children. E. B., the oldest, was seventeen; Ben, the youngest, was just four months old; Henry was eleven; Robert, nine; Tilford, seven; Stella, five; and Fannie was three. Aunt Adelaide took Ben, the baby, home with her and reared him there.

Mary had been a very devout Catholic and had always told Montford that if anything should ever happen to her, he should turn to the church for help. A very broken man, he went to Denison, Texas, and made arrangements to place all of the children in the convent, except E. B., whom he decided to send to live with Montford's father, Boggy Johnson, in New York. Later that fall, in October, after getting all his children off to their various schools, Montford had another flare-up of his malaria that laid him up for a few weeks.

Notes

1. Couch, Edna. Unfinished manuscript. Edna Couch Collection, Oklahoma Historical Society.
2. Hoig, Stan. 1980. *David L. Payne*. Oklahoma City: Western Heritage Books, p. 214.
3. Steele, Aubrey L. 1944. "Lawrie Tatum's Indian Policy." *Chronicles of Oklahoma*, Oklahoma Historical Society. Vol. 22. p. 93.

School in New York

hen Boggy Johnson, Montford's father, heard of Mary's death, he insisted that E. B. come to New York at once. Montford took E. B. to Atoka to board the train, and as he bade him good-bye he said very soberly, "Son, I want you to go to school with white boys and learn the white man's ways."

E. B. often thought of his father's good sense and judgment and often contrasted it with the policy of the federal government in educating the American Indian. More than one hundred years ago, Montford, a poorly educated Indian himself, saw that if the younger generation was to live and compete with white people, these Indian youngsters should be thrown together with the white children during the formative period of their school days. The government, on the other hand, continued to segregate the Indians, educate them in Indian schools, and graduate them with an inferiority complex. Montford thought that if the Indian schools could not do a better job preparing the Indian children to live in the white man's world, then they should be abolished, and the young Indians sent to the state colleges and universities on an equal footing with the whites.

Here is a letter that E. B. had submitted to the *New York Times* a few years later, when he was twenty-one. It appeared in the *Cheyenne Transporter* on August 30, 1884.

EDUCATION OF THE INDIANS

The following is a letter to the *New York Times* written by Ed Johnson, son of Munford Johnson, who is well known here:

"Having a desire for a long time to visit the Indian school at Carlisle during a sojourn through the state a few weeks ago, I had the pleasure of gratifying my yearning. Being acquainted with Capt. Pratt's (at St. Augustine) ability to manage the red man successfully, I must confess I was not disappointed in the least, but, on the contrary, no more commendable tribute could be offered to the public than the fruits of his humane toil. As a preparatory school for enlightening the Indian for the various duties of daily life, viz.: giving them a primary education and a fair knowledge of manual labor, this institution is perfect, so to speak. And in fact the manual department both for boys and girls, would serve as a creditable example for many of our public institutions. Having accomplished so much in the judgement, and I think it a practical one, there should be a special appropriation or some immediate means whereby students showing the capacity and having a desire for a higher education, should receive it. In this case, in a very short time we will have native teachers, physicians, and if their condition require it, representatives of law who will know the inmost characteristics of the race, and unquestionably will have more influence than one of different blood. Trusting all institutions organized for the advancement of the Indians will continue more successful in the future than in the past, I remain in behalf of the cause.

Edward B. Johnson, of the Chickasaw Nation, Indian Territory,
New York City, Thursday August 21, 1884

Upon E. B.'s arrival in New York, he was met by his grandfather, Boggy, who took him to his home in Bay Ridge on the western tip of Long Island, in Brooklyn. The house was the finest E. B. had ever seen, but the household was rather confusing. Living with Boggy, who was a widower the second time, was Aunt Belle, a daughter by his second wife. She was a half sister to Montford. Aunt Belle had married a Jewish businessman, Edward Simpson, who was a tall man, six feet four inches, and as dark as any full-blood Indian. Besides Aunt Belle and her husband was Mr. Becker, a nephew of Boggy's, who was a partner with Boggy and Edward Simpson in the wholesale liquor business. Aunt Belle had two boisterous children, Coody, a girl, and Pax, a boy.

After visiting with these newfound relatives for a few days, E. B. insisted that he should live someplace else if he expected to study any at school. Boggy arranged for him to live with Mr. Thomas D. Ormiston, who also lived in Brooklyn, and as soon as E. B. was settled in his new surroundings, he enrolled in the School of Civil Engineering in the Brooklyn Polytechnic Institute.

E B.'s schoolwork was very interesting, but he found himself lonesome for home and found it difficult to adapt himself to his new surroundings. He had a letter from home that told about the death of Aunt Eliza, Jack Brown's wife. She had served as midwife and granny for Montford's whole family. Next to his mother, E. B. felt that Eliza was the dearest person, black or white, that he had ever known. Montford's letters indicated that he was lonesome and quite discouraged; he also complained about the continued intrusion of the Long O steers drifting in on his cattle at the Pond Creek ranch.

Toward the end of April, according to the May 10, 1881, *Cheyenne Transporter*, while Montford and a group of his cowboys sat around at camp, two men rode by with an unusual amount of ropes with them. Montford, knowing that one of his neighbors had reported the theft of some ropes, became suspicious. After the two men passed the camp Montford had his men mount up and pursued these strangers to question them about the ropes. When Montford's party reached the two men and hailed them to stop, the rope-heavy duo opened fire on Montford and his men. A fire fight followed and some sixty shots were fired before the two men fled. The only casualty at the time appeared to be a pack pony belonging to the strangers, but three days later, one of the suspected men was found shot through the hips. He was taken to the hospital at Reno where he claimed that he was not a thief, putting all the blame on his former partner. The paper concluded, "As to this man's character, we know nothing, but certainly the circumstances are not such as to prejudice to his favor."

E. B. remained in Brooklyn all that summer of 1881 without any visitors from Indian Territory. In September, however, E. B. was overjoyed when he learned that Montford had given in at last to Boggy's insistence and was coming to New York. He arrived along with C. B., who was recovering from typhoid fever, and Ella, Aunt Adelaide's two children. Aunt Belle greeted her half brother, Montford, with open arms and made a great fuss over him. During his visit, which lasted several months, Aunt Belle and Boggy showed the sights of New York to Montford and the two children, for which Montford footed the bills. Montford was not accustomed to so much flattery and attention, and in a short time this Chickasaw Indian, whom his father had abandoned and neglected for so many years, was so gullible that he was a fit subject to the taken in.

Before Montford really knew what was happening, he had been persuaded to buy Becker's one-third interest in the E. Simpson and Company wholesale liquor business. He agreed to pay twenty-five thousand, ten thousand of that up front, for this interest in a business that was barely paying expenses. Before he left for home, he purchased for Aunt Belle the house in which they lived. He paid five thousand dollars down

E. B. Johnson (right) *and first cousin, C. B. Campbell, circa 1880–1882. Neil Kingsley Collection.*

and signed a note with Boggy and Aunt Belle for the balance. He also purchased three hundred dollars worth of fashionable clothes for Ella. Montford had a good time on this visit. Boggy saw to it that his best brandy was close to Montford's elbow most of the time, and Aunt Belle continued to shower him with attention. E. B. was very much relieved when Montford finally decided to end his trip and return to the Chickasaw country.

After Mary's death in his home at Silver City, Montford, like most Indians, wanted to get away from his old surroundings and memories of his wife. He decided to build a new home on a hill overlooking the intersection of Beaver (Snake) and Buggy Creeks. This new site was a little less than two miles west of Aunt Adelaide's home.

The plans for the house called for eight large rooms with fireplaces in four of them. Basically, there were two multiple-roomed houses connected together by two large adjoining rooms. The south building contained the kitchen and dining room, and the north building consisted primarily of bedrooms. The southern building also had a room to the west for the dust-covered cowboys to clean up in. The two middle rooms could be opened together as one by folding back four doors that divided them. This large room could then be used for dances or other gatherings, and it had screened porches on its east and west sides. The entire house was probably a little under two thousand square feet, quite a step up from his sixteen-by-fourteen log cabin on Caddo Creek. A cellar for storage was dug under the dining room, but another large dugout was made west of the house to be used as a cyclone cellar. Also on the west side was a well house with a hand water pump and dinner bell out in the yard.

Montford sent his wagons to Hunnewell, Kansas, for the lumber and hired a Mr. Chilton to build it. A large barn and corrals were built in the valley north of the house on the west bank of Beaver (now Snake) Creek. West of the corrals, Montford planted a large vineyard and orchard. Since no one paid any attention to section lines, because all the Chickasaw land was held in common, it was later discovered that Montford's barn, corrals, vineyard, and orchards were located in the corner of four different sections (T 10 N, R 6 W, Secs. 17, 18, 19, 20). [This site is now occupied by Braum's massive dairy farm complex.–C.N.K.]

On May 8, 1882, shortly before E. B. returned from New York, the town of Mill Creek was all but destroyed by a four-hundred-yard-wide tornado. Fortunately, only one fatality was reported among the thirty-five wounded. Montford received a letter from former Chickasaw governor Cyrus Harris asking for help and assistance for the families at Mill Creek. A copy of the May 1882 issue of the *Chickasaw Academy Leaflet* followed shortly with a more complete description of the damage:

The school house and church was completely demolished. The upper story of Gov. Harris's residence was torn away, but none of the occupants were injured.

The barn belonging to the stage company was blown away, and scarcely any fragments were left to mark the place where it stood. George Taylor, the stage driver, in attempting to run from the barn to Mr. Heald's house, was struck by a piece of flying timber, and was instantly killed. . . . Four horses were killed. One horse was carried in the air by force of the wind four hundred yards. Onions, and other garden vegetables were blown out of the ground.

The prostrate fences, the trampled grass, the torn and shattered trees, the dead horses, the groans of the wounded, the open grave, and the sympathetic tear in the eyes of those whose hearts are not stone—these were at Mill Creek the day after the Cyclone.

We have often been at the field hospital where the wounded and dying soldiers were gathered from the battle field, and even then, in those days of carnage, it made our heart feel sad to see men, even soldiers, groaning and weltering in their blood, but when we saw fair women, and tender children crowded into a storm shattered house, with broken bones, and sore bruises, it was more that we could bear.

Such a scene as this met us when we reached the house of our old friend, Gov. Harris, at Mill Creek. In every room came the sound of suffering.

The article went on to appeal for aid and assistance for the people and community: "Come to the rescue! And come quickly, come cheerfully, come liberally. . . . and in the mean time let contributions continue to flow into Mill Creek until comfortable homes shall have arisen on every heap of ruins." Many of Montford's, Mary Elizabeth's, and Aunt Adelaide's old childhood friends lived in that area, so they were quite concerned when they received these reports and contributed what they could to this devastated community.

When E. B. came home for his vacation in the summer of 1882, they were still building these new headquarters. He spent most of that summer riding with his father and visiting the various ranches. In late August it was time for the girls to return to school. Montford loaded the two Campbell cousins, Ella and Addie, along with his two daughters, Stella and Fannie, in the family hack to take them back to the Sacred Heart Mission School in the Pottawatomie country. He was driving a young and high-spirited team. When they started down the steep hill leading from the house, a pole strap broke, which allowed the hack to bump the horses from the rear. This immature team began to plunge, run, and pitch down the hill with the carriage careening from side to side. The carriage finally turned over and threw them clear, except Addie, who was caught under the carriage and was dragged a short distance. Montford was bruised and cut but managed to hang onto the team until some of the cowboys were able to catch and hold them. Montford turned the team over to the men and stumbled back to see how badly the children had been injured.

All were shaken up and skinned, and Addie was sprawled out on the ground and complained about a severe pain in her hip. After the damage to the hack was repaired and the harness fixed, they loaded in again and resumed their journey. Addie suffered with her hip all the way and when they arrived at school, the doctor discovered that she had dislocated and fractured her hip. She was confined to her bed at the convent for several months, and even after she was able to get up, she walked with a slight limp and found out that the injury was to be permanent. Addie's mother, Sallie, blamed Addie's injury on Montford and never let him forget it.

Shortly after E. B. returned to New York that fall, he went to bed with typhoid fever. He was placed in the Catholic hospital in Brooklyn and was confined there for several months. Montford came to see him and at the same time tried to straighten out the finances of the E. Simpson and Company, which no longer had any credit. By the time E. B. recovered it was too late to enter the first term of school, so E. B. let Montford and Boggy persuade him to go on the road peddling whiskey. He went on one trip and received many complimentary orders because his grandfather, Boggy, had written ahead to all the customers. When he returned to New York, E. B., disgusted, turned in his sample case. He had seen enough drunken sots, poor half-starved women, and neglected children hanging around saloon doors to last him a lifetime.

Shortly before Montford returned to his home in the Chickasaw Nation, he surprised E. B. by telling him that he was going to marry his brother-in-law Charley Campbell's daughter, his second cousin, Addie Campbell. Since Addie was so much younger than Montford, E. B. objected to the marriage and tried to dissuade him. Montford told him, "Edward, what you are saying to me has no more effect than if you threw paper wads at that big stone building. I am going to marry her." E. B. realized that Aunt Sallie, Addie's mother, had schemed the whole thing. By suggestions and hints, she had made Montford feel that since Addie had been permanently injured in the runaway hack accident, he was obligated to look after her. E. B. suspected that Montford had come to New York to get away from Aunt Sallie's domineering influence, but he had come too late. The wedding date had already been set for early June. When E. B. realized that it was useless to try and talk his father out of this marriage, he helped Montford buy his wedding clothes and promised that as soon as school was out, he would return home in time for the wedding.

One of E. B.'s New York friends, John E. Dockendorff, went home with him. When the wedding day arrived, there was a huge rain that had all the creeks and rivers on a rampage. The wedding guests began to arrive at Aunt Sallie's from all over the Chickasaw, Cheyenne, and Wichita Nations in wagons, hacks, and buggies and on horseback. They went to Montford's former home at Silver City, which Montford had given to Aunt Sallie and Uncle Charlie Campbell.

On the day of the wedding, Indians, Negroes, and whites rubbed elbows in the yard as they watched the ceremony take place on Aunt Sallie's front porch. When Ella, Aunt Adelaide's daughter, started the wedding march, E. B. and his friend John Dockendorff slipped away and rode over to Aunt Adelaide's, where the reception was to be held. John and E. B. were dressed in Prince Albert suits, like the groom, which made quite a contrast to the rough garb that was worn by most of the men guests. By the time Montford and his bride arrived, E. B. got himself together and was able to congratulate them. When the music started, which consisted of a piano, violin, banjo, and guitar, E. B. took his father's bride on his arm and led the first dance. While they were dancing, Montford settled himself in a comfortable chair on the east porch, bummed a chew of tobacco, and visited with his old friends who gathered around him.

Addie, his bride, spent the evening on the floor, dancing with the younger generation. During the evening Ella introduced E. B. to many newcomers in the country, among whom were three popular girls, Fannie, Mollie, and Callie Graham, who lived with their parents on Bob Curtis's place northwest of Silver City in the Caddo country. E. B. and his friend John danced with these girls and arranged to call on them. At daybreak the dance broke up; E. B. and John helped the Graham girls and their brother Isaac into their wagon, said good-bye, and again promised that they would see them at an early date.

Besides wanting to see the girls, E. B. was curious to see how people from the States adapted themselves to this wild Indian country. The Graham family's original home was in Missouri. A few days after Montford's wedding, E. B. and John saddled their horses and rode the eight miles to the Graham place.

As they rode up they looked over the house and grounds. The house was of four rooms. It was made of pickets, the space between chinked with clay, and the roof was made of clapboards. Some logs extended above the roof that were coated and chinked with clay, making a wooden chimney like the one Montford built on Caddo Creek before the family

Graham family in front of their home on the Bob Curtis Farm west of Silver City, Indian Territory. Courtesy, Oklahoma Historical Society, #1730 OHS, Archives and Manuscripts Division.

moved to Camp Arbuckle. Through an open glass window, the end of a bright cloth curtain flapped in the breeze. They had one long living room and a "lean to" kitchen and dining room combined. These rooms had pine floors, but the girls' bedroom floor was dirt, so they used the wooden crate that the organ came in to floor their room. Mollie said, "If it had not been for that organ, I don't know what we would have done out there on the prairie. Fannie was the most accomplished player, but we all learned to play a few tunes; for example we learned songs like ' Kathleen,' 'Blue Eyed Mary,' and 'Southern Home.' "

Surrounding the house was a flower garden, and on the east side was a scraped and swept croquet ground. Behind the house was the usual windlass with rope and bucket hanging over the well. A wire-netting fence enclosed a chicken yard, and beyond this was a small shed and corral for the livestock. The vegetable garden nearby looked clean of weeds and thriving, while in the new field beyond was a beautiful dark green field of corn that was beginning to tassel. Most of these pioneers made sure that the grounds around their homes were scraped clean, hoping to minimize any chance of a wild prairie fire destroying their houses.

John and E. B. dismounted and tied their horses to the pole hitching rack, noticing that the holes under the rack, made by pawing horses, indicated that there had been numerous callers before them. A slender, tall, quiet-mannered woman opened the door at their knock and introduced herself as Mrs. Graham. She invited them in after they had presented themselves. They entered a medium-sized room with a homemade rag carpet on the floor and what appeared to be bleached flour sacks sewed together and tacked on the walls and ceiling. There were two chairs, an organ, a sewing machine, and a double bed in the room.

While they were visiting with Mrs. Graham, the three girls came in and with them a younger sister, Hattie, who had not been to the dance. The mother and girls told of their coming to this part of the country. They had first moved from Chillicothe, Missouri, to Winfield, Kansas. Not long after moving to Winfield, they were visited by Henry Williams, Caddo Bill's brother, who told them of the great opportunities in the Indian Territory. The oldest son of the Graham family returned to the Caddo country with Henry Williams and worked several years on George Washington's ranch. George was a Caddo chief. Isaac had rented this place from Bob Curtis and sent for his brother, George Graham. The two boys built the house, then went to Kansas for the rest of the family.

The girls said the worst experience coming out was running into a severe blizzard near the Darlington Agency. When they got ready to set out the next morning, the wind was blowing such a gale that they could not start a fire, so they ate a breakfast of cold leftover biscuits. They crawled into the wagon and huddled close together under the feather beds and headed across the windswept prairie. After a long cold day of shivering and bumping along, they reached their new home early in the afternoon on February 17, 1882. Their brother, Isaac or Ike, and their landlord, Mr. Curtis, had a warm crackling fire roaring in the fireplace and a big hot pot of beans with ham waiting for them. That meal was indeed a tasty pleasure for the two weary parents and their cold and hungry children as they put a little life back into their numbed extremities.

After recounting their frigid ordeal, the girls suggested a croquet game, and they hurried to the yard to get mallets and balls. Fannie and E. B. were partners, John chose Mollie, and the two younger girls, Callie and Hattie, played together. During the game there was much talking about nothing in particular, and the girls teased each other about the cowboys from the Hobart and Montgomery ranches. These cowboys were frequent visitors. By the time they tired of the croquet game, the six of them were on a friendly footing, and when E. B. and John took their leave, they promised to call again soon.

About a week later they all got together at a dance at "Caddo Bill" Williams's place. When E. B. and John rode up, the prairie around the corrals was lined with wagons, buckboards, hacks, and a few buggies. A number of saddles lay where the riders had dumped them and spread their blankets over them, while others were perched on top of the rail fence. Children were yelling, running, and playing among the rigs. A short distance away were the tepees of the Caddo Indians who had been invited to the party. Most of the older people were carrying baskets and were headed toward the barbecue pits. By the time the two young men had turned their horses into the corral and joined the crowd, tablecloths were spread on the ground and little groups assembled around them to eat their picnic dinners.

After dinner several good horse races were run. This was a treat for the Caddo Indians, who loved horse racing, and their decorated clothing added color and excitement to the proceedings. E. B.'s friend John was fascinated by a shawl worn by Mrs. Polecat. The shawl was covered with beadwork, and the border was lined with elk's teeth. In this colorful shawl, with her cheeks painted crimson, Mrs. Polecat made a striking picture. In the evening the Indians presented several of their dances, and after that, the square dancing on the newly constructed platform began. The whole affair was typical of Caddo Bill Williams and his hospitality.

All day and all night the long table in his dining room was heaped with food, ready for anyone who wished to eat. In the house and on the porch, beds and pallets were spread for those who were too tired to dance or even watch. Extra fiddlers were on hand to rest the ones that had been playing. Anytime during the day a man thought that he had a fast horse, there was always someone to accept the challenge, and a race was run. Indians, cowboys, ranchers, and farmers joined in and had a glorious time. When anyone felt that they had been entertained enough, they headed for home; some of the guests stayed four days before they were satisfied. By the time the Graham girls left for home, John and E. B. were on very friendly terms with them.

There were several other parties that summer. Soon after Caddo Bill's party, Bob Curtis gave one at his place. John and E. B. and the Graham girls attended this party, which was spoiled a little because some of the men had too much whiskey to drink. After the Curtis dance, everyone in the neighborhood got busy training their top racehorses for the big celebration of the summer, the Fourth of July celebration at Fort Reno. E. B. planned to meet with Mollie at this celebration.

The Fourth of July in 1883 dawned a fine summer day. By midmorning all the roads leading to the fort were crowded. It looked as if everyone in the country had decided to come. Old friends who had not seen each other in a year or so visited and exchanged news as they gathered on the main grounds where the entertainment was to be held. The races were, as usual, a big attraction. The first races were footraces at a distance of one hundred, two hundred, and last, four hundred yards.

To get ready, the contestants just pulled off their boots or shoes and ran barefooted. The excitement ran high, however, with the friends of the runners screaming encouragement to them. Following these real tests of speed were the sack, wheelbarrow, and three-legged races. In the first the racers' feet were tied in sacks, and they ran or hopped along a fifty-yard course, with many of the runners taking several tumbles as they hopped along. The wheelbarrow race was a kind of free-for-all affair. The contestants were blindfolded and pushed the wheelbarrow ahead of them. They shoved them in many different directions, which resulted in collisions, spills, and skinned shins. The three-legged race was more a test of teamwork, where the right and left leg of each pair of runners were tied together. To make any headway, the runners had to perfectly coordinate each step they took.

The next two events were the running broad jump and the high jump. This was followed by a half-mile bicycle race. This last event greatly amused the Indians, and they whooped and laughed to see these white men pedaling their strange machines. After that race was over, families and friends joined their own parties for the picnic dinner. John and E. B. hunted up Aunt Adelaide's layout. She had a large tablecloth spread on the ground, and it was completely covered with pans and dishes of food. It looked as if there was enough to feed the whole fort. After satisfying their first hunger, John and E. B. strolled around and honored most of the good cooks of the country by visiting with them and sampling their food.

After dinner the leftovers were stored away and all rushed to the horse racetracks. The first race was for Cheyenne Indian horses, the second was for Arapaho, and in the third both tribes entered their best horses. The fourth race was between the winners of the first and second races. Then the Fort Sill army horses ran. The soldiers from the different companies were betting and backing the horses from their respective troops. During all these races, everyone was excited and yelled for their favorites, but the Indians made more noise than all the others.

Following this group of races, there came a hilarious diversion, the slow mule race, a free-for-all affair. Many of the cowboys borrowed mules in advance for this. Others dashed to nearby wagons, where mules were tied, threw off the harness, and saddled them. Many a mule owner was surprised to see his faithful old mule led to the starting line, but most of them entered into the spirit of the race and cheered on the mules and riders. Mules that appeared docile enough when hitched to a wagon objected to their saddles and riders, especially with a big crowd of yelling spectators looking on. At the command to mount and go, many of the cowboys found themselves on kicking, pitching animals that went in almost every direction except around the track. As they got them headed in the right direction, the judges watched closely to see that the riders didn't pull back on the reins and that they were actually trying to let them run their best. The last mule across the finish line was the winner. Some of the mules never finished because they threw the rider and saddle both. The race provided a lot of fun and excitement for everyone, except perhaps for the mules.

The last group of races were the half-mile horse races in which the ranchers entered their fastest horses. Caddo Bill Williams's horse won the main event and beat Montford's fine horse. John and E. B. lost their money when they backed Montford's horse. In the evening there was an exhibition of fireworks, followed by square dancing that lasted until daylight.

Horse racing was one of the principal sports of the Indians, and the custom was continued by the ranchers. Matched races were held frequently at Silver City, Bitter, Walnut, Johnsonville, and Stinkin' Creek. Notices of these races were published in the *Cheyenne Transporter* and the word was passed along by the cowboys as they traveled across the country. In the spring of 1884, there was a matched race at Silver City between a bay mare from Kansas and a sorrel that Caddo Bill had raised and sold. Over three thousand dollars was bet on this race by Caddo Bill and the Chickasaw backers. The Chickasaws lost their money and Caddo Bill was one of the heaviest losers. In this race the jockey who rode the Caddo Bill horse was a little fellow and wanted by the U.S. marshals for peddling whiskey in the Indian Territory. When one of the marshals in the crowd identified and started to arrest the jockey, it looked as if the race might be called off. The marshal was persuaded to let him ride and to arrest him after the race was run. When the horses crossed the agreed upon finish line, the jockey rode on as if he could not stop his horse. After he got out of rifle range, he rode over a little knoll and exchanged his racehorse for a fresh one that had been planted there for him. He made his getaway on this second horse.

At a celebration held by the Negroes at Walnut Creek, Charley Brown, a nephew of Jack Brown, created a lot of excitement. He had been drinking and decided to show off what a good rider he was. After the races, most of the celebrants were gathered around the dance platform. Charley lit up a big black cigar, mounted this green bronc that he was riding, and thumbed the bronc in the shoulders, which sent the wild bronc pitching and bawling straight for the dance platform while Charlie calmly stayed in the saddle, fanning himself with his hat while he puffed on his cigar. The intoxicated guests, seeing this bucking horse bearing down on them,

took to the blackjack trees like flying squirrels. As Charley and the bucking horse passed the platform, the blackjack trees were so full of people,
they looked like a crow's roost. One of the Negroes yelled, "Say, look at
that boy ride, smoke that cheroot, and never miss a puff."

Negroes, Indians, white men, and women were all the same when it
came to their interests in horses and horse racing. Aunt Adelaide and
many of the other women in the country attended the races regularly.
These women had watched the progress of many of these horses from
the time that they had been foaled and were just as interested in them as
the men. To get a bet out of Aunt Adelaide, all a person had to do was
pass her buggy and make some slight remark about her horse, and she
would bet as long as her money lasted.

The rodeo, which now seems to be a typical western exhibition, did
not come into being until some time after the opening of Oklahoma. To
the old-timers and early settlers, racing was their principal sport, while
roping and riding were just a part of their everyday life. Now that the
cowboys are disappearing, the descendants of those original settlers and
ranchers like to see part of this early frontier life exhibited at these modern rodeos.

A close second to horse racing in popularity about this time was
baseball. It was introduced into the Territory in the 1880s by two Indian
boys who had been attending school at Carlisle, Pennsylvania. On their
way home to the reservation for the summer, they played catch at various places along the way where they stopped for the night. Many of the
cowboys tried to catch and throw the ball. Once they got their hands on
it, they too caught the baseball fever. Baseballs and bats were ordered
and neighborhood teams sprang up, with the players ranging in age
from thirteen to sixty.

One of the earlier games was played at Cook's store, which was
owned by Mr. Carey, who advertised that they would have a big celebration on July 4, 1883. Several large steers were butchered and barbecued
for the event. Wagons from Purcell hauled lumber for the dance platform, along with some ice for the church ladies to make ice cream. A
straightaway racetrack was measured off and, finally, a baseball diamond.
Carey had become a great baseball fan, organized a team, ordered baseball uniforms for his team, and had issued a challenge to a team that had
been organized at the Alex store. This was owned by W. V. Alexander.

On the Fourth the cowboys who made up the Alex team rode up,
dressed in their Sunday best, checked wool breeches, high-top boots,
and fancy shirts. When they saw the Cook's store team resplendent in
their new uniforms, they no longer wanted to play, but Carey and the
excited crowd insisted that they do so. The Cook store team took the
field, and Willie, Carey's son, warmed up in the pitcher's box. All the

players, even the catcher, played bare-handed because they thought it was sissy to even wear their work gloves. When Henry Thomas, one of the Alex players, stepped into the batter's box, Carey yelled, "Willie, throw him a dew drop in." The ball came floating up to the plate, Henry met it with a full swing and knocked a home run. That blow was the beginning of a comedy of errors, which was finally ended on account of darkness. The score was ninety-six to sixteen in favor of the Alex team. This celebration came to an abrupt end the next day when Charley Burch, who had been holding an old grudge, shot at John Davis. When Burch jerked his gun to fire, Davis jumped, threw up his hand, and dodged. The bullet nipped a finger, cut his tie in two, rolled up the skin under his throat, and finally hit an old man who was sitting some distance away on the edge of the barbecue pit talking to George McLaughlin. That was the last straw, and everyone headed for home.

It was at one of these parties that Mollie told E. B. about an accident on the South Canadian River that nearly killed her father. While taking a load of ripe watermelons to sell to the troops at Fort Reno, a roaring head rise on the South Canadian caught Robert smack dab in the middle of the riverbed. The wagon was so heavily loaded, he knew there was not enough time to get to either bank of the river. So, as the water and logs came rolling down upon him, he quickly unhitched the team, jumped on one of the horses, and made a run for it. Getting to the other side in the nick of time, he could only watch as his load of watermelons bobbed and weaved down the raging riverbed never to be seen again. After the water receded, he located his wagon downstream, hitched up his team, and headed for home, a wet, but very lucky man.

Toward the end of the summer of 1883, another unwelcome event happened. One afternoon, Ella, Aunt Adelaide's daughter, suggested that they ride over to Silver City and Aunt Sallie Campbell's place to play a game of croquet. John and E. B. were boarding at Aunt Adelaide's, since Montford and his new bride had returned home to Beaver Creek. When they arrived at Aunt Sallie's, William Rennie, Ella's sweetheart, was already there. While some of them were playing croquet, Ella and William went for a buggy ride. It began to get late and time to be getting home when E. B. asked Aunt Sallie what she thought about Ella being gone so long. At first she said that it was all right, and that Ella could spend the night with her when she came home, but she finally confessed that Ella and William had eloped and that she had engineered the whole thing. Ella and E. B. were like brother and sister, and this turn of events was a bitter pill for him to take. E. B. did not want to be the one to tell Aunt Adelaide that her little girl had eloped. Of course when E. B. did tell Adelaide about the elopement, she let out a bloodcurdling squawk, then screamed for C. B., Ella's brother. She ran to where C. B. was sleeping under a big elm tree and urged him to get his horse, overtake them, and bring Ella back. C. B. just rolled over and growled, "To hell with them, she is of age, and if she wants to run off, let her go."

Besides attending dances and parties and courting the Graham girls, E. B. rode the range with his father. He noticed that a number of small ranches, belonging to intermarried white men, had sprung up along the edge of Montford's range, and that beef contractors, who furnished beef to the Indians on the reservations, used their contracts as an excuse to graze and occupy part of the range that Montford formerly used. Many farmers, like the Graham family, had also drifted into the Chickasaw country and were farming lands for Chickasaw Indians or intermarried citizens. In addition to this encroachment, Montford was worried about the carelessness of the farmers and hunters in burning his ranges. In checking the accounts at the Silver City store, Montford found that a large number were long past due and that the store's accounts were in poor shape. E. B. suggested to his father that he quit school and help him, but Montford insisted that he return to New York and to continue his education.

In September E. B. returned to New York and took his brother Henry and his sister Stella along with him. The three lived with Thomas Ormiston in Brooklyn and continued with their educations. The younger children returned to the Sacred Heart Mission in the Pottawatomie country.

Snowstorm

In May 1883 Silver City had its mail service initiated when Phil Smith was made postmaster, operating out of Montford's store.[1] Within a year their deliveries from Darlington increased from once to twice a week. Early in February 1884 Montford wrote to his son, E. B., an urgent letter that his health was failing and that he was anxious for his son to return home. E. B. wound up his affairs in New York and left for Atoka, where he arrived about the middle of the month and stepped off the train into a raging blizzard. The snow was already up to his knees and a cold, piercing wind from the north was piling the snow into huge drifts. He had difficulty in trying to hire anyone to drive him to Stonewall, the first leg of his journey home, but by tipping a man twenty dollars above the regular price, he hired a man to drive him there. This initial leg covered a distance of about thirty-five miles. The man drove a team of small mules up to the store and they loaded the hack with some emergency rations, a small cooking outfit, several heavy blankets, a lantern, and some bricks to put around the lantern, which was placed by their feet in the hack under a robe.

They soon started out and made very good time for awhile by following the road, which had been opened by a large wagon that had preceded them. After the wagon turned off of their road, they were reduced to a slow walk and had a very difficult time as the small mules floundered through the heavy drifts, and oftentimes the men walked behind the hack to lighten the load. They had about decided to make camp for the night when they came upon another intersection, where a wide-wheeled wagon had entered the road also headed for Stonewall. They finally arrived at Humphus Colbert's hotel long after dark. The hotel was nothing special, but after they had thawed out and eaten a hot supper, it looked mighty good to the two weary travelers.

The next morning E. B. hired a liveryman to take him to Johnsonville, a distance of about forty-three miles, for twenty-five dollars. This team was shod, and the snow quickly balled up on the horses' feet, making it very difficult for them to stand up. They made very slow and slippery progress. When they arrived at John Bradley's place on Big Sandy Creek about noon, Bradley said that he was going to Johnsonville as soon as the weather cleared, which was good news to the liveryman, who had battled the storm all he cared for.

E. B., who was still very worried about the condition of his father, persuaded Bradley to drive on to Johnsonville that afternoon. They caught his team, removed the shoes, and hitched them to a light Indian wagon. They made good progress for a short time. It then started to snow, which soon turned to sleet, hitting the horses squarely in their faces. The horses kept trying to turn tail to the storm, making E. B. afraid that they would leave the road and get them all lost. When they passed near the home of their old neighbor, Alec Cochran, they decided to turn in and spend the night. Alec and Arnaca Cochran were delighted to see them and made them comfortable in front of a big roaring fire. They slept well, while the sleet continued to patter down on the roof and the wind howled throughout the night.

When they arrived at Johnsonville later the next day, they drove up to Hill Phillips's home north of town and found Gus Leslie, one of Montford's men, staying there. By this time the sleet had turned to a slow drizzle that froze on top of the snow and sleet. This turned the whole country into a sheet of ice. Gus had his horses shod with protruding metal horseshoes called ice calks, and they started out for the last leg of their journey. By the end of this third day, they finally reached Jack Brown's old place up on Walnut Creek, a distance of about thirty-five miles. The horses' legs were in bad shape from the cuts and bruises caused by the horses' feet continuously breaking through the top crust of ice. It felt almost as good as getting home when they finally arrived at Jack Brown's place.

Jack had remarried after Aunt Eliza's death, and his new wife, Suka, was a fine woman and proved to be equal to Eliza in the cooking department. She fixed a fine meal for the exhausted travelers. After supper they sat in front of the fireplace and discussed the storm. Jack said that if this storm did not let up and thaw out real soon, many stockmen would be put out of business. While they talked, they sewed together leather boots to protect the feet and legs of the horses from the sharp cutting edges of ice that awaited them in the morning.

The next morning they drove straight north to the South Canadian River bottom, hoping it might be warmer there. Gus Leslie had suggested that they might go to the Graham farm or Mark Brittain's place, but E. B. was determined to get home as quickly as he could. They came in close to the Adkins' cabin under Adkins' hill and drifted up the flats to the Red Branch. There they made a good fire and had lunch. After some good hot black coffee, they were good to go on.

The leather boots they made for the horses seemed to work wonderfully. They continued northwest until they reached John Worley's dugouts late in the afternoon, having covered another twenty miles. John's cabin had burned some months before, and the two cowboys they found staying there were holed up in a small dugout like a couple of prairie dogs. They put their team under an old hog shed and fed them some corn and a little hay, which they dug out of a small protected hayrick near the shed. Bill Story, one of the cowboys, said they had not seen John Worley in over two weeks. He had apparently taken his family to some relatives right after the cabin burned down.

The cowboys also reported that they were having trouble keeping themselves and their horses alive and that a great number of the cattle had drifted south with the storm toward the Washita. They had tried to hold the herd back the best they could, but the storm had made it impossible. E. B. and Gus commented that they had seen a few dead steers along the river and many of the cows were hovering in the brush along the creek bottoms and were keeping alive by eating small twigs and brush. Seeing that these two cowboys were very low on food, E. B. broke out what food he had with him, and they all had a decent supper.

The next morning Gus and E. B. headed out for their final leg home. A crust of sleet and ice still covered everything. The creeks were frozen solid enough to hold up the team, and they made very good time. They reached the Silver City store a little after noon, and got a little can lunch with plenty of pepper sauce on it and some hot coffee from Phil Smith. Shortly before dark they drove into Montford's place and E. B. rushed in to see him and found his father sitting up in a chair and feeling much better. Montford was surprised to see his son and could scarcely believe that he had driven all the way from Atoka in the worst storm that he had ever seen.

There was very little to be done until the storm blew itself out; in fact, it was ten days before Gus Leslie could head back home to Johnsonville. As soon as it began to thaw, E. B. and Montford's cowboys rode out to cut the ice for water and check over the range to estimate their losses. The cows, well located, had come through the storm very well. Many others, however, were not so fortunate. A number of areas were located where the cattle, having found no shelter from the storms, were piled up so thick, one could walk on them for a distance without ever having to touch the ground. The largest loss for Montford was among some Arkansas steers that they had moved into Oklahoma, late in the fall, to winter. Matters were only made worse when the Boomers set fires and burned the range in the Oklahoma territories almost bare, so Montford took his remaining cattle in his northern range and drifted them back south across the Canadian Rivers back into the Chickasaw country.

These fires were becoming increasingly dangerous. Although these fires were not uncommon in the Indian lands, the problem was especially acute in the Oklahoma Territory, where these fires were costing the cattlemen heavily in cattle and sometimes in men. With the Boomers, nesters, and hunters wandering over the country, the number of fires was on the increase. A cloud of smoke in the fall or winter was a signal that these early ranchers dreaded because in this high grass a fire traveled very rapidly, and if it was not brought under control, it might burn out the entire winter range.

The ranchers began to protect themselves from these fires by building fireguards. In the late summer when the grass was still green, a furrow was plowed across the range to be protected, with the two ends of the furrow winding up, whenever possible, at bare creek banks. Then a back furrow was thrown up against the first one. About fifty yards from this furrow a similar one was plowed parallel to it. A mower was used to cut the grass along the inside of these furrows and as soon as the grass dried it was burned. This made a firebreak or barrier about fifty yards wide, and was usually effective in stopping most of the prairie fires.

Robert Graham, the father of the Graham girls, was seriously burned while working on one of these fireguards. He had been hired to burn the middle of the fireguards by Hobart and Montgomery, one of the beef contractors for Fort Reno. The guard extended across the divide between the North and South Canadian Rivers. Mr. Graham had fitted up a camping outfit: a wagon and team, bedding, a barrel of water, some sacks, a sprinkler, and regular fire-fighting equipment for prairie fires. The working party consisted of Graham, his son, Isaac, and a young Negro farmhand. When they were ready to leave home that morning, Graham's youngest son, Bobbie, aged twelve, cried to go along and Graham finally gave in, putting him in the wagon. They started at the South Canadian River bottom and began burning the tall grass. By noon they had reached higher ground. While they were eating lunch, a smoky, blue haze banked in from the north, which indicated a norther might be on its way, but no one took it seriously or gave it a second thought. Up to that point, their controlled fire was breezing along very nicely, when suddenly the wind changed and the norther hit them hard. The shift of the wind came so quickly and so strongly that the fire jumped the small fireguard and furrows and headed directly toward the entire party. In the twinkling of an eye, the head fire leaped toward them. Sheets of fire seemed to fly through the air. Isaac rushed to the wagon and filled the sprinkler and tried to dampen the grass around the wagon and team. As the fire bore down upon him, he jerked his hat over his eyes and face, ducked his head, stuffed his hands in his pockets, and holding his breath, ran right through the charging flames of the head fire. He ran forty-two steps before he felt cool air and knew that he was behind the fire wall. Other than his scorched ears and singed hair, Isaac was unhurt.

The young farmhand, frightened by the flames and commotion, jumped from the wagon and started running ahead of the flames. Luckily he stumbled and fell, rolling into a small wash, which was deep enough for the flames to pass over him. Little Bobbie Graham jumped out to follow him, but losing sight of the farmhand, Bobbie turned back and ran toward the wagon. When Isaac turned after running through the head fire, he saw Bobbie, running and screaming toward the wagon with his clothes on fire. Isaac ran to him, grabbed him, wrapping him in a blanket and plunged him into the water barrel.

Mr. Graham, who was driving the team, tried to hold the horses as the fire swept past them. In spite of the fact that he was dressed in heavy underwear, wool-lined pants, and a jumper of ducking with a wet blanket over his shoulders and head, he was burned terribly and large blisters covered most of his body. Finally, unable to hold the team any longer, they bolted and ran parallel to the fire until one of the horses dropped dead. The other horse was burned severely and lost all of its hair. This horse survived, but never fully recovered its health.

Bill Barnard, working for Uncle Jim Bond on the south side of the river, saw the flames leaping and the smoke now billowing toward the southeast, and knew that the fire had gotten out of control and had reversed its direction. He jumped on his horse, crossed the river, and riding up the west side of the fireguard that had been burned earlier that morning, found the stricken party. As soon as he saw their condition, he knew that they needed medical care, so he rode back to Uncle Jim Bond's for a team and hack to take them to the hospital at Fort Reno. While he was gone, Graham and Isaac sprinkled a mixture of soda and molasses over Bobbie and themselves. Bill returned with Uncle Jim Bond and several other men to put out the fire, which had roared on to the banks of the river, while the burned fire crew was taken to the hospital at Fort Reno. Little Bobbie Graham was burned so terribly that he died the next day. The soldiers at the fort gave him a military funeral and buried him in the soldiers' cemetery at Fort Reno. [His grave lies in the northwest corner of the cemetery, before you reach the separate section for the World War II, German P.O.W.– *C.N.K.*]

Graham was burned about the face so deeply that he was unable to move his jaws. His whole face was cooked, and the lower lids of his eyes so badly burned that the doctors tried to graft some skin on them, but without success. The muscles and tendons of his hands and fingers were seared into the closed position that they were in while he gripped the reins of the runaway team. All of his burns were so serious that the treatment by the doctors seemed to have very little effect. When "proud flesh" or abnormal growths around the wounds began to develop, Isaac, who had partially recovered, decided to try an old-fashioned remedy. He had cured proud flesh in wire cuts on horses with burned alum, so he pounded some to a powder and burned it on the top of the stove. This remedy helped kill the proud flesh, and Graham began to improve. After being in the hospital about two months, Graham was placed on a bed that was rigged up on a spring wagon and brought home. He had been home about a month when E. B. called on the family. E. B. was not permitted to see him because the family thought that his appearance was too frightful, and he still could not move his jaws to talk.

Mollie, his daughter, explained to E. B. what she was doing to care for her father, because she had become his principal nurse. She forced a small round stick that was clamped to the palm of his hand through his fingers; then she massaged the fingers to bring some life back into them. As the fingers slowly began to loosen, she forced a larger stick into his hand. When some life finally showed up in his thumb and forefingers, he was then permitted to sit up. Mr. Graham treated himself by rubbing his hands on the rungs of the chair. Mollie told E. B. that just a few days earlier her father had been able to bite a small piece out of a doughnut. She said that he was so happy to be able to move his jaws that much, that big tears rolled down his cheeks from behind the smoked glasses that he wore. In the retelling of that moment, tears began to form in Mollie's eyes too and she was soon at a loss for words, so E. B. politely excused himself, said goodnight to Mollie and the rest of the Graham family, promised to return soon, and returned to Montford's.

Once Montford began to recover from his illness, he insisted that E. B. return to New York and try to work out some kind of a settlement with E. Simpson & Co. on the wholesale liquor business. E. B. spent almost a year working on improving the business, then realizing it was a lost cause, gave it up as a complete loss. Out of the twenty-five thousand dollars invested in E. Simpson & Co., Montford received five notes of $1,721.89 each, payable in five years. None were ever paid. The loss of the twenty-five thousand dollars, the purchase of the Brooklyn home for Aunt Belle and her mixed household, and the extended credit that Montford had allowed his customers at the Silver City store had stripped him of all his cash.

When E. B. returned home from New York City, as noted in the February 15, 1885, *Cheyenne Transporter*, he came home to stay. To celebrate his homecoming, Montford, with the aid of Sarah Short, Uncle Jim Bond's niece from Leavenworth, Kansas, gave a big dance for E. B. and all his friends. C. B. and his new bride, Maggie Williams, a daughter of Caddo Bill Williams, whom C. B. had married on December 16, 1884, were among the guests. C. B. had built himself a new home on the south side of the South Canadian River and about five miles west of Montford's home. C. B.'s range extended west to the edge of the Chickasaw Nation, with his headquarters just west of what is now Pocasset, Oklahoma.

Another old friend of the Johnsons had moved to Silver City and built a home a few hundred yards east of the store. Jane Shirley, who had the store at Cherokee Town with her husband, had moved to Silver City in the early 1880s. Her husband, John, had died in March 1875 due to an accidental poisoning, according to the *Caddo Oklahoma Star* dated March 19, 1875. Along with his brother William, they had operated the Shirley Trading Company. They were involved in a hotel, a ranch, and a toll bridge at Cherokee Town, along with their store. Their bridge was the first to span the Washita River. Besides their other businesses, Doctor Shirley had been partners with Jim Bond in a number of cattle deals over a number of years. John had also worked for Caddo Bill Williams in his youth. John left nine children, many of whom married into other pioneer families around Minco.[2]

Notes

1. Munn, Irvin. 1984. *Chickasha . . . A Journey Back in Time.* Chickasha, OK: The University of Science and Arts Foundation, p. 13.
2. Tower, Michael. 1987. "Traders Along the Washita." *Chronicles of Oklahoma,* Oklahoma Historical Society. Vol. 65, pp. 4–15.

Saving the Silver City Store

fter the dance celebrating E. B.'s return, Montford and his son got down to the business of straightening out Montford's business affairs. The unpaid bills at the Silver City store amounted to more than fifteen thousand dollars, which did not include eight thousand dollars that Montford and his numerous partners in the cattle business owed. It was a good time of the year to work inside, so E. B. had his father give him written authority to check the accounts and to take an inventory of the store. When E. B. presented the letter of authority to Phil Smith, the manager, Phil flew into a rage and his face blazed up as red as fire, exclaiming, "I guess your father wants a New Yorker to take charge here. If so, I am ready to step down and out. The store owes me one thousand dollars. If I can get five hundred dollars in cash, you can have the damn store." When E. B. reported to his father that he had stirred up a hornet's nest and that Phil wanted to quit, they managed to come up with the five hundred dollars, had him sign a receipt in full settlement of all wages and interest in the store, and paid him off.

After Phil left, Will Sawyer, one of the clerks, helped E. B. take the inventory. The assets, including merchandise, freight wagons, teams, and open accounts, amounted to forty-five thousand dollars, which did not include the accounts receivable of fifteen thousand dollars. Because of the Montford's Silver City store's "easy credit," it seemed as if everyone in the surrounding countryside and as far south as Johnsonville owed bills. Montford gave E. B. a half interest in the store and 50 percent of whatever he could collect from the old accounts, if he would take over the management of the store. E. B. agreed to this arrangement if he

Page from Montford Johnson's ledger book from his Johnsonville store, Dick Tuttle account, circa 1877. University of Oklahoma, Western History Collection, E. B. Johnson Collection

could hire Joe Lindsay of Atoka to take over the day-to-day running of the store while he worked on collecting from the overdue accounts. Joe was an experienced merchant and was also able to communicate fluently with most of the Indian tribes. He also agreed to put thirty-five hundred dollars of his own money into the new business, bringing in some much-needed stock.

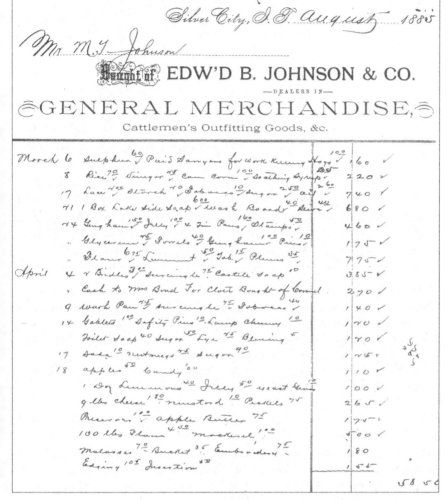

Silver City Store, statement of account for Montford Johnson, August 1885. E. B. Johnson and Joe D. Lindsay, proprietors. [Note prices for various items on statement– C.N.K.] E. B. Johnson Collection, Western History Collection, University of Oklahoma.

Due to the harsh winter weather and the freezing of so many cattle, the store had taken in trade many cowhides that were now piled up ready to trade off, so one on E. B.'s first jobs was to load them up in wagons and haul them to Atoka where he could exchange them for the essential goods that the Silver City store had run low on. Upon arriving in Atoka, E. B. and Joe finalized their agreement and headed back to Silver City together with their wagons reloaded with fresh supplies. While

Silver City (Store), Indian Territory, May 6, 1888. Courtesy, Charlotte Peavler Collection. Left to right: Charley Morrison, in vest; Walter Harding, in short sleeves; boy standing in doorway, H. M. (Bunt) Lindsay; man near horse unknown; second from horse Lon Gray; next unknown; Walter Morrison; boy; John Pinkay; Bill Nelson, blacksmith; John Hennessey; J. D. Lindsay in door; F. E. Clayton in front of Lindsay; W. L. Sawyers. Picture identified by H. M. Lindsay of Anadarko. Courtesy, Oklahoma Historical Society, #1624.1R OHS, Archives and Manuscripts Division.

all this was going on, back at Silver City the rumors spread that E. B. was going to take over all of Montford's businesses, which would include all of his ranches too. One day, while Joe and E. B. were working on the inventory and the old books, Hy Downing, a plain and gruff-spoken foreman of Uncle Charley Campbell's ranch, came in and said, "Hello, dude, I understand your dad wants you to run his ranches, too. You are a hell of a smart kid if you think you can give orders to men like C. B. Campbell, Jim Bond, and John Worley, who have forgotten more cow sense than you will ever know. How about it? If it is true, my time is up right now." This sudden attack from a man E. B. had always considered his friend almost took his breath away, but E. B. knew this was a showdown and that he had to stand his ground before Hy and the bunch of leathernecks who had followed Hy into the store. As calmly as E. B. could control himself, he walked slowly up to Hy and said, "You have made a good guess, but it is ridiculous to call me a dude. I was born and raised between cow legs and on horses' backs and have followed cattle up and down trails all my life. I am back from school and a grown man; my father has asked me to help him and by the eternal, I am going to do my damned best to do it. I expect to treat everyone as I want them to treat me, and I want you to know that. I have done nothing to offend you or any other cowman. I consider everyone in this country to be my friend. I intend to be square with them and I expect the same treatment in return." This was a long speech for E. B. to make, and when he had finished the room was very still. Without a word Hy and his henchmen filed out of the store.

This was the first outburst against E. B., and there would be many others to follow. When debtors of long standing came into the store to make new purchases, E. B. insisted that they pay, either in cash or livestock, and requested that they make notes for the old accounts at 10 percent interest. Many of the customers became very angry when their credit was stopped. Montford's partners called on him in a bunch and said that if they were going to have to make notes for their old accounts that they were ready to quit. Montford called E. B. in for the conference to explain what he was trying to do. E. B. told them, "Men, I see no reason for you to be so hasty and want a change. I know that many lost money last year, but these losses can be whittled down by preparing in advance of these severe storms. By working together, putting up hay in the summer, building earthen dams to provide water during the dry spells, we can insure ourselves against some heavy losses. Since father has asked me to take over his affairs, I want to make some changes that will be beneficial to you as well as to him." C. B. spoke up, "I have all the cattle of my own that I want to look after, and I am ready to close out the partnership business." Uncle Jim Bond said that he felt the same way, and John Worley said, "I have to put my children in school and will move them to my relatives on the Washita. My home at Pond Creek has burned, and I don't have the money to rebuild. Besides, I have heard that E. B. intends to build a holding pasture with barbed wire. I can't afford to have my horses cut to pieces by barbed wire, so I guess that I'll quit, too."

Montford and E. B. disliked breaking up the relationship with all these men, but E. B. felt sure that he was correct in the changes that he intended to make to save his father's business and allow it to be profitable again. Montford supported him wholeheartedly. E. B. told the men that he was first going on a trip and try and collect on the old store accounts, and as soon as that was finished, he would collect a branding crew that would move from one ranch to another branding the animals intended for payment. He said, "When I brand, you can turn over the selected stock at each ranch, in turn, to me."

As soon as he could, E. B. hired a crew of three good men, rigged up a chuck wagon and camping outfit, and headed for Johnsonville to start collecting on the old accounts. At each place he presented the letter from Montford, which authorized him to act as his agent, then he asked for payment, first in cash, but if he could not get that, he took cattle, oxen, horses, hogs, hides, chickens, furs, or almost anything of any value. By the time that he had worked Johnsonville and the Negro settlements that were nearby, he had taken in another wagon, which was loaded down with assorted articles. He left this collection at Jack Brown's place, went down to the Washita, and returned via Walnut Creek to Brown's place again. At Jack's he left this second load too. E. B. and his crew then started working up the Canadian River to John Worley's place, where John had left the two cowboys living in a dugout. He established a head-quarters there at the Pond Creek ranch for the livestock that he had taken in as payment and left them there. He returned to Silver City with the various other items that he had collected.

During his stay in the East, E. B. had observed the advantages of fenced enclosures. When he sent the wagons to Atoka with his tradeable collections for more supplies, he also included in his order some barbed wire. When they returned with the wire, it was left at the Pond Creek ranch. E. B. got a fence-building crew and they built a four-wire fence, with two wooden staves between each two posts. The fence enclosed a pasture about a mile square. While they were putting up the fence, many of the neighboring cowmen came by to watch and comment on what they were doing. When the fence was finished, John Worley, one of the men who had objected the most about the wire fences, helped E. B. drive about two hundred of their good cow horses through the west gate of the pasture and turned them loose. As they watched, it soon became evident that the horses were going to stay away from the fence, and it was much better than herding the horses all the time on the open range. It also gave them a small trap to hold and locate cattle.

By the time the fence was completed, it was late enough in the spring to start branding and closing out the partnerships. Since many of the cattle had drifted south with the Long O steers, and had drifted as far as the Washita River, several of the ranchers joined their wagons and crews. Starting at the Washita, they worked back north, gathering the cattle as they came. When E. B. and his crew reached Pond Creek, they cut out John Worley's cattle, which he then moved to a ranch on the Washita. E. B. left two men at that camp, one to ride the river and pull cattle out of the bogs, while the other was to reestablish a line camp at the spring on Bishop's Creek, now known as Norman's Camp after surveyor Abner Norman, and ride line on the cattle between the headwaters of the Little River and the South Canadian River. A few years later, Norman's Camp became Norman Station as the Atkinson, Topeka, & Santa Fe Railroad extended their tracks north from Purcell in the spring of 1887. The railroad provided its laborers with a cafe during the construction and it didn't take long until all the cowboys turned up there for their meals too.

From Pond Creek, E. B. moved his crew and branded, in turn, the Bitter Creek and then the Salt Creek ranches. He delivered their cattle to Uncle Charley Campbell and Uncle Jim Bond and put some of his proven crew in charge of these ranches. He returned to Silver City via C. B.'s ranch and brought in Montford's share of that herd, then worked what they considered their home range. By this time, the change in management was completed.

During the summer E. B. had his hay crews cutting and stacking hay. He also hired men to make and burn fireguards between creeks and hired two men to break out three hundred acres of land at the Pond Creek ranch. Fortunately, they had taken in a few oxen as payment on the old delinquent accounts, making the plowing much easier. Meanwhile, Joe Lindsay became the new postmaster at Silver City in July 1885.

Montford usually sold his steers to contractors who trailed them to market, but by early fall E. B. had assembled a very fine crew of men. The two of them decided to use this crew to gather the steers and drive them to the Kansas market themselves. It might be of interest to tell just how a crew works to gather a herd. During breakfast, E. B. gave orders and directions to the cook and horse wrangler about the distance and place they were to travel for the noon camp. The bedrolls of the riders were tied and carried to the chuck wagon. As soon as it was light, the horse wrangler drove up the moveable corral or remuda of horses.

This remuda was put together as four of the cowboys placed themselves in a square, holding the ends of the rawhide ropes, which lay flat on the ground. As soon as the horses entered the square, the ropes were raised; this made an enclosure that held the horses as well as if they were in a corral of high-rail fence. The boys called off the names or pointed out the horse they wanted to ride. E. B. eased into the rope corral and, without swinging the loop, tossed the lasso on the horses called for and led them out to each rider. Several called for young horses that they were breaking in while on the roundup. Often, when these broncs were caught, a man already saddled had to ride up next to the bronc, dally the rope around the saddle horn, and drag the uncooperative horse from the herd. These wild broncs would often set back, forcing the rope to tighten on their necks until their wind was cut off. Then, rising on their hind feet, they lunged, striking at the rope as they came forward.

If a bronc was too mean for the rider to saddle by himself, another went down along the ropes, got the horse by the ears and twisted, holding him until he was saddled and mounted. As soon as all the mounts and chuck wagon team had been collected, the ropes were lowered and the remainder of the horses were turned loose to graze. The men mounted their chosen steeds and usually a number of these broncs pitched or broke in two. The bawling of the horses and the pitching lasted a short time, during which the men on broke horses herded the pitching broncs away from the wagons, loose horses, or any other object that might cause the bronc to fall. When the horses had settled down, they rode off into the early morning haze.

At different intervals men were assigned a certain part of the range to work and to drive all the cattle to the designated roundup ground. The first man to arrive at the roundup spot held up his cattle; then, as the others came in, they took their places around the growing herd. When the drivers were all in, a few were left to hold the herd while the rest went to the new camp to catch fresh and more experienced horses to work the cattle. They usually ate their dinner at the chuck wagon, which was nearby, then returned to cut out the steers that were to make up the herd to be driven to market. Usually they cut the steers into the wind, because cattle naturally head into the wind, and as they were cut out, one man held up the cutouts until they had finished. After that herd was worked, they grazed the cut group into or near the camp that the cook and horse wrangler had established for the night. When the cutouts neared the camp, they were held up but allowed plenty of room to graze.

As night began to settle in, two riders were left to loose-herd them and bed them down, while the rest of the cowboys returned to camp, caught fresh night horses, staked them near the chuck wagon, and ate their supper. While they were eating dinner they were assigned their night guard duties. The first shift left immediately to relieve the two that had been bedding down the herd. The rest soon grabbed their bedrolls and turned in until they were called on for their guard shifts.

The cook, after cleaning up, filled his lantern, cleaned the globe, and hung the lighted lantern on a forked stick above the wagon to serve as a beacon to the men going and coming from the herd. Even with this lantern as a guide, guards sometimes got lost and did not find the wagon until daylight. When the guard was to be changed and while the herd was staying quiet, one of the guards loped to the wagon and woke the men who were to take their place. They slipped quietly out of their bedrolls, dressed, and drank a hot cup of coffee from the pot that was on left on the waning fire. Then speaking softly or quietly whistling to their horse so as not to startle him, they approached and mounted their morning ride, and the two new guards rode off to relieve the lone guard left behind with the herd. This last rider generally gave a report on the actions of the herd and how they had behaved so far that night, and then returned to the wagon. The new guards rode in opposite directions around the herd, singing or whistling softly as they rode; when they met, they visited a short time, turned back and rode back until they met each other again.

The last guard saw the day break and the morning come to life. When the relieved guards came to the wagon, they woke the cook, who got up and started the crew's breakfast. First, he stoked up the smoldering fire and placed on it the five-gallon can of fresh coffee; then he cut steaks from a quarter of beef that he had hung in the tree for the night to cool. After placing several Dutch ovens on the fire to heat, the cook filled his dishpan with flour, hollowed out the center, and in it placed the sour dough, baking powder, salt and some lard, and water. When the dough was ready, he placed the rolls in the Dutch ovens, set them over fresh coals, put on the lids, and placed a shovelful of coals on the tops. The cook then put the steaks into another Dutch oven and placed it on the fire.

Finally, he hollered for the men to wake up and to come and get their breakfast. By the time the men were fully awake and had their boots on, a good hot breakfast was prepared. There is nothing that tastes better than a good breakfast eaten out-of-doors on the prairie at dawn. The air is cool and fresh, and the scalding hot coffee is fragrant, tasty, and appreciated. The cattle get up, stretch themselves, and begin to graze. It is another day on the trail.

When E. B. and his herd reached headquarters on Beaver (Snake) Creek, Montford, riding Caddo, his coal black horse, came out to meet them and rode through the herd. The cattle were in excellent condition, fat and glossy. After riding around through them for some time, Montford rode over to his son and said, "Edward, turn them loose–they are too pretty to sell." E. B. was a little more practical than his father, who needed the money, so E. B. finally persuaded Montford to let the men take the herd of approximately twenty-five hundred on to Hunnewell, Kansas. After they crossed the river, the men on the point or lead held the cattle up and let them spread out to graze. Following the actions of the men on the point, the men on the flanks spread out and, not hurrying or driving the steers, kept them moving and grazing in the direction they wanted them to go. The men in the rear or on the drag kept the stragglers moving, but did not crowd them on the steers ahead. In this way the cattle walked, grazed, and fattened as they drove them north to market.

The usual custom was to try and water about noon, then let them graze along slowly toward the bed-ground, which they tried to reach about dusk. The men on the point would check the leaders, and the rest of the herd would drift in and, with their paunches full from grazing, the steers soon found a place to lie down. The steers were never crowded on the bed-ground, because a steer usually gets up at least once during the night, grazes a little, fools around, and then lies down again. The cattle handled in this manner do not disturb the others when they get up.

Each morning E. B. would ride to the lead; the point would be drawn in closely by the two point men, and E. B. counted them. If the number

"Cowboys Eating," cowboys seated around the chuck wagon and the cook. [Note the moveable horse corral, or remuda, in right background–C.N.K.] Texas-Oklahoma Panhandle, circa 1885. Courtesy, University of Oklahoma Press, #3 Forbes Collection, Western History Collection.

was correct, the herd usually drifted along at a good fast walk for some time until they began to graze again, then they let them spread out and take their time. Handling the herd in this manner, they averaged about ten miles a day. One day was very much like the day before. Each morning the herd was counted, and the chuck wagon went ahead to prepare the noon meal; after that was over, the wagon moved on ahead to get the camp and supper ready by the time the herd came in for the evening.

During the noon hour, after they had eaten lunch and caught their fresh horses for the afternoon, the boys not needed to hold the herd often took a short nap. To get out of the hot sun, they might crawl under one of the wagons and doze off with their heads out of the sun and their feet protruding from the sides. A peaceful sleeping scene like this was too much for Henry McLish, who was a great practical joker. Occasionally he would get the cook to shake the wagon while he rattled the trace chains of the harness and yelled, "Whoa." The men, half asleep, would think that they were under a runaway wagon and make a break for the open. Many a skinned and bumped head resulted from Henry's pranks as he would roar with laughter. Fortunately for Henry, the crew could take a joke in good humor, but they did not take in good grace the boneheads that a greenhorn can cause. Henry always had a few pranks up his sleeve. On another occasion, while conducting some business in

El Reno, he rode right into one of the local saloons, leaned over in his saddle, and ordered a drink to quench his thirst. The bartender drew out a beer from the keg and raised it up to Henry, who then cheerfully slurped it down while perched on his horse, paid up, rode back out through the swinging doors, and set off for home.

One day as they arrived at the wagon for lunch, most cowboys loosened their saddles and dropped the reins so the horses could graze. By the time they had finished eating, one of the horses had rubbed off his bridle, but was grazing with the rest of the saddled horses. Before the crew realized what had happened, a young rider from another outfit, who had stopped to eat dinner with them, caught his horse, uncoiled his rope, and threw it at the horse he presumed loose. The horse saw the rope sailing toward him, jumped, and the loop caught the horn of the loosened saddle. Of course, the horse started to run, and when he hit the end of the rope, the saddle turned under his belly. The surprised young man, excited, turned the rope loose, and the boneheaded play was fully under way. The rope now was dragging between his hind legs, along with the stirrups' sweat leathers and flapping saddlebags.

This really spooked the horse, causing it to bolt straight into and through the remuda, which scattered the remaining horses in all directions. The hind feet of the horse finally stepped on the stirrups and saddlebags, which were then jerked off. After a long chase, one of E. B.'s men caught the horse after he had kicked the remains of the saddle loose and finally brought him back to the wagon. The horse was wet with sweat, his legs and body were bruised and cut so badly that it was several months before he was well again.

E. B.'s crew was well seasoned and unafraid of being mistaken for a group of sissies when they brought out one of the few creature comforts they had on the drive. Years of experience had taught them to make themselves as comfortable as possible in this hostile environment. Many of the veteran cowpokes carried mosquito bars in their bedrolls, which they put over themselves at night to protect themselves from the millions of mosquitoes that swarmed from the buffalo wallows during the wet season. The less provident of the crew, who had no mosquito bars, could only pull the end of their tarpaulins over their heads and swelter through the night.

One of the most irritating things that can happen to a herd is to find a "bullin' steer." Bullin' steers, although they have been castrated, have retained some sexual smell and the other steers like to ride them. The worst of it is, if one bullin' steer shows up and they start to ride him, it seems to be contagious, because many others that crowd around to lick and ride him soon get wet on top of their backs and they become bullin' steers, too.

About the third day from home, one of these bullin' steers showed up. They had just watered the herd at noon at a stream, using the usual method of throwing the leaders in downstream and easing the rest of the herd above them so that they could have clear water to drink. About half the herd had crossed the stream when they noticed that one of the steers that had just crossed was being ridden by another steer. They dropped him out of the herd to let his back dry off, and one of the men held him back until the herd had passed him, then let him trail along behind. When they stopped for lunch, several of the men told about remedies that they had heard of for curing bullin' steers, so after lunch they caught this troublesome steer and tried out one of these cures.

They smeared axle grease on his hips and back, and on top of the axle grease they sprinkled liberal quantities of cayenne pepper. The theory was that if one of the steers getting ready to ride the bullin' one licked him before trying to ride him, that he would get his mouth burned and would go away. They put the steer back in the herd to see how it was going to work. The other steers seemed to be attracted by the grease and pepper. Instead of running away, they came back for more. The cowhands once again cut the steer from the herd and in the afternoon let him follow along behind. When they reached the bed-ground that evening, they roped him and took him over near the remuda of horses, put hobbles on him, and left him to graze and bed down with the horses.

During the night he learned to take short steps, slipped away from the horses, and joined the steers. Immediately the herd began trying to ride him again and although the men on guard cut him out, the herd milled around most of the night, looking for him. After that, when they hobbled him at night, they staked him by the hobbles near the wagon. They found a use for him when they approached the stockyards at Hunnewell. They put him in the herd and let them get the smell of him, then tossed a rope on him and led him to the pens. The rest of the herd soon followed in after him.

When they arrived they discovered that ten carloads made up a train. They found several other outfits waiting to ship when they arrived, so E. B.'s crew had to wait their turn for cars. It took them almost a week to dispose of the whole herd. While they were waiting, E. B. purchased two good jacks or donkeys and bought and packed fresh supplies for the chuck wagon. As soon as they finished shipping the cattle they headed for home.

Returning home, he took the jacks to the Pond Creek ranch and hired John Bilby to look after them. He built a donkey lot, corrals, and a breeding chute. In addition to the yelping of coyotes at night and the answering barking of their dogs, they had some new ranch music from their braying cornfield canaries.

Changing Times in the Chickasaw Nation

Although Montford did not realize it, many events were taking place that were changing the social and business life that he and his friends had developed. When the Chickasaws moved to the Indian Territory, they followed the tribal custom of holding all their lands in common. Montford had built his big ranch on this Chickasaw principle— that a man could use this land as long as he did not encroach on someone else. As a stockman, he had always been very progressive by improving his cattle, horses, and hogs, and he had broken out a lot of land to make sure of supplies of feed. He still carried on his business in the free and easy style of the early pioneers. His partnership and other contracts were just oral agreements between old and true friends. He had run his store accounts on the idea that a man who needed supplies should have them and that the man would pay for them as soon as he was able to pay. When E. B. returned from New York in 1884, he saw at once that he must make use of his education in the white man's ways, which his father had known years before. E. B. saw that with many more people and strangers moving into the country, a better business practice had to be adopted. Montford backed him up.

By the time E. B. had run the Silver City store about a year, Joe Lindsay had educated his customers that they had to pay either cash or the equivalent. To accomplish this, Joe took in a lot of cattle in payment for bills. To take care of these store cattle, they fenced a pasture two miles square that was located just southwest of Silver City. They hired a man to receive, brand, and look after these cattle, and as soon as they had a hundred or so on hand, E. B. bought them from the store and moved them to the ranch on Pond Creek.

With the coming of so many strangers who were overrunning the country, ranching on the Oklahoma side, or east side, of the South Canadian River had became very hazardous. It was not unusual to find a bawling cow, with her udder badly swollen, as she hunted for her calf, which some Boomer had thoughtlessly butchered. In Washington, D.C., many representatives shouted and protested against cowmen using the Oklahoma Territory at all.

The propaganda and trouble that these Boomers created caused some ranchers to give up and sell out. Cass Wantland, who ranched east of Council Grove on Crutch Creek [between present-day Midwest City and Del City– *C.N.K.*], was in the midst of these encroachers. The Boomers hunted, prowled, and staked claims on his ranch. They killed his cattle for beef and set fire to his range before they were forced out. He shipped his three- and four-year-old steers to market and started to Red Fork with them. In a stampede, he lost about a hundred head, but found a large number of them when he returned home. He sold this remaining big steers to Henry Johnson and Sam Clayton. He sold his Crutch O brand, stock cattle, yearlings, and two-year-old steers to Montford, who moved them to the Pond Creek Ranch. They did not rebrand these cattle, but did bob their tails. This was done by crowding about thirty head at a time into a small corral. The cowboys climbed into the corral, caught the closely packed cattle by the tail, and cut off the bushy end. After bobbing the tails, they herded them rather closely for about two weeks with their home cattle, then turned them loose.

Johnson and Clayton worked for the Long O outfit and lived just a few miles north of Montford's Pond Creek ranch. They rebranded their steers with AB on the left shoulder. As they gathered these big steers, they collected some of the two-year-old steers with their tails bobbed that E. B. and Montford had bought and paid for. When E. B. heard of it, he took his crew over, rounded up their steers, cut out his bobtailed steers, and told them that they had better stop it or he would come back and bob the big steers' tails also and claim each of them as a two-year-old, because he had a bill of sale for the brand. Henry Johnson and Sam Clayton promised to be more careful in the future.

During these years some pretty hard outfits established ranges and camps that bordered Montford's range. At every roundup they found some of their cattle that had had their brands tampered with. The outside riders, who worked through the neighboring outfits all the time and especially during the roundup season, had the most dangerous jobs. Montford always picked his top hands for this work, men who were absolutely loyal, level-headed, and who could be depended upon. On July

10, 1885, as reported in the *Cheyenne Transporter*, C. B. Campbell lost one of his men, Adam Ward, who was killed in a dispute over a steer. Ward was working with an outfit owned by a man named Frank Murray. C. B., Montford, and several others were at the roundup when Ward got into an argument over the burned-over brand on a steer. The EC brand had been blotted out to make a jail-door brand. Two of Murray's men, Williams and McCracken, shot Ward from his horse. Then Murray and all of his crew immediately opened up on C. B.'s outfit. Ward, as he fell from his horse, managed to pull out his revolver and get three shots off before he hit the ground. C. B.'s horse was shot out from under him and Montford had a hole shot through his hat, but they finally managed to escape.

In a separate incident, a cowboy named Harvey Lucas was shot by a cowboy named Brown, who was also with the Murray and Willams outfit. A month later, the Murray and Williams crew had another gunfight out on the range reported in the *Cheyenne Transporter* from August 15, where there were three casualties. Dick Cavat was shot dead from his horse, while Dick Jones was wounded three times, and Bob Woods was shot in the arm.

During October 1885, Montford had a more peaceful visitor travel through his range when Father Hilary Cassal from the Sacred Heart mission visited the family at his Silver City ranch. Two of Montford's and his late wife Mary's boys, Robert and Til, were attending school at Sacred Heart, along with Stella and Fannie, their two youngest daughters. Montford, his second wife, Addie, and the children threw a big watermelon feast for Father Hilary. He remarked that it was the first occasion that he had ever used a spoon to eat watermelon. Addie, herself a Catholic, as were many of the Campbell's, had gone to school at the convent of the Sisters of Saint Mary at Denison, Texas. Father Hilary said Mass for the family, and then went on to visit Addie's parents, Charlie and Sally Campbell, and their children at their ranch before heading off to Cherokee Town and other stops on his way back to the mission.[1]

Earlier in his trip around the Chickasaw Nation, Father Cassal had been told a story about an encounter with Father Robot by Captain Jack Stilwell while the two of them enjoyed a hearty breakfast with the Comanche chief Quanah Parker at Mrs. Tieman's hotel in Anadarko. Some years earlier, as the Captain recalled, while returning to Fort Sill, he overheard some singing off in the distance. He could not figure out what language these men were singing in. He ruled out Indian funeral chants, Spanish, French, or German, too. Finally he came upon these two men who were lying on the ground, apparently asleep or ill. He inquired if they were sick, but they replied no, saying only that they were starving. They had lost their way in this open country and had run out of food two days earlier. The Captain then asked them if they were the singers he had heard earlier and, if so, in what language were they singing. Father Robot replied that they had been singing the "Salve Regina" (a prayer to the Blessed Virgin) in Latin.[2]

Having had his curiosity satisfied, Jack handed them some cheese and crackers out of his saddlebag and then proceeded to ride into the nearby timber to hunt up something a little more substantial to eat. He soon returned with a squirrel that he had shot, skinned, and cleaned for them. He then roasted it Indian-style for the two hungry priests. After their meal the grateful priests thanked him most heartily. "You have saved our lives," said Father Robot and Brother Dominic. "We shall never forget your kind deed." The Captain accepted their praise thinking, "Indeed, I did save their lives, and I believe if it had not been for that strange song, I would have ridden on by and they most certainly would have died." Finally, before he bid them good-bye, he set them back on the trail to Fort Sill. He had not seen the two priests since.

Meanwhile, conditions continued to deteriorate for the ranchers and some of Montford's old friends. Bill McClure, who ranched east of Wantland's place, also decided to get out of Oklahoma. His cattle were of an inferior grade and Montford wasn't too keen on buying them, but McClure was insistent that E B. take them all at $18 a head. Reluctantly, E. B. gave McClure $1,780 in cash and his note for $20,000 at 6 percent interest, payable in two years. They all had a cross on the left jaw and some had an O on the left shoulder and a C on the left hip. E. B. relocated these cattle south of the Pond Creek ranch, but some of them wandered south of Walnut Creek and were picked up by a man named Cooper, who had a rather questionable outfit adjoining Bob Love's range.

Cooper took some of the steers that just had a cross on the jaw, put a circle around the cross and called it a wagon wheel. Bob Love sent word to E. B. that Cooper was burning some of E. B.'s newly acquired McClure steers. E. B. had his top men working at Pond Creek at that time, so he just moved the whole crew to Cooper's range and began rounding up his cattle. E. B. was cutting all the steers that had a fresh wagon-wheel brand on their jaw and resembled the McClure steers, when Cooper rode up. He wanted to know what E. B. was doing by cutting out his steers and threatened him if he did not get off his range. He was trying to run a bluff, which made E. B. very angry. He told Cooper that he had a thousand head of the same steers just ten miles north of him that were originally branded with a cross on the jaw, that it was evident that the brands had been tampered with, and that he was going to take his cattle. E. B. jerked his rope from the saddle horn, doubled it, and gave Cooper a good beating over the head with the doubled end of his rope. Fortunately, Bob Love intervened before things got out of hand with this six-shooter man. Also, E. B. was backed up by ten good men who went prepared for trouble, and Cooper knew it. Later, he told E. B. that he would have killed him, but that he was such a green kid that he let it go. The crew then cut out the rest of their steers, returned them to the ranch, and located them with a bunch of stock cattle until they were satisfied to stay at home.

In the fall of 1886 E. B. rounded up for market about two thousand head of fat dry cows, several old bulls, and about two hundred head of the Silver City store cattle. He passed the headquarters at Beaver Creek and headed for Hunnewell, Kansas. Montford came out and rode through the herd and wanted E. B. to cut out and leave some of his old native Indian cows. E. B. knew that this was just sentiment, so he talked his father out of it and took them along. This was to be their last trip to Hunnewell because the railroads were extending their lines into the Oklahoma and Indian Territories. This trip ended in tragedy and a killing. The cowboys had been working at top speed for some time and had become exhausted and oversensitive. They resented any kidding and had grown quite tired of each other's company. Ed Pickens, a Choctaw Indian, fell out with W. S. Green over some "rawhiding" remark that Green had made about Pickens's saddle and blankets. One night when they were camped near a nester's farm, Green told Pickens that he had better stake out his old "kack," or saddle, to keep it from stealing all the farmer's chickens. This remark, along with what had gone before, continued to prey on Pickens's mind.

After penning the cattle at Hunnewell, the crew all headed for the saloon. They took a few drinks to get the dust out of their throats, bought some new clothes, had their faces shaved, hair cut, and their boots shined. They returned to the wagon to finish slicking up and getting on their new clothes so that they could take in the sights after dinner. They returned to town and continued their drinking. Pickens got crazy drunk that night and became very jealous of Green, who he noticed was receiving all the attentions of a faded blonde at the end of the bar. Brooding over all of the past insults, Pickens could not stand this final conquest of Green's, so he jerked out his pistol, shot Green, returned to the wagon, caught a good horse, and under the cover of darkness headed back for the Indian Territory. The next morning, October 2, 1886, E. B. bought Green a new suit for his burial that cost eighteen dollars and they had a very decent kind of funeral for thirty dollars. The remaining twenty dollars and seventy cents still owed W. S. for wages was given to his brother J. N. Green. E. B. then gathered up his saddened and fairly sober crew and headed for home.

By this time the Graham family with all the girls had moved from Bob Curtis's place in the Caddo country, to what was known as Sutton

Flat, which was about four miles north of the old Jack Brown's place and about three miles west of the present town of Noble, Oklahoma. Mr. Graham was developing the land under a regular Chickasaw lease contract. He was sponsored by his brother-in-law, Perry Froman, who had married Lavina Colbert Pitchlyn, a Chickasaw widow. In 1882, Perry Froman who, like Noah Lael before him, was also an intermarried Chickasaw, bought "Lael's Sulphur Spring" place for three hundred and fifty dollars. Noah had married Lucy Harris, a daughter of Cyrus Harris, a Chickasaw governor. Perry Froman maintained possession of this land until he sold 547 acres to the Sulphur Springs Development Company in the 1890s for twenty-five hundred dollars. The sale was later rejected by the Chickasaw tribe.[3] In 1903, the federal government bought up all the lots around the springs, including E. B.'s, and made that area into Platt National Park, currently known as the Chickasaw National Recreational Area.[4]

In the meantime E. B. was courting Mollie Graham, and at every opportunity he dropped by the Graham farm to see her. Now busy with his father's business, his visits were short and far between. Luckily, he was able to see her at the few dances that were given at some of the neighboring ranches and to which everyone in the country was generally invited. These dances, without a doubt, were the main social activities on the prairie. Chincie Ross, Alec Cochran's granddaughter, related a story that her father, Turner, an Indian neighbor and friend of Montford's, recalled. "In those days, the boys and girls thought nothing of riding 25 miles to a square dance. They would dance all night and get home at sunrise, in time to cook breakfast. There were very few activities to spend money on, no picture shows, no gasoline; the motive power was grass and that grew free. The only amusement was square dancing and that was also free."[5]

Women were scarce and the Graham girls were in great demand at these dances. Since hacks and buggies were very scarce, too, one man in the neighborhood was usually detailed to take a hack, gather up a load of girls, and bring them to the dance. Montford was giving a big dance at his place on Beaver Creek, and Jim Tuttle, foreman of the Long O ranch, got the detail to go after the Graham girls. He went after them and when he reached Whorley Creek, he found that it was up and the red muddy banks were slippery from the recent rains. Jim and the girls were anxious to go to the dance and so decided to risk crossing the stream. They made it through the water, but when the horses started up the slick west bank, their unshod hoofs slipped out from under them and one of the horses fell down. This twisted the hack around, and it backed off into the stream again. Mollie Graham and Sarah Short, who had been visiting the Graham girls, jumped out into the water, which reached up to their waists.

Fannie Graham fell down in the bottom of the hack, and the seat fell on top of her. She was almost drowned before she came sputtering and gasping to the surface for air. Jim got the horses up, righted the hack, and managed to get the wet and soaked belles to Aunt Adelaide's, where the girls dried and ironed out their clothes. Once they were dressed, they hurried on to the dance at Montford's, which lasted until morning.

Chincie Ross related another incident that her father, Turner, had told her that took place at one of these parties. He said it was a common practice to put the children to bed in the wagons and hacks, as these dances continued into the wee hours. At one of these dances, a couple of intoxicated cowboys decided to play a trick on the party revelers and switched the sleeping babies amongst the wagons. After the dance finally broke up early the next morning, most of the tired dancers were well on their way home before they discovered the baby swap. None of the recipients of this joke were very happy with the surprise they received when "their" respective children woke up on the way home. Needless to say, these two cowboys kept a pretty low profile for some time after that prank.

The next time E. B. saw Mollie was at the first "invitation only" dance given in the country, by a family named Stovall. In the past it had always been the custom, when a dance was given, that everyone in the country was invited. The Stovall family decided that it was high time to step up things in a social way. The result of this "invitation only" dance was that the people who did not get invitations had their feelings hurt and felt terribly slighted. Rumors began to float around that the uninvited boys were going to come anyway and try to break up the dance.

Henry McLish had the privilege to drive the hack with the Graham girls, who were all excited and expecting some kind of trouble. When E. B. and the rest of the invited men arrived, Mr. Stovall insisted that they place their guns under one of the beds and not drink any liquor. The music started, and in a short time the dance was in full swing. Just as the musicians and dancers began to really get warmed up, one of the uninvited cowboys dropped an old rooster through an open window. The rooster had been plucked of most of his feathers, except one lone feather in his tail, which waved in the breeze. As the rooster hit the floor the cowboy shouted, "There's your damned picked party," and bang, bang, went several shots in the air outside the house. The girls screamed, the music stopped, and everyone huddled in a corner of the room and waited for the next outburst. Mr. Stovall quickly stepped outside to see if he could make peace with these uninvited interlopers and was immediately surrounded by a group of half-drunken men, including his son, Wade. It seemed that a whiskey peddler had slipped into the Territory and had unloaded his entire inventory on these boys. These young men insisted that Mr. Stovall take a drink with them to show that he had nothing to do with the invitations. While he was protesting and finally taking a drink, an innocent dog trotted by in the moonlight. Young Wade Stovall took a shot at the dog and immediately all of them started shooting, some at the dog and some just about any direction. E. B. and Henry McLish went out to see if they could stop the shooting. When Henry stepped outside, Bob Bean, one of Henry's friends, shot between Henry's legs. Henry told him to cut it out, but Bob was in a playful mood and shot again. The bullet whistled through one of Henry's trouser legs. Henry rushed back in the house to get his gun from under the bed and swore that he was going to kill the drunken fool. Callie Graham threw her arms around Henry's neck and hung on to him for dear life. Several others came to her aid and they managed to hold Henry until he cooled off and, no doubt, saved Bob Bean's life. When the shooting finally let up, everyone began slipping away from the house and leaving the dugout filled with the cooked food, untouched. So ended the first "picked" party in the Territory. And as Mollie Graham later remarked, "This was our introduction to society in the far west."

During January and February 1886, 1887, and 1888, E. B. spent much of his time collecting permits from the white people living in the Chickasaw Nation. The January 7, 1888, issue of the *Purcell Register* commented that "Ed Johnson has been here this week rustling the boys for their permit money," while paying for a few subscriptions to the paper. Many settlers had come into the Chickasaw country and were working the land for some Indian citizen, who became the sponsor for the white man. Usually the only requirement for holding the land was to break out the land, make certain improvements, and pay the five-dollar per capita tax on every adult male each year. The fee originally, in 1876, was twenty-five dollars, but that fee had dropped as farm wages in Texas had become more competitive. This fee was also levied on any other non-Indian professional people, such as dentists, pharmacists, or newspaper publishers. The appointed collectors each received one dollar and twenty-five cents for each five dollars collected.

As the Santa Fe Railroad built northward through Ardmore, Pauls Valley, Purcell, and other new towns, it gave easy access to thousand of whites to move into the Chickasaw Nation. By the 1890 census, the entire Native American, intermarried white, and freedman population represented less that 10 percent of the Chickasaw Nation's inhabitants; the rest were white.[6]

E. B. drove a buggy and team for this work and met many new people that he would not have met in any other way. Sometimes it was impossible for the Chickasaw sponsor to pay this fee in cash, so E. B. traded for one thing and another to help them out. The mobility of this job also made it possible for him to court Mollie a little more often. Finally, in early 1887, E. B. proposed to Mollie, asking her, "if she would take a chance and embark with him in his canoe." She accepted immediately.

E. B. sent Lyman Leader to Stonewall for the marriage license, which cost fifty dollars since he was marrying outside of the tribe. When Leader returned from Stonewall, Mollie and E. B. left for Johnsonville to be married. They were accompanied by Mollie's parents, Montford, and Lon Gray, who were all present at the ceremony, as well as the Hill Phillips's family, in whose home they were married on February 17, 1887. Mrs. Phillips was the former orphan, Sally (Thompson) Walker, who had remarried after her husband, William Walker, died. Mollie's sister, Callie Graham, was already boarding at the Phillips's house since she was teaching school in Johnsonville at that time.

Mollie wore a grey silk wedding dress that her uncle, A. R. Froman, had given her. Parson L. D. Holsonbake, a combination preacher and blacksmith, married them in short order. He had a small church a little west of Johnsonville, on the north side of the Canadian River. Some of the Johnsons' old friends got wind that Ed was to be married, so a few of them showed up too. Gus Leslie came down from his place near the present-day Noble area. Gus confessed to one of the Grahams that his best trousers had holes in them and he had to keep putting his hand on one knee to cover the holes up. As Mollie later recalled, "Times did not demand announcements, parties and showers as they do now. It was a blessed thing, as we had no money and no place to buy anything, so my trousseau was pitiful to behold. If anything could have stopped this wedding, it would have been the lack of clothes." Mollie also remembered, "Ed did not have a ring, only one made of his father's and mother's which I wore throughout our engagement. I wore this one until time came when Ed bought me a broad band of gold, which grew so heavy I had it cut in two and wore it from then on. We were married on the fifth anniversary of the Graham family arriving in the Indian Territory." Their wedding gifts amounted to a pig and pillow. After the ceremony, E. B. and his young wife returned to Montford's home on Beaver Creek, where they lived until a new home could be built for them at the Pond Creek ranch.

E. B. hauled the lumber for their new four-room house from Purcell. According to the *Purcell Register*, E. B. hired Bob Woods and some additional carpenters to build their new home, and they had it completed in time for Mollie and E. B.'s first anniversary. Their first daughter, Veta, would remember the house as having three bedrooms, one of which was used as the living room, a small hall, dining room, and kitchen. E. B. had a sawmill cut some oak, walnut, and cottonwood lumber for a big barn, numerous corrals, and a round house over a cellar for the ranch crew. South of the house, which sat on a high hill, he constructed a large earthen dam that soon filled with water, and it was kept fresh by the spring-fed creek that flowed into it. Veta remembered also "the cooling breeze that always kept the house comfortable in the summer evenings, coming from the pond. The pond was soon stocked with fish and big green bullfrogs." There was still plenty of deer, wild turkey, quail, and prairie chickens in the area, so E. B. felt that he could provide very well for his bride. Ed and Mollie moved into their new home on February 17, 1888, their first wedding anniversary. In honor of this day, one of Ed's farmhands, who was an Indian boy and a great hunter, shot a big wild turkey for their first supper.

Mollie gradually took over the cooking chores, but she was inexperienced and lacked confidence. One day she tried making some sourdough biscuits. They failed to rise and turned hard as stone, so she threw the rest of the dough over the fence before anyone might have sampled them. The sun's heat soon made that dough start to rise and shortly thereafter, their recently healthy wedding pig was found dead near the forgotten pile of dough. At least that was the way E. B. liked to tell the story.

Notes

1. Cassal, Rev. Hilary. 1956–1957. "Missionary Tour in the Chickasaw Nation and Western Indian Territory." *Chronicles of Oklahoma*, Oklahoma Historical Society. Vol. 34, no. 4, pp. 413–414.
2. Ibid., pp. 408–409.
3. Boeger, Palmer. 1987. *Oklahoma Oasis: From Platt National Park to Chickasaw National Recreation Area*. Muskogee, OK: Western Heritage Books, p. 41.
4. Conlan, Czarina C. 1926. "Platt National Park." *Chronicles of Oklahoma*, Oklahoma Historical Society. Vol. 4, p. 12.
5. Lee, Virginia, and Chincie Ross. 1990. Grady County Genealogical Society. Vol. 7, no. 3.
6. Littlefield, Daniel F., Jr. 1980. *The Chickasaw Freedmen.* Westport, CT: Greenwood Press, pp. 44, 45.

Fort Reno Contract and Chickasaw Politics

N ow that barbed wire was coming into general use, E. B. hired some neighboring farmers to break out and fence some fields on the flats east of his house. He farmed out many of his young mules to be broken, and in this way got more land broken and his mules tamed at the same time. E. B. had also hired Will Partridge out of Purcell to do some tin work around the Pond Creek ranch. Montford was busy too, increasing his farming acreage and hog production at the Beaver Creek ranch, so that in the fall one could see long ricks of corn piled up in the stack lots. Along with the increased hay output, these cornstalk fields helped the thin, fire-sale cattle that the Johnsons had been buying up winter better than they would have otherwise.

At the Silver City store, Joe Lindsay said that he could increase their trade if he had an outlet for their fattened trade cattle. E. B. contacted his friend Cornelius W. "Neal" Evans, a brother of the well-known Fort Sill sutler, John S. Evans. Montford had known the Evans brothers since his days at old Fort Arbuckle. Neal operated the sutler's store at Fort Reno. Neal Evans was highly thought of among the settlers, soldiers, and Indians alike. He was affectionately given the name "Little Buffalo" by his Indian customers, according to a memorial piece in the April 22, 1934, issue of the *El Reno Tribune*. E. B. and Joe received one of the contracts to furnish beef to the fort. The post at the fort required a higher grade of beef than that provided by D. R. Fant for the Cheyenne and Arapaho Indians' rations at the Darlington Agency. E. B. and Joe were to receive eight cents a pound for the dressed beef. In order to keep on hand the quality of cattle that would meet this contract, E. B. and Montford both

The traders store at Fort Reno, Indian Territory, July 1885, with an assemblage of Cheyenne and Arapahoes present. [Neal Evans, proprietor and author's namesake— C.N.K.] Courtesy, Oklahoma Historical Society, #9529 Hickox Collection OHS, Archives and Manuscripts Division.

increased their feeding operations and enlarged their feedlots. They also purchased fat cattle from neighboring ranchers. E. B. bought four hundred head of fat dry cows from Mark Brittian, Jack Brown, Nute Burney, and Mr. Goldsmith. These cows were dehorned and placed in the feedlots, where they were fed chopped, snapped corn. The cows ate the corn husks for roughness, and hogs followed the cattle and ate up the remnants. During the fall and winter, the hogs had rivals for this food because ducks and geese flocked to these pens to feed. They moved about a hundred head at a time west of Fort Reno, where they were herded until it was time to butcher them.

They rented a two-room shack from Red McAfee and hired Billie Frass and E. B.s brother-in-law, George Graham, to handle the camp and to keep the fort supplied with beef. They usually slaughtered about ten head at a time and butchered twice a week. The army supplied inspectors to pass on the beef, but the young officers assigned to the job knew nothing about beef. One morning one of these dumb inspectors condemned a hindquarter because, he said, "There is too much neck." This was too much for Billie Frass, realizing that the inspector could not tell the difference between a loin and a neck. Billie pulled a gun and ran him off the place. They ran this slaughterhouse about two years, and their profits just about offset the depredations of the Indians.

Joe Lindsay, partner with E. B. Johnson in the Silver City Store, later became the sole proprietor. Courtesy, the family of Robert A. Johnson.

This shack or slaughterhouse was located about three miles west of the fort in the Cheyenne and Arapahoe reservation. The Indians soon learned which days that they butchered the cattle and drove their wagons

Waiting for the beef issue on the Cheyenne-Arapahoe Reservation at Cantonment, circa 1890. Courtesy, University of Oklahoma, #456 Division of Manuscripts, Western History Collection.

to the slaughterhouse. This scavenging of the fort's beef issue helped augment the Indians' own meager rations. In an excerpt from an article in *Harper's Weekly*, Richard Harding Davis made a few observations about the Indians' beef issue:

> Those (cattle) I saw had been purchased in October, and had been weighed and branded at that time with the Government brand. They were then allowed to roam over the Government reservation until the spring, when they had fallen off in weight from one-half to one-third. They were then issued at their original weight. That is, a steer which in October was found to weigh eleven hundred pounds, and which would supply twenty or more people with meat, was supposed to have kept this weight throughout the entire winter, and was still issued at eleven hundred although it had not three hundred pounds of flesh on its bones.[1]

The whole family came, with the father driving and the wife and children sitting on a wagon bed of platted green willow shoots. The Indians preferred this springy wagon bed instead of the regular wagon boxes that were issued to them by the government. They just threw the issue box away, and one could see them scattered all over the reservation.

Butchering on the reservation. Courtesy, University of Oklahoma, #28 Irwin Bros. Collection, Western History Collection.

When the Indians rebuilt their wagon beds with willow, it left the wagon without a brake beam. They did not seem to mind however, because as a rule, they would not drive a team that could not outrun a wagon.

The Indians were usually dressed in leggings, moccasins, with a blanket over their shoulders. As soon as the butcher finished with a beef, they crowded in to salvage all the waste. The guts were a special delicacy. They cleaned them, as discussed earlier, by pulling them through their fingers, and then tossed them on a smoldering fire of coals. They would only leave the guts on the fire for a few seconds, just enough time to warm them up, then they would jerk them off the coals and quickly eat them. The unborn calves, which they found in the cows, were placed in their wagons and taken home.

At the start of Montford's ranching, through his friendship with Jesse Chisholm, he had always felt free to use all the country that he wanted, while many of the rest of the Chickasaws were afraid to encroach on the hunting grounds of the wild Indians. It was very different now because other Chickasaws and intermarried citizens took up claims and ranches on or near his various ranches. Montford decided that he would rather pay to lease this tribal land if he could be assured the exclusive use of it. He wanted to lease the country along the Bitter and Salt Creeks, where there were no settlers. He sent E. B. to Tishomingo to discuss it with

Governor William L. Byrd, and suggested to him that he recommend a bill that would provide for the leasing of specific land to ranchers for a period of years. The governor thought that it might be easier to get the bill passed if E. B. were in the legislature and introduced the bill himself, so the governor urged E. B. to run.

The voting in E. B.'s district took place at Stonewall, Indian Territory. E. B. remembered his initial introduction to political campaigning: "I rigged out two chuck wagons, one went to the Washita to round up supporters for my election. I took the other myself. We had plenty of good beef and food. I rounded up all my Chickasaw friends as we went along. It was a kind of Roman Holiday until we got to Stonewall, the county seat of Pontotoc County." He quickly discovered that it was the custom to keep your voters well supplied with whiskey, but sober enough to get to the polls and vote, while his supporters tried to get the opposition so drunk that they could not vote. The whole campaign was a nightmare, with sick, crazy drunk Indians, reeling and staggering around, smelling of sweat, booze, and vomit. E. B. was elected, but he was already disgusted with everything he had seen in his brief political life.

When the legislature convened, E. B. introduced the bill. Lobbyists began to work on the legislators and started pouring whiskey into them again. E. B. said he'd never seen such a drunken mob; they could hardly do any kind of intellectual business. As soon as he introduced his bill, it seemed that everyone in the Chickasaw Nation wanted to lease the Bitter and Salt Creek country. Frustrated, E. B. withdrew his bill and decided to just continue to hold his range under the old policy of use in common. By the time the legislature ended, he was tired, worn out, and disgusted with his office. He returned home to the Pond Creek ranch, where there were plenty of doable tasks waiting for him.

Each year in the early part of April all the ranchers in the area, calling themselves the Chickasaw Stock Association, held a meeting and planned their spring roundup. They agreed on the starting date, where the different outfits would assemble, and the general direction that each wagon would take, and the wagon boss for each one was designated. The spring work began on April 10, 1886. Three wagons assembled at the Long O headquarters and spread out and worked the country east of Shawnee Town. When they reached that point, the wagons separated. One went up the North Canadian River, one took the Little River, and the last took the South Canadian River. Another separate group started at C. B.'s ranch. They worked the country west to Bent's ranch along Boggy Creek and the South Canadian River, thence north to the North Canadian. The third group assembled on the south side of the Washita River, worked down to Cherokee Town, thence back to the Bitter and Salt Creeks.

Each big outfit transferred one or two of their men to these other wagons. These outside men were to gather any of their own cattle and look after the interests of their employer. They took their own bedrolls, equipment, and their own string of horses, and reported to the wagon boss to whom they had been assigned. When the wagon showed up near the home ranges, these outside riders turned over the cattle that they had gathered to their line riders. It was these line riders' job to relocate them back on their home ranges. These outside men, when they were not working with some wagon crew, prowled through neighboring ranches and picked up any other stray cattle they could find bearing their own ranches' brands.

The big job in the fall, after rounding up and penning the horses, was branding and castrating the male colts. Most of the horses ran in bands of twenty to thirty mares and a stallion and ranged in the Oklahoma Territory. Montford had a corral built on the Oklahoma side of the South Canadian, on a high hill north of Little River. He also used a special type of horse, which he called a "Red Buck," to round up these bands. These Red Buck horses were long-legged, slender, sorrel, and the toughest and swiftest that he raised. Rounding up these mares was exciting work. They posted riders along the route from the corral to the range that a particular band used; one of two riders circled around each band and when they were flushed, the race was on. They ran like the wind and as one relay team began to tire, the others that had been posted along the route took up the chase, until they finally wound up with the wild horses in the corral. Sometimes an old mare became such an outlaw and so difficult to pen that they either shot her, or if they could catch her, they would cut a leader in the knee, which would slow down her considerably.

After these horses were penned, the older horses were cut into another pen, and the teams got ready to work on the excited colts. One man would rope one by the neck, then another would rope the same one by the forefeet, jerk the colt's feet out from under him and throw him on his side. As soon as the colt hit the ground, one man got on its head and another grabbed the tail and bent it back over its croup. If the colt was a filly, as soon as it was branded it was turned loose; but if it was a young stallion, the hind feet were brought forward and tied to the forefeet. This left the sheath exposed and ready for the operation. The purse was opened, the membranes scraped back, and a wooden clamp was fastened around the cords, which were burned into with a red-hot iron. After the wound was swabbed with a mixture that acted as an antiseptic and fly-repellent, the colt was turned loose and another was caught until they had finished. While the branding was going on, others cut out the young horses that they wanted to take into headquarters and break.

When the bronc riders had them gentled, with some of the fight taken out of them, they were turned over to line riders, who continued to ride them during the winter. By spring they were broken enough to be used in full service.

In this time frame Montford lost an entire band of these Red Buck mares and the stallion that ran with them. The offending Indians ate the horses and stole the colts, which had not been branded. Later that same winter, Montford's riders found some of the colts in the winter camps of the Indians, but could not prove that they belonged to him. These winter tepees of the Indians were covered with swamp grass and were much better insulated than the canvas that they used during the summer. The government refused to pay anything for these depredations, because they claimed that they took place on the Indian reservation.

During the winters of 1885 and 1886, after the government had forbidden ranchers to use the Cheyenne and Arapahoe reservation for range purposes, thousands of those cattle on the reservation just drifted. Montford moved many of his horses and cattle out of Oklahoma and the line riders were kept busy trying to keep these in the Chickasaw Nation and trying to keep out the reservation cattle that wandered hungrily over the burned Oklahoma Territory. A large number drifted past the line riders and survived, but thousands piled up along the South Canadian River and died. The cowboys exaggerated, but it shows the number that perished when they said that they could walk on dead cattle from one end of the river to the other, where it crossed the Chickasaw Nation, without putting a foot on the ground.

After the experience of the winter of 1886, and the continued trouble with the Boomers in Oklahoma, Montford decided to try and keep most of his cattle in the Chickasaw Nation by building a drift fence along the river. The Chickasaw law prohibited the fencing of the public domain, so Montford began lobbying for a fence bill, which was not passed until April 6, 1889, less than two weeks before the "Run of '89." This bill permitted ranchers along the South Canadian River to erect drift fences to protect themselves from the livestock that ranged north of the South Canadian River. In the meantime, Montford started the construction of large earthen dams on his ranges bordering the river. He hoped this would provide an ample supply of water if he had to cut the cattle off from watering at the river.

Their cash business had increased by selling to Boomers and families wandering through the country. A large surveying crew of the Santa Fe Railroad had become another steady customer. When the construction crew came after the surveyors, E. B. and Joe arranged to put in a branch store on the South Canadian River near the railroad crossing and several miles south of Camp Norman. They built a good dugout for living quarters, and adjoining this, a room fourteen by twenty in which they kept their groceries and sundry supplies. They carried a good stock of groceries, overalls, slickers, and other work-related items. Bob Love, who had built a small slaughterhouse about half a mile east of the store, delivered fresh beef each day. They ran this store until Purcell was built up a little and had opened up some stores of its own.

One day in the spring of 1887, while visiting with E. B. at the store, Bob Love suggested to him that they go into the townsite business in the town to be established south of the river in the Chickasaw Nation. They engaged a surveyor from the railroad who was to lay off the principal streets in Purcell. Bob borrowed a plow from Mose Pugh, and they hitched E. B.'s chuck wagon, loaded the plow, and drove to the townsite. After they hitched the team to the plow, E. B. drove the team and Bob held the plow as they marked off two streets. They named them Main Street and Chickasaw Avenue. E. B.claimed four lots across the street from where Bob said that he was going to build a bank and a hotel. E. B. fenced his four lots and later, when the town began to grow, rented the site for a lumberyard. By June of that year, trains were regularly running to Purcell.

Now that the Santa Fe Railroad was running trains to the east of Silver City in Oklahoma, and it was rumored that the Rock Island and Pacific Railroads would soon be built to the west, E. B. could see no reason to continue their dry, inland store at Silver City. During the summer of 1888, he sold out his interest to Joe Lindsay, who within two years moved the store into Minco when the railroad extended there. Minco's post office was activated on June 30, 1890, in Joe Lindsay's store; the new postmaster was Frank E. Clayton.[2] E. B.'s deal with Joe Lindsay also included the two-section fenced cattle pasture on Store Creek, west of the store. This pasture was later turned over by Joe Lindsay to Henry McBride, his brother-in-law, who had married a Colbert, making Henry an intermarried citizen. Years later, Henry McBride took this land as his allotment.

Notes

1. Savage, William W., Jr. 1977. *Indian Life: Transforming an American Myth.* Norman: University of Oklahoma Press, pp. 131–133.
2. Munn, Irving. *Chickasha . . . A Journey Back in Time.* Chickasha: University of Science and Arts of Oklahoma Foundation, p. 1.

Oklahoma Run

In the spring of 1889 E. B. was busy farming, constructing new ponds, and hauling wire from Purcell to be used in building their drift fence along the river. They had been assured that the legislature was going to pass the bill that authorized the fence, but they had decided to build it whether the legislature passed the bill or not. It was a matter of necessity.

Montford preferred the old-fashioned open-range idea, but he, too, was adapting himself to the new conditions. He had increased his farming at Beaver Creek and had large fields of rye, oats, wheat, and corn. His headquarters looked more like the home of a Southern planter than that of a Chickasaw rancher. John Fowler, who visited the headquarters as far back as 1885, told E. B. many years later of the deep impression it had made on him. Fowler had gone with Henry Courtney to see a Chickasaw Indian at Silver City about getting an Indian lease. According to the February 21, 1896, *Minco Minstrel,* Henry farmed outside of a small town called Courtney after him, just north of the Red River, near Mud Creek. Fowler became the postmaster there in August 1886.[1] When they arrived at Silver City, Fowler learned that Montford was the Indian that they were going to see.

At the store in Silver City, Joe Lindsay referred them to the place on Beaver Creek, where Fowler expected to see an old full-blood Indian living in a dugout. He was greatly surprised when they topped the rise overlooking Beaver Creek and saw, on the hill of the opposite bank of the stream, a large house, big barns, corrals, and farmland in the bottom. Courtney stopped the team at the bottom of the hill, left Fowler in charge, and walked to the house. Montford welcomed his old friend Henry Courtney and broke out his best bottle of imported whiskey as they caught up with each other's lives. A short time later, one of Monford's Negro farmhands came down and took charge of the team and told Fowler to go on up to the house. Montford was always stranger-shy and quickly put the whiskey bottle up when John Fowler came walking up on the front porch. The two were invited to eat with the family and that afternoon were entertained by the efforts of Tilford and Henry. Henry had just returned from a trip to see his grandfather, Boggy, in New York, and brought back a pair of roller skates. So the two boys had the group in stitches as they slipped, slid, sprawled, and fell all over the place trying to learn to roller skate in the combined living and dining rooms.

When Montford learned that Fowler was an experienced farmer, he questioned him very closely about the various farming practices in different parts of the country. Fowler exchanged ideas with Montford on the many things that he had seen on his buying trips in Kansas, Missouri, and Kentucky. Fowler was pleasantly surprised to see the variety of crops that Montford was raising as they toured his river-bottom fields. The two were soon fast friends, and the next time Fowler showed up at Montford's he was treated as any old friend.

Once Aunt Adelaide was informed of Montford's new guests' arrival, she gathered up her family members and brought them over for the noon dinner. The folding doors were pushed back, and the two families and their guests all ate together at a long table. In the afternoon several of the girls played the piano for everyone's entertainment. Montford enjoyed much more the antics of a purebred Durham bull that was staked a short distance from the house. The bull lunged against the rope and found out that he could not jerk up the stake or break the rope, so he started walking round and round the stake, and wound the rope around it until the rope was real short. Then the bull stood over the stake and jerked his head from side to side, which loosened the stake. He seemed to know exactly what he was doing. After the stake was loosened in this manner, he raised his head, pulled out the stake, and headed for the gate into the cornfield. Montford jumped out of his chair and ran to catch the rope before the bull reached the gate, knowing full well that the bull would walk right through the gate as if it were not there. He was a beautiful animal, and Montford kept him close to home to breed a special group of purebred cows.

The news that Oklahoma was to be opened for homestead settlement came as a great shock to all the ranchers, but Montford was better prepared to meet it than most of them. In the closing days of Congress a rider had been attached to the Indian appropriation bill that provided that 2 million acres be thrown open for settlement. On March 2, 1889, in the last few weeks of his term, President Grover Cleveland signed the bill and it became law. On March 23, shortly after his inauguration, President Benjamin Harrison issued a proclamation that stated that Oklahoma would be opened to homestead settlement at noon on April 22, 1889.

Prior to this, on March 10, Lieutenant Colonel E. V. Sumner, who was in command at Fort Reno, had ordered all cowmen to remove their livestock from the Oklahoma Territory. This order gave the ranchers in the Chickasaw Nation a little over a month to roundup their cattle and horses in Oklahoma, move them to the south side of the South Canadian River, build dams and ponds, and put up drift fences. Many others less fortunate had to find new ranges entirely. Fortunately, there was plenty of help as the homesteaders poured into the country. They were happy to find work while they waited for the eventful day. E. B. hired many of these men to do the work at home and assembled his experienced cowboys to make one more roundup into the Oklahoma Territory.

E. B. and his crew first removed the stock horses. The mares were turned out to pasture at the Pond Creek ranch, and the stallions were placed in stalls in the barn. He then joined forces with all the other ranchers in Oklahoma and along the South Canadian River to make a clean sweep at one time, moving everything ahead of them. They started at the southern end of Oklahoma and threw the cattle into one slow-moving herd that was grazed north, while riders on the flanks combed the country for any additional livestock. When they found calves too young to follow their mothers, they were carried on horseback until they caught up to a wagon that had been assigned to haul them. The cows usually followed along behind the wagon, and when the herd stopped the calves were let out to feed.

Outlaw steers, which had been getting away into the blackjacks to the east, were roped and driven out of the woods. One horn was sawed almost in two, then cracked back so that it dangled loosely from its head. This horn became so sensitive that the steer would no longer have any desire to run through the woods; fearing even the slightest touch, he quickly reverted to following the herd. A few outlaw cows were mean enough to hook and fight a horse. These cattle were roped and soon controlled by placing small green sticks, about two inches long and flat on one side, upright in their eyelids. With these serving as a blinders, they could not see anything directly in front of them, and only got glimpses of objects to the side. They followed along behind the herd, walking rather hesitantly along and carrying their heads lifted rather high in the air. A few of the old bulls were often in the habit of breaking out of the herds, especially when a young bull charged them. They returned to their old haunts in spite of being whipped over their heads with a bull whip. They just shut their eyes and walked away from the younger bulls. These stubborn old bulls were not worth the effort it took to contain them, so they were left behind to greet their new landlords, the eighty-niners.

By the time they reached the mouth of Pond Creek, they had a herd of about twenty-five hundred head of grown cattle. They left the herd in charge of a few riders, while the flankers were going to comb the Chickasaw country for Oklahoma ranchers' cattle and gather as far north as the Long O ranch. While they were eating lunch, one of the men, whom they had left with the herd, charged into camp and said that about thirty soldiers and some Indian scouts had taken over the herd, arrested the riders as trespassers, and had headed toward Fort Reno with the cattle and men. This boy had managed to slip away. The soldiers claimed that they were going to hold them for a trespassing fee under an old law that applied to the reservations of the wild Indians. This Federal Act, 2117, could not apply to Oklahoma because it was not an Indian reservation, and it had never been enforced in that country.

All of the ranchers were terribly upset over this high-handed act of the troops, since they had been given a specified time period to remove their cattle. Some of the Cherokee strip outfits wanted to recover the cattle by force, if necessary. E. B. was very angry, too, but felt sure that there must be some mistake, because Lieutenant Colonel Sumner was a good friend of his father's. E. B. felt sure that he would have notified him if he was intending to try and enforce this old act. After he had cooled off a little, E. B. told them that they could not afford to attack the soldiers, if it could be prevented, and that he would take full responsibility to recover the herd. He asked for the ten most level-headed men to accompany him. Some of those taken along were John Reed, Lon Gray, Henry McLish, and the two Dalton and two Turnbull boys. All of them were excellent, tried and true cowmen. The Dalton boys, however, later turned into bank robbers.

The horse wrangler brought up fresh horses, each rider cleaned his Winchester and six-shooter, got plenty of ammunition (which E. B. did not intend to use if it could be avoided), mounted, and set out to recover the cattle and their arrested men. After crossing the river it was easy to pick up the fresh trail of the herd. They came to a place where two calves had been butchered. The only things that were left at the spot were the heads, the feet, and a small pile of grass that had been emptied from their paunches. It was a typical Cheyenne or Arapaho butchering that had been done by the scouts.

When they sighted the herd, it was strung out for about a mile. The soldiers and scouts were riding the flanks, shouting and shaking blankets at the cattle and crowding them along as fast as possible. They undoubtedly had scouts placed at the rear, because they must have been expecting the ranchers to overtake them. As soon as the soldiers sighted the ranchers, they came to the rear and left the herd in charge of the Indian scouts. They dismounted and deployed in a line as if they expected to fight a battle. E. B. moved his men up a shallow draw until they were within a half mile of the soldiers. He stopped his men and gave the horses a chance to blow, while they mapped out their plan of taking the cattle. He said that he would take the lead when they came out of the draw and for the rest of them to ride single-file behind him until they reached the right point of the herd so that they could turn it. They were to ignore the soldiers, be perfectly quiet, and not shoot unless they were fired upon. In the event the soldiers fired on them, they were to drop off their horses with their Winchesters and pick the soldiers off, because they were deployed in plain sight and without any cover.

When the cowboys rode out of the draw at a lope, they could see the guns of the soldiers glistening in the sun. As they neared the herd a white flag went up, which was ignored by the cowboys because the soldiers suddenly ran to their horses, mounted, and rode like scared rabbits toward the fort. The Indian scouts quit the herd and followed the troopers. The sudden flight of the soldiers was such a comical ending to what might have been a very serious affair that one of the Dalton boys let out a wild cowboy yell as if he were chasing coyotes, which was taken up by the rest of the men. As an added incentive to the flight of the soldiers, they shot into the air a few times, loped to the head of the herd, and turned it back toward the Chickasaw Nation, where they crossed the river by dark, and held it on the Chickasaw side.

Since all the soldiers had fled, they had been unable to find out why they had seized the cattle, but they went ahead that evening and planned their work for the next day. The men were to ride their fastest mounts and if they ran into soldiers to light out for the Chickasaw country. The horse wranglers were instructed to keep their remuda along the ridges where they could see what was going on and be ready to supply the riders with fresh mounts at a moment's notice. The cooks were to have the dinner ready, promptly, at noon and to locate their chuck wagons near the river. Their plan was to work the range between the two Canadian Rivers as far north as Council Grove and to do it as quickly as possible.

The next morning E. B. took the west flank of the drive, and they saw a troop of cavalry coming. While most of the cowboys headed back to the river in a long lope, E. B. and two of his men rode to intercept the soldiers. When they drew near, one of the soldiers came forward and ordered them to halt. Then they ordered E. B. and his men to lay down their arms, to which E. B. replied sharply, "You can go to Hell!" One of the scouts then attempted to grab the bridle reins of E. B.'s horse, which wheeled away from him as E. B. brought the butt end of his heavy cow whip down on his outstretched arm. The soldier let out a wild yelp, and the whole troop, headed by the Indian agent Major A. E. Woodson, rode up and surrounded them. Woodson had a high shrill voice and said that E. B. and his men must consider themselves under arrest, and to ride with a detail at the rear of the column. They headed back toward the fort and in a short time Major Woodson sent for him so that he could question him. He particularly wanted to know where the rest of the men could be found. E. B. told him that part of the men were holding the herd that the soldiers attempted to take the day before and that they were in the Chickasaw country and that the rest of them would show up at the chuck wagons at noon. Captain Woodson changed his course and headed for the noon location of the wagons. Out of the fifty men that had started out that morning, only eight showed up at noon.

The cooks fed the officers while they discussed the events of the preceding day. Major Woodson's chief complaint was that E. B.'s cow-hands had fired on government troops. E. B. and his men denied firing at the soldiers. He then surprised Woodson with the letter from Lieuten-ant Colonel Sumner, which gave them several more days to clean out any cattle still in Oklahoma, completely contradicting Captain Woodson's orders to round up all the cattle in Oklahoma immediately. There was a definite conflict in orders, so Major Woodson ordered E. B. to go with him to the fort to appear before the Colonel. He arrested the eight men that showed up at the wagon, and they all headed toward his camp to spend the night. They did not arrive there until after dark, and when the detail started checking their prisoners they discovered that the eight men whom they had taken at the wagon had all slipped away in the darkness. Woodson was so angry that he threatened to put E. B. and his two men in irons, but E. B. finally convinced him that he did not intend to escape and wanted to be taken on to the fort that night.

Major Woodson finally cooled off and offered E. B. a toddy, but he was so disgusted with the Major's decisions that he declined. Shortly thereafter, the Major picked a detail of some twenty men to take them on to Fort Reno. When they arrived at the high picket fence that en-closed the guardhouse, E. B. demanded to be taken before Colonel Sumner at once and was finally taken to the Colonel's house. E. B. shouted his name out to the darkened house and in a few moments Colonel Sumner came out of his front door to see what all the shouting was about. E. B. said that a widower's son was in distress. After explain-ing the situation to him for a short time, Colonel Sumner told the detail to take E. B. to the hotel for the night and that he would discuss it in more detail the next morning.

As soon as E. B. had breakfast, he called on his old friend at the sutler store, Neal Evans, asking him to go with him before the Colonel and intercede for him. When they appeared before Colonel Woodson, the Colonel said that he had a very bad report and asked E. B. why he had fired on the soldiers. E. B. said that they did not shoot at them and if they had, the fort would be holding some funerals, and then proceeded to explain the whole affair. In addition, E. B. told him that, since he was a native Chickasaw Indian, he expected the government to protect them from the Boomers and wild Indians instead of confiscating their cattle for grazing fees, which they did not owe. The Colonel closed the affair by giving them until the day of the opening to get their cattle out of the territory and ordered the troops to leave the cowmen alone.

E. B. and his men headed for Montford's headquarters to report the incident to him before they rode back to rejoin the wagons. They met Montford in a buggy on his way to the fort. One of E. B.'s riders had all ready reported to him what had happened to E. B. and his crew. After explaining the situation to his father, E. B. rejoined the rest of the wagons, and they continued their drive, knowing there was no time to waste.

On April 21, 1889, they bedded the herd down near Cow Creek (southwest of Will Rogers Airport) in Oklahoma for the night, and the next morning crossed into the Chickasaw country with about four thousand cattle. There were so many landseekers along the south bank of the river that they had to get the soldiers to get them to move back and make a lane so the cattle could pass through. They turned them loose in a holding pasture and put up the gate of the newly made drift fence. The cowboys looked over their new neighbors who had drifted into the country since President Harrison's proclamation. While rounding up the cattle, they had jumped a few Sooners, homesteaders who had slipped by the soldiers and intended to come out of hiding and file on choice land as soon as the signal was given. Several cowboys caught fresh, fast horses from the remuda to make the run just for the fun of the thing, because they did not think that it was possible for a family to make a living on one hundred and sixty acres.

At high noon on a beautiful spring day, the country having been burned clean, with new green grass and wildflowers making a gay carpet, the soldiers along the river shot their guns, which was the signal for a wild stampede. As the smoke from the guns drifted away in the gentle breeze, a mighty shout went up and down the river. The riders on the swiftest horses took the lead; they were followed by men on slower mounts, workhorses, mules, and burros. After them came wagons, buggies, carts, and buckboards, which rattled and twisted behind the faster-moving horses that had disappeared in the initial cloud of dust stirred up by the earlier riders as they crossed the riverbed. Last, but just as determined as the

Run of '93 into the Cherokee Strip, September 16, 1893. [Similar to the Run of 1889–C.N.K.] Courtesy, University of Oklahoma, #184 Cunningham Collection, Western History Collection.

fastest rider, came a few stragglers on foot. Out in front of this chaotic charge ran deer, coyotes, and animals of all kinds trying to stay clear of this encroaching mob. In the wild rush, many drivers hung the wheels of their wagons, which sometimes caused a wreck and a runaway that scattered parts of the wagons and the passengers over the sandbars. The homesteaders were excited, desperate people, taking a big gamble in a new country.

The Sooners who had escaped the soldiers patrolling Oklahoma came out from their burrows and staked claims. Bands of them stood by each other and swore that they had made the run. Many of the best farms were taken in this manner because they were the first ones to stake their claim. The homesteaders came into Oklahoma from all directions and it was difficult to prove whether a person was a Sooner, which was illegal, or not. Many of the cowboys who had made the run for the fun of it sold their claims for whatever the market would bring before returning to the wagons. Fees ranged anywhere from a shotgun to one hundred dollars cash.

The land had been surveyed many years before in the early 1870s and rock markers set up, but many of those had been moved or destroyed in the intervening years. These homesteaders had no idea where the markers were or in what section they might have staked their claims. Oftentimes a settler was on one corner and another on the other side. Considering the haphazard manner in which the whole thing was run, there were few disputes that were not settled amicably.

While this run was taking place out of the Chickasaw country and across the South Canadian River from the west, similar groups were charging in from the Pottawatomie-Shawnee country on the east, the Cherokee Strip on the north, and the Cheyenne-Arapaho reservation on the west. Trains on the Santa Fe were loaded with homesteaders and townsite seekers at the north and south borders. Twenty minutes after the signal was given, a Santa Fe passenger train arrived in Norman from the south. It unloaded many homesteaders, who were ahead of the horse drawn mob that had crossed the South Canadian River from the west. The train ran on north, unloading passengers as it went, until it met the train coming from the Cherokee Strip to the north.

There have been many stories told about individual experiences that happened on that eventful day. One of the stories was about a young man who liked the looks of the country through which the train was speeding and who leaped out of the window of the train. His companions, looking out the window, saw that he was able to get up and threw his baggage out after him. Shortly after the train left Guthrie, a young woman who was riding on the pilot of the engine and who had arranged for the engineer to slow the train down at a certain point, jumped off and took possession of an excellent quarter section along the railroad right-of-way.

Captain Stiles, who was stationed at Oklahoma City and who raised his telescope and looked over the country as far as he could see at two minutes of twelve, said that he saw nothing except the rolling green prairie. He did not expect to see any homesteaders for at least a half hour, but a minute after twelve, more than five hundred men sprang up from the prairie, dropped from the branches of trees, and crawled from beneath freight cars and out of ditches. They ran like a pack of beagles trying to pick up a lost trail. At twelve fifteen, the men of the Seminole Land and Townsite Company were dragging steel chains and staking off what they hoped to be the townsite. Five minutes later more than forty tents were pitched on the newly surveyed lots. This was the work of Sooners, who had slipped into the Territory to stake out a claim for friends or employers who were actually making the run.

Chris Madsen, a soldier at Fort Reno during the run, recollected two other stories showing the general madness of the time. He remembers arresting two Boomers turning themselves in for arrest who had been riding around for days in a buggy in anticipation of the run. Unable to find any food for themselves or their horses, they turned themselves in in the hope of getting a free meal or two. Madsen also remembered two German men heading west the day before the run carrying only the clothes on their backs and pushing a wheel barrel that only cradled a full keg of beer. They were seen again the next afternoon headed back east, having finished the beer but missed the run.[2]

At Norman, where the townsite seekers jumped off the train with a plat in their hands, they found a tent had already been set up and the town had been surveyed and staked by some Santa Fe engineers. They had run the streets parallel and at right angle to the railroad track. The townsite seekers accepted it and started staking lots. D. L. Larsh, who had been station agent at Purcell and who had filed on a quarter section just south and west of the freight depot in Norman, was one of the far-sighted homeseekers. He had the lumber already cut and loaded on the first freight. His carpenters accompanied the lumber, and the next day he was living in his own house.

Many homeseekers were not so fortunate with their freight. The run came at the same time as the southwestern movement of cattle to the Cherokee Strip. Because of the steep grade south of Noble, only twenty cars could be hauled by a single engine. These cattle had to be moved and they had the preference, while the freight of the homesteaders jammed the railroad terminals.

At last, when the supplies did arrive and were unloaded, there was no place to store them, and much of it was ruined by exposure to the weather. The people were treated to a sample of Oklahoma's unusual climate when a norther blew in three days after the opening. They were chilled to the bone; then the spring rains set in, which filled the buffalo wallows with water and made an excellent breeding ground for mosquitoes. It was too late in the season to break the sod, work up the land, and plant a crop, so many of the settlers nearly starved. They remained undaunted, however, and their cowmen neighbors realized that these homesteaders were here to stay.

Mollie's brothers, Isaac and George Graham, and sisters, Fannie and Callie, also made the run across the river from their farm in Indian Territory. They staked out their four claims off of one section corner south of Noble and built four small houses on each of their respective corners. They spent a few days fending off a would-be claim jumper who kept blowing up holes near them with sticks of dynamite. Eventually they took the long wagon trip up to Guthrie to file their claims. Since she was a young woman, officials made Fannie swear with both hands held high before they would accept her claim. Callie, not old enough to hold a claim yet, had Lafayette Tackett, a hired hand, make her claim. In August, Callie turned twenty-one and Tackett relinquished his claim to her.

Cannon house, cabin, and dugout, December 25, 1901. [The two primary building styles other than sod for settlers in the Indian Territories—C.N.K.] Courtesy, University of Oklahoma, #445 Phillips Collection, Western History Collection.

Shortly after registering their claims, her father, Robert Graham, and brother George, along with Tackett, crossed the river from the Graham farm and built a three-bedroom house on the site where the other three quarter sections joined the fourth. The home had one unique design to it. Each claimant's bedroom was built on his or her own claim, thereby fulfilling the homestead requirement.[3] [Their claims were in Section 15, Township 8 North and Range 2 West, sometimes referred to as "Boomer Hill," a little northeast of Noble.—C.N.K.]

Notes

1. Shirk, George. 1948. "First Post Offices Within the Boundaries of Oklahoma." *Chronicles of Oklahoma*, Oklahoma Historical Society. Vol. 26, p. 196.
2. Madsen, C. Cassette interview #cLL 90, Oral History Collection, Oklahoma Historical Society. May 28, 1938.
3. Womack, John. "Claims During Run of '89." *Norman Transcript*, April 26, 1981, p. 5.

Pond Creek Ranch, Newcastle

21

In the meantime E. B. was enlarging his personal operations and entrenching himself on Pond Creek. He traded many of his extra stock horses to C. D. Adkins for his ridge-fenced pasture that joined E. B. on the south. He took in a little extra country, built two large dams, dug a good water well, and put up a windmill. He increased his farming operations until he had about two thousand acres in cultivation. In addition to the crops that he raised, he purchased most of the crops of his neighbors. He paid about fifteen cents a bushel for corn. He enlarged his hog pasture and feedlots to include a whole section. During the early fall and before he started feeding his cattle, he usually started fattening his hogs by unloading the corn for the hogs into the large ponds. The hogs would swim out and get the corn, which kept them washed and cleaned and soaked the corn. After he started feeding his cattle, the hogs followed the cattle and cleaned up the leftovers. During the winter months, after the crops were gathered, he turned his range cattle once again into the fields to clean up anything that the harvesters had missed. These cattle did so well that the next year he planted millet, cane, and kaffir to supplement the fields and stacked hay. With this extra feed the cattle wintered much better and fattened more quickly than when they were turned out to grass in the spring.

Montford's father, Boggy, also came to visit in October 1889 and stayed with his son at his Beaver Creek ranch. During this trip Boggy also stopped in Fort Smith, presumably to collect nearly four thousand dollars that had been in the Chickasaw Orphan Fund in his late wife,

Rebekah's, and her deceased brother, Peter's, names. This money had apparently been collecting 6 percent interest for many years according to the General Laws Regulating Indian Affairs, revised statute, Section 2108.[1] Boggy assigned this money, principal plus interest, to (Daniel) Saffarrans and Lewis, a firm that often acted as an agent for the Chickasaws, especially in the removal days fifty years earlier. It is not known if Montford or Adelaide, the legitimate beneficiaries, received any of this money.[2]

Late in the summer of 1889 one of Silver City's and the Indian Territory's finest benefactors, Meta Chestnut, first arrived in the Oklahoma Territory. As a ten-year-old girl in North Carolina, Meta had told her mother that she planned to move to the Indian Territory and open a school. By the time she had graduated from college, she had lost both her parents in death and knew that the time was right for her move west. So in August 1889 she headed west with only the name of a schoolmate's friend, the W. J. Erwin family, who had recently moved to Silver City from Texas. After arriving in Oklahoma City, Meta spent one frightful night at the Grand Avenue Hotel. She was exhausted from her journey, but she slept very little due to the howling and groaning of a tethered wolf in the room below her. She wondered whether this first night in the territory might well be her last.[3]

The next day she hopped a lumber wagon and made her way across the river to Silver City, where she found the Erwins, with whom she would board for the next five years. Meta arrived on a Friday and by the following Sunday had organized a Sunday school class. On the next day, Monday, September 8, she took over the teaching duties and opened school with seven students. This small schoolhouse, dedicated to Nora Bond Tuttle, had been built shortly after Montford arrived in the area. The schoolhouse originally was built on a hill just west of the house Montford had traded out with Caddo Bill Williams, but it was soon moved a little further west. With the establishment of the new cemetery after the deaths of Muggs McLish and Montford's wife Mary, it was agreed to move the schoolhouse further west. Montford wanted that nearby knoll to be the burying place for his family, so with the help of drovers from the Chisholm Trail, they put sixteen oxen to work and pulled the schoolhouse to its permanent location.[4]

Meta Chestnut remained the schoolteacher until she, along with the rest of the Silver City residents, packed up and moved to the newly established town of Minco where the Rock Island Railroad built a depot. A small portion of C. B. Campbell's Chickasaw land was used for the townsite. With the railroads taking the place of the cattle trails, towns such as Silver City and Fred (a little further south) were no longer needed and were quickly moved to the new railroad hubs or deserted. J. D. Lindsay moved his Silver City business to Minco, and C. B. Campbell soon opened up his own clothing store there. Many of the towns' leading citizens, including the Tuttles, Campbells, Johnsons, Williams, Bonds, Erwins, McLishes, and Smiths, pooled their resources and built a new twenty-four by thirty-six-foot schoolhouse, which they called "Sunny South." Ms. Chestnut then went to both the Chickasaw and Choctaw councils, requesting and obtaining financial assistance for her school within their nations. The federal government also allowed two dollars a month for each Indian student after inspecting her fine school.[5]

Four years later Meta opened up a larger facility, the El Meta Bond Christian College, named for herself and Adelaide "Grandmother" Bond, who Meta referred to as the "dear old Aristocrat of the Plains." The students ranged in age from five to thirty-five and came from all over the Territory. The school stayed opened for thirty years, finally closing in 1920. Even then, the school had twice the necessary applicants for full enrollment, but it could no longer compete with the state-funded schools that had opened up after statehood. She was always a strong proponent for Oklahoma statehood and made a point of telling Teddy Roosevelt about it when she met him at a prohibition meeting in 1904. She told him, "Mr. President, I am not here in the interest of prohibition but I want statehood for Oklahoma." He gave her an interesting look and his own wide smile and said, "Yes madam. It'll come in time."[6] Meta married J. A. Sager, a music professor, in 1901 and after closing the school moved to Chickasha, where both she and her husband continued to teach for many years.

While the more fortunate homesteaders who had filed claims were taking possession of Oklahoma's prairies, the ones that lost out poured into the Chickasaw Nation and began hunting up Indians to lease some land. They poured into the nation so fast that the old Chickasaw permit law could not be enforced. In desperation, the governor of the Chickasaws, on July 2, 1890, appealed to the United States government to free the Chickasaw Nation of the intruding white settlers. This intrusion was a violation of the Treaty of 1866, which provided no white people should go into the nation, except in accordance with the laws and usages of the nation. The government ignored this plea and claimed that the Chickasaws themselves were responsible for the encroachment.

The cattle that had been gathered in Oklahoma were sorted according to ownership. The various outfits either shipped their cattle to new ranges or shipped them to market. Montford found his ranges overcrowded and constantly reduced by the claims of intermarried citizens, who claimed land on or along the border of his ranches. Finally he turned to his old friends, the Caddo Indians, who had a large country just west of him. He arranged to lease two hundred thousand acres for his cattle and horse operations.

El Meta Bond College at Minco, Indian Territory, circa 1893–1894. Courtesy, Norma Jean Gambil.

When the Indians started fencing lands that had been open for years, many disputes arose as to the boundaries of their old range. One of E. B.'s old friends, W. P. Leeper, became involved in one of these fence-line disputes with Ben Freeney, who shot and killed Leeper in April 1892. A short time later, Freeney rode up to E. B.'s house late one evening and shouted, "Hello." From the tone of his voice E. B. could tell that it was Freeney and that he was upset about something. In spite of his reputation as a killer and ignoring Mollie's cautionary pleas, E. B., bare-headed, in his shirt sleeves, and unarmed, walked out to discuss a fence line with him. They came to an amicable agreement causing Mollie and E. B. to breathe a sigh of relief when Freeney rode away. If he had come out with a six-shooter hanging from his hip, the result might have been different, but E. B. figured that Freeney would not shoot down an unarmed man in cold blood.

Leeper, before he was killed, was grazing some cattle for Briggs and Runyan, who, after his death, were anxious to dispose of them. They were small Arkansas cattle, and E. B. bought eight hundred head of them and fed them out in his feedlots. They did so well that he decided to send a man to Arkansas with some of his extra horses to trade for cattle. This man was referred to as Sly Burr because he turned out to be a crook. E. B. received a letter from Sly, stating that he had traded off the horses and had seven hundred head of cattle but needed one hundred dollars for expense money for the return trip. After sending this money, a month passed and E. B. received another letter, stating that his herd had been caught in a flood and scattered and that he needed two hundred and fifty dollars more money. He enclosed in the letter a mortgage on his home in Norman. E. B. began to get dubious of these stories, and he knew that cattle could go a long ways without drowning because he had seen them go twenty miles down the Canadian River. He sent the money to Sly by one of his trusted men, Marshall Hallmark, who also had a note to Sly from E. B. saying that Marshall would assist him. Sly told Marshall that he did not need his help and to return home. Marshall looked over the herd to see what he had and check the tally brand, then left, presumably for home, but took a back trail and found out that Sly had been peddling cattle along the route.

Marshall wired E. B. that he had better meet Sly, who was headed for his brother's place with the herd. E. B. got his good crew together and set out to meet Marshall and the herd near Purcell. When Marshall rode into camp, he was on an old pot-bellied horse and told them that his fine horse, Ginger, had been taken from him by some bank robbers that had held up the bank at Greenville, Texas. E. B. and his men caught up with Sly's herd shortly after it had left his brother's place. He was very surprised to ride up and see E. B. counting the cattle. Marshall rode through the herd with E. B. and after the count, E. B. figured that Sly was short a hundred head of big steers that he had when Marshall checked him in Arkansas earlier. E. B. then told Sly that he was receiving some other cattle and had to leave. E. B. left two men behind to help Sly reach his home without any other detours. E. B. then backtracked to Sly's brother's place, where they found a large number of big oxen that Sly had left. E. B. took these steers with him to the Pond Creek ranch and had them waiting in a holding pasture when Sly arrived. When Sly saw those oxen that he had left with his brother, he went all to pieces and confessed to everything that he had done. In settling up with Sly, E. B. gave him two hundred dollars more and took title to his home in Norman. E. B. told his father the trouble that he had with Sly. In spite of that, two years later, Montford entrusted him with six hundred and fifty head of stock and cow horses to trade. Sly sold them all right and skipped with the money to Old Mexico.

A few of the ranchers had moved their cattle to the Pottawatomie country after the original opening of Oklahoma, but they soon learned that they would have to move off of this range too, because it was scheduled to be opened for settlement on September 22, 1891. On July 14, 1890, a Mr. Townsend, who was ranching on the Iowa reservation, just north of the Pottawatomie reservation, told E. B. that he had to remove himself and his cattle by August 1 and inquired if E. B.'s crew might be available to help him.

He told E. B. that he had attempted three times to move a herd of fifteen hundred three-year-old steers that had been running in the same pasture as his cows, and each time they had stampeded and returned to the ranch. Townsend was at his wits' end as to what to do with these steers, which were as flighty as calves that had never been weaned. He offered two propositions: first, he would pay E. B. two dollars a head for steers and one dollar seventy-five cents a head for all cows that E. B. could deliver in the stockyards at the railroad head; second, he would sell the cattle to him for eighteen dollars a head, and throw in about eight hundred head of calves. He also offered to sell forty head of cow horses at twenty dollars a head. If E. B. purchased them, he would still be responsible for getting them off the ranch.

It was very hot and dry and a very poor time to try to move cattle, but it looked like a good buy, so E. B. assembled his crew, went by Norman, filled his chuck wagon with supplies, and the next day arrived at Townsend's ranch. His men were sitting around with a frustrated look, so E. B. took charge and put them to rebuilding and enlarging their corrals so that the big steers could not possibly get out. The next morning at daybreak they combined their forces and rounded up all of the cattle. They cut off a small bunch of about fifty head that included cows and steers and started cutting the rest of the steers in the main herd to them. After the steers were cut, they cut out the cows that had been left in the original little bunch that they had pinched off. They shoved the steers to water and, while they were filling up, they moved the cow herd over the hill and out of sight. After lunch they grazed the big steers toward the corrals for the rest of the afternoon. They arrived at the corrals shortly before dark and penned them without incident. Although the steers were penned, they put two men at a time on night guard just the same as if they were holding them in the open.

Townsend rigged up a wagon to haul the young calves, and E. B. instructed him on how to handle the cow herd and move it off the reservation. E. B.'s crew helped them most of that day and received eighteen hundred and nine dollars for assisting him in removing the stock cattle. E. B. took twenty head of his best cow horses as part payment and credited Townsend with six hundred dollars.

When E. B. and his men returned to the corrals, he found the outlaw steers still inside milling around, bawling, and looking longingly through the fence with their bloodshot, dust-filled eyes. A few bullin' steers had developed, and they were cut out into a separate pen. After being off water for a day and two nights, they were getting lank and drawn. They divided the steers into four groups and took about a fourth of them to water at a time. When they opened the gate, the steers tore out for the tank and swam out in it and let the water just run down their throats. As the group was watered they were grazed back toward the corrals and thrown into the pen again. It took most of the day to complete this task. The next morning they planned to start back to the Chickasaw Nation with them.

When they let these steers out the next day, they first let them water again before letting them spread out and graze in the general direction of Noble. By nightfall they had a good fill, and the cowhands held them up in the open prairie for the night. They bedded down, seemingly contented and chewed their cuds. About midnight the men at the chuck wagon and in their bedrolls heard the steers bawling, and they knew that the men on guard were having trouble. So the whole crew caught their night horses, rushed to the bed-ground, and found the steers milling around, bawling for the cows, and looking for bullin' steers to ride. There was nothing to do but let them mill, although they did drop out a few of the worst bullin' steers that hung around close to the herd, and when they counted them off the bed-ground after a long sleepless night, they had their exact count.

E. B. sent a rider ahead to look over the chances of watering the herd on Dave Blue Creek, but he came back with a report of small homesteaders' fields along the way and no fences to keep the cattle off the crops. Since they were just east of Norman (long before the creation of Lake Thunderbird), E. B. sent for Chief Big Jim Wapameepto and the renowned hunter Little Axe, two of his absentee Shawnee friends. After explaining the predicament they were in, he asked them to bring back about ten of their tribesmen to help them water the herd. The two Indians went home and came back with twenty-five men. With all this extra help, they cut off small bunches of the steers, watered them, and let them graze in a loose herd while they watered the rest of the herd. E. B. gave the Indians a beef for their trouble and they returned the next day to help them through the nesters' small farms. They managed to keep the herd on pastureland most of the time and saved the crops that were almost burned up anyway, but the stacked prairie hay was not so fortunate. The steers seemed to delight in shoving their long horns into the small stacks of loose hay, and tossing it high into the air, where it was caught and carried away by the wind.

After feeding so many Indians that had come to help, E. B. had to send the chuck wagon ahead by Noble to get more supplies and directed his men to cross the herd at the Old Cabin Crossing, which was northwest of Noble. While the cook was making his purchases, Isaac Graham came into the store and reported that a head rise was coming down the river.

They loaded their wagon quickly and hurried out of town to try and cross the river ahead of the rise. When they crossed the railroad tracks, they could see the water rushing slowly over the sandbar. The cook crowded the team and managed to get across ahead of a rolling, swirling wall of water that was rolling trash and logs along with it. E. B. returned to the herd and had them spread out and let them graze toward the river. E. B. rode ahead of the herd and when he topped a small rise, he saw that the head rise had passed, but smaller walls of several inches were following along like stair steps. There was a damp, musty smell that drifted to him, which was peculiar to the river when it was up. He knew that as soon as the steers, with no rest for several nights and as dry as they were, got a whiff of this water that there was nothing to stop them until they plunged off the bank into the river. They gulped the muddy red water as the cowboys shoved them across the river. Within an hour of their crossing, the river became a raging torrent, and yet there wasn't a cloud in the sky for as far as anyone could see.

They grazed them until late in the evening and then penned them up at the Graham farm. The next day they drove them up to the newly acquired and fenced Adkins pasture to the north, where they settled in for the night after some real rough handling. After the river went down, Townsend came to Pond Creek to close the deal. He gave E. B. a credit of thirty-two hundred dollars for moving the steers off the reservation. E. B. paid part cash and gave a note for twenty thousand dollars payable in one year, without interest. Townsend was so pleased in getting rid of the steers that he gave E. B. ten more cow horses. E. B. put the steers in the feedlots that fall, fed them out, and made a handsome profit.

When the Pottawatomie lands to the east were actually opened, E. B. lost one of his finest men and best ropers, A. L. "Doc" Rowntree, when he made the townsite run to Tecumseh. According to the plan, the claimants were to ride from all four sides to file on their lots. Doc urged the officials to let them all enter from just one side or to draw lots for them, because, he said, "If you permit the claimants to charge in from all sides, someone is going to get run over and injured." The officials ignored his sensible suggestion and went ahead with their original plans.

When the signal to start was given, Doc, who was riding a very fast Red Buck mare, jumped to the lead. He had tied his rope to his bridle reins, which he was holding in his left hand, while in his right hand he carried a light hatchet and a small stake to which was attached a red flag. When he reached the lot that he had selected, he stepped off his running mare and held onto the rope. He was squatting on one knee to drive his stake in the ground when he was run over by a wild charging horseman who had entered from the south side. In the mad scramble other riders rode over and trampled his body as if it were a log. When the excitement died down, they found his mangled body. The very situation that he had warned the officials about had come to pass, and Doc Rowntree was the victim. He left an expectant widow and a small child, and E. B. lost one of his top cowhands. [He was buried in the Liberty Cemetery, now the Warren Cemetery, located in the early Brookhaven additions of Norman.–*C.N.K.*]

While E. B. was engaged in all this trading and working the ranges, he hired additional men to make a great many improvements at his headquarters on Pond Creek. He built a large barn, smokehouse, oat bins, corn cribs, put in a blacksmiths shop, and added many miles of fence. He planted an orchard of twenty acres and constructed two tenant houses and a tall picket fence around his yard to keep out the hogs, cattle, and horses, and to protect the cedar trees. He also put in a new chicken coup for Mollie's chickens. The tenant houses cost about two hundred dollars each, a dug water well about thirty dollars, and a rock chimney about twenty-five dollars. He paid two dollars an acre to break out about two thousand acres that he had under cultivation, and he had enclosed about another two thousand acres that he intended to cultivate.

Mollie was delighted with the improvements and at having a few more people living close at hand. Their Pond Creek ranch had become quite a little settlement in its own right. Being so close to the new town of Norman was a mixed blessing. On one hand, merchants and hired hands were now very accessible, but on the other, every insurance agent, lightening-rod salesmen, and anyone else trying to sell something stopped at E. B.'s and Mollie's home hoping to get free room and board. After some prodding from Mollie, E. B. built another small house just for the cowhands and these extra visitors. They hired John Zimnier and his wife to cook for the extra mouths, with Mrs. Zimnier also helping out with the growing family. Mollie appreciated having this older woman around, who was especially skilled when dealing with sick children.

Mollie was having other reasons for wanting help around. On July 13, 1888, their first child, a daughter, Veta was born. There were no doctors, nurses, or midwives available to help, so they got an old doctor from one of the Boomer camps near the river. This doctor seemed only to be interested in his little bottle of red medicine as he propped himself up in a chair, waiting for the baby to come. As Mollie reflected later, "That medicine was the only thing that the old doctor had that stood between me and the Heavenly Gates and the opportunity to leave a handsome widower and a new born darling girl." Fortunately, Mollie's mother arrived and took over the delivery with no more than five minutes to spare. Years later, Mollie reflected, "I had a fat little black haired girl, which I thought was the prettiest baby in the world, and as I have often said, that this was the happiest hour of my life." Veta got to sit on

E. B. (Ed) Johnson and his wife Mollie with their first two children, (left to right) Veta and Ina. Circa 1890–1891. Courtesy, Phyllis and Ron Murray.

Mollie's lap the next year as they watched from their wagon while the '89ers made their run.

Next came Ina, on April 6, 1890. She was named for a German woman, whose father E. B. had helped out with a job when they were close to starvation. Neil R., the first boy, was named after Neal Evans, E. B.'s friend who ran the sutlers store at Fort Reno. He arrived on July 3, 1893. E. B., the proud father, preferred to call him "Spurs." Two years later, on July 20, 1895, Montford T. was born and named after his grandfather. Then came Graham B., born at the Graham farm during a blizzard on January 25, 1897, with Doctor M.T.J. Capshaw arriving too late from Norman for the delivery. Little Graham weighed in at a hefty eleven pounds. The last three children were born at their first house in Norman. Their old friend and Confederate veteran of the Civil War, Doctor Calvin Polk Kelly, having survived being wounded at Gettysburg, did make it for Froma's arrival on May 15,1899. His skills were very much needed, as she was not in the proper position for delivery. Arline was next in line and was delivered by Doctor C. S. Bobo on July 18,1900. Edward Jr. came last, and Doctor Davis assisted him into the world the day after Christmas 1902.

The improvements on their homestead were located where E. B. wanted them, without any regard whatsoever to section lines. When the lands were allotted several years later, this haphazard building caused a lot of problems. In the meantime E. B. took advantage of the Chickasaw open-domain system, which allowed a Chickasaw to use all the land that he improved. He had several farms that were to revert to him when the tenants had finished out their ten-year leases. In addition he bought out the rights of other Chickasaws who were tired or fed-up with farming.

He purchased the rights and improvements from Perry Froman on the Sutton, now Graham farm, which the Graham family had worked and improved under a lease made in 1884. Mollie's father, Robert M. Graham, continued operating the farm through the remainder of the original ten-year lease and for some years more until both parents moved to Norman. South of this farm, just west of Purcell, was a tract farmed by two old friends of E. B.'s, Isaac and Frank Harness, that covered two square miles and which was to go to him. He also had the reversion rights to the Cushman farm southeast of Purcell with some South Canadian bottomland, along with the use and control of most of the blackjack country west of his Pond Creek ranch.

Among the many white people that now made their home in the Chickasaw country was E. B.'s friend, Doctor C. P. Kelly. Besides being a doctor, C. P. was also a preacher and encouraged the building of a new combination schoolhouse and church around the Pond Creek ranch. On January 13, 1894, a meeting was held at the Pond Creek ranch to decide on the specifics of this new building. Besides Doctor Kelly and E. B., R. Clopton and J. W. Greely were on the committee, along with help from Mr. Lusk, Mr. Jones, Mr. Leslie, and Mr. Barrow. The building was twenty-four by forty feet, with three windows on each side, two doors at the front, and one door ar the rear. It would also have a rock foundation and be painted with three coats of white paint.[7] Doctor Kelly also organized a Ladies Aid society. One of their first projects was to make cushions for the wooden benches in the new building. E. B. had one of the local boys bring in some hay to fill up the new cushions. Unfortunately no one noticed that the hay concealed a great deal of needle grass.

The very next Sunday the entire community assembled at the church to worship and hear Doctor Kelly's sermon. Sadly as the service continued the needle grass began to work through the thin covers on the cushions. Soon the congregation, one by one, started to squirm, twist, and fidget, which only made matters worse. It finally became unbearable and the entire congregation began leaving, quietly slipping out the back door, regrouping outside to discuss the calamity that had overtaken them inside.

Doctor Kelly, realizing that he was now speaking to a nearly empty house, cut short his sermon to find out what happened to his audience and followed them outside. When they told him what happened, Kelly roared with his infectious laugh and decided to leave his sermon for another day. More importantly they now had a schoolhouse for the local children around what would become Newcastle later that same year in 1894.

E. B. was raising and fattening many more hogs than they could dispose of locally, and it became quite a problem to move these fat hogs to the railroad to be shipped to market. They generally kept the hogs until the cattle were shipped out, so they were not sold until late in the winter. When they drove them to Norman, they drove them to one of his tenants, Mr. Clifford, and spent the night. The next day they crossed the river and drove on into Norman. This was a slow, tiresome, irritating job because the hogs moved so slowly. Sometimes a hog would break back and several times riders received hard falls when the running hog darted across in front of the horse, knocking his forelegs out from under him and turning him end over end.

When they reached the river, it would very often be floating with ice and deep enough to swim the hogs. They surrounded the west side of the bunch with wagon sheets so they could not see a crack through which they might run and break back. They forced them down to the edge of the water, a cowboy roped a hog around the neck and one foreleg and dragged him, squealing, into the stream. Some of the hogs took after the caught one and, once they started, the cowboys kept the bunch moving together and forced them across.

One cold day as they were nearing Norman, several drunk Chickasaw cowboys met them in the section line and rode into the bunch of hogs. George Foster, especially, made a nuisance of himself by trying to reach off the horse and grab the hogs by the tails. When he caught the hog's tail, he was either jerked off or fell to the ground. His horse stopped when he fell off, and twice they put him back in his saddle, took the horse outside of the bunch, and started him back toward home. However, George would stop the horse and ride back into the hogs and fall off again. E. B. finally got tired of fooling with him, put him on his horse, took a rope, tied it across his legs and to the rings in the cantle of the saddle, hit his horse across the rump with his quirt, and sent him in a dead run for the river. The last they saw of him, his horse was still running, and George was trying to fall from the saddle again.

After the hogs were penned in the stockyards and the horses and teams were left at the wagonyard, many of the men headed for the saloons to get warmed up after their chilling ride. There was usually a group of practical jokers who were always framing these gullible cowboys in one way or another. One of their favorite tricks was to invite a cowboy to sit down in a stairway for a confidential talk about something. Beforehand, the prankster had one of his friends at the head of the stairway with a barrel filled with tin cans and bottles. Just as this private conversation was about to get started, this loaded barrel, making a terrible din, came rolling down the stairs toward them. Simultaneously the man at the head of the stairs would scream, "Run for your life!" The cowboy, not having the least idea what was descending upon him, tried to follow the warning and bolted for the door. Many in the saloon had been tipped off and were out in front to see the fun. They usually yelled, sometimes shot a few times to add to the excitement, and if horses happened to be tied to the hitching rack, they either broke loose and ran, or at least started to run away. Not all of the cowboys got drunk because they still had to load the hogs into the freight cars before they could call it a day. After making quite a night of it, the rest of the cowboys were rounded up the next morning. The wagons were then loaded with supplies, and this hung-over bunch of cowboys rode, not so comfortably, back to the ranch.

One of the cruelest pranks pulled was perpetrated on Dave Brindle after he had stopped a runaway team that belonged to the Norman Mill & Elevator Company. This team of horses occasionally just ran for the fun of it. On this particular morning they came charging down the street with the wagon rocking from side to side. Dave, who was a tall awkward youth, stepped out and as the team rushed past, vaulted into the wagon, took the lines that were tied to the dashboard, and brought the team to a stop. It was really quite a feat and those in the saloon congratulated him on his daring and filled him with several rounds of drinks. While the celebrating was going on in the saloon, some of the other patrons slipped out the door and borrowed the team again away from the company driver. They then borrowed the scavenger's or "honey" wagon, which was used to clean out the refuse from the outhouses. They proceeded to shovel half of his load into the other wagon. With their wagon and team prepared, they took it down the street to turn loose again. George Giles, who had appeared so proud of Dave, managed to get him back out in front of the saloon. The stage was set.

As the team came tearing down the street again, George Giles said, "David, you had better stop that team, they're liable to hurt some women and children." David, bursting with pride from the praise that had been showered on him, vaulted once more into the wagon as the team sailed by. As soon as he hit the inside of the wagon he knew he had been set up. Everyone in the saloon came out and roared with laughter. David tied up the team, jumped out of the wagon with the spoils of his folly dripping from his boots, and came back to the saloon and called everyone there every kind of name that he could think of, but they all just bent over and laughed as he ranted and raved.

The Chickasaw Nation was dry, but a person only had to cross the South Canadian to find a saloon. As a matter of fact, a few of these whiskey bars were built right in the middle of the river to provide easy access to their patrons from either side of the river. One such saloon was the Sand Bar Saloon, which stood on stilts about two hundred yards from the Santa Fe Railroad station in Purcell. A rickety footbridge led from the saloon to the Chickasaw side of the river to enable residents of the Indian Territory and travelers on the eight daily passenger trains that stopped in Purcell to get a drink.[8] These saloons were obviously subject to the whims of the river, and after each significant head rise came downstream the saloon would have to be rescued by horse or mule teams and literally dragged back upstream and set up for business again.

The papers of the time always had a few stories about the locals getting inebriated. One such story from the July 18, 1899, *Norman Transcript* goes as follows, "Three roosters from the Chickasaw Nation made ex-county attorney Andy Hutchin dance in a dusty road near Lexington. Filled with Lexington tanglefoot (liquor) and armed with a violin and a gun, the three made a number of people get off the road en route to Noble, where they (the three) were (later) arrested."

On a more serious note, it is clear that "from the first Jefferson administration to the capstone (prohibition) law passed in 1892, it may at least be said that drinking for most Indians was a learning experience, that Indians drank because non-Indians drank, that the post removal liquor trade was socially and economically devastating to most western Indians while at the same (time) providing considerable economic resources for the white invasion of the trans-Missouri West, and that, with few exception, prohibition failed to discourage either Indian drinking or the interdiction of alcohol in Indian country." Basically, much of the white man's advancement through the West was made off selling whiskey to the Indians for their annuity money, animals, crops, and later their allotted land.[9]

Silver City remained a busy town up until the railroad reached Minco in 1889. As late as the summer of 1888, the town was still throwing an incredible Fourth of July extravaganza. Here is a sampling of the ad that ran in the June 16, 1888, *Purcell Register*: "An Indian dance in the afternoon and night in which the Kiowas, Comanche, Cheyenne, Arapahos, Wichitas, and Caddos will engage. The old-time "war dance" will be rendered by the above tribes at night by fire light in which all of their old-time ferocity will be exhibited. A large and commodious platform will be erected for those who desire to try the light fantastic. Good music will be furnished." Transportation to the nearest train line was also available. Once the town of Minco was established, the Campbell and Johnson families often paid for show troupes to perform in that town too.[10]

1888 was also the year that Billy Nelson apparently took over the blacksmith shop at Silver City, answering E. B.'s help-wanted ad in the May 24 *Purcell Register*. The last line of that ad reflected the tough spirit of these frontier people, in which E. B. simply stated, "No slouch need apply."

The Johnsons and Campbells also put in a livery stable at Minco, which Walter Atwood managed. It was a very popular activity to rent a hack on a warm Sunday afternoon and go riding around to see all the ranch houses in the area and maybe even mosey on down to the river if the trails were dry. One of these after church buggy rides could easily encompass the whole Minco, Tuttle, and old Silver City area in one pleasant afternoon.[11] The Silver City post office closed on August 14, 1890.

Minco was now the end of the railroad line for the next two years, until the Rock Island started to expand again to the south in 1892. The railroad installed a Y switch in the northeast corner of town to enable the trains to turn around during that two-year period. According to the April 5, 1927, issue of the *Chickasha Daily Express*, Montford was the first cattleman to ship his cattle out of Minco. Another significant change had come to the Indian Territory as the Chisholm Trail, once "the great highway between the states north of the Indian Territory and Texas and Mexico on the south," was now obsolete and discarded.[12] "With the coming of the steam engine to Minco, the inhabitants of Silver City folded their tents like Arabs, and silently stole away, and the traces of the pioneer trading post were soon lost and forgotten."[13]

By 1891 the Rock Island Railroad had reached Chickasha, which gave Montford and his family's ranches another handy shipping point along with Minco on the western side of his range. Montford now, in addition to all his other enterprises, joined with some of his friends and neighbors to organize banks in these two towns and placed a number of his sons and cousins in charge of the their active management.

Notes

1. *Indian Affairs Laws and Treaties*, Vol. 1, 1904. Compiled by Charles J. Kappler. Washington, DC: Government Printing Office.
2. Johnson, E. B. 1950. E. B. Johnson Collection, Western History Collection, University of Oklahoma at Norman.
3. Holshouser, Nelle. 1928. "Only Memory of Christian College Is Left." *Daily Oklahoman*, September 9, p. 7.
4. Sager, Meta Chesnut. 1931. "Dedication Speech for Silver City Monument." *Chickasha Daily Express*, November 30.
5. Bailey, Mary Hewett. 1937. "History of Grady County, OK." Master's thesis, University of Oklahoma at Norman.
6. Holshouser, Nelle. 1928. "Only Memory of Christian College Is Left." *Daily Oklahoman*, September 9, p. 7.
7. Johnson, E. B. 1950. E. B. Johnson Collection, Western History Collection, University of Oklahoma at Norman. Not yet classified.
8. Gumprecht, Blake. 1996. "Oklahoma Whiskey Towns." *Chronicles of Oklahoma*, Oklahoma Historical Society. Vol. 74, no. 2. pp. 147–148.
9. Unrau, William E. 1996. *White Man's Wicked Water*. Lawrence: University Press of Kansas, p. 116.
10. Underwood, Virginia L. 1991. Grady County Genealogical Society, Vol. 7, no. 3.
11. Robbins, V. A. "Do You Remember?" *Chickasha Star*, December 19, 1983.
12. Williams, Thomas Benton. 1948. "Reford Bond at the Silver City and Chisholm Trail Monument dedication, November, 1931." *Orations of Famous Indians*. Self-published, p. 36.
13. Ibid., p. 3.

Wichita Indian Lease

ontford's main interests remained in his cattle and horses. He had been forced to remove his livestock from the non-Indian parts of Oklahoma because of the opening of that territory for settlement. He was being encroached upon along the entire eastern side of his range by settlers, so he turned to the west and south in a final attempt to find land that could be used in the manner to which he was accustomed.

On April 4, 1889, he leased two hundred thousand acres from the chiefs and headmen of the Wichita, Delaware, Keechi, Towaconie, Caddo, and Waco Indians. The land included in this lease extended west from Montford's range between the South Canadian and Washita Rivers and was part of the Wichita reservation. It was also part of the lands formerly owned by the Chickasaws and Choctaws and was referred to in the Treaty of 1866 as the Leased District. He paid six cents an acre per year, payable semiannually beginning June 1, 1889. The money was to be paid to the United States agent for the Kiowa, Comanche, and Wichita reservations. In comparison with present-day pasture rentals, the sum of six cents an acre seems like very little rental, but it should be remembered that the government had paid only five cents an acre for the entire Leased District and had used it for twenty-three years without paying any more for it.

Montford paid a bonus of one thousand dollars to Baldwin Commander for his assistance in getting the Indian chiefs to execute the lease. When subsequent payments were made, Baldwin Commander demanded that he be paid another bonus, but Montford refused to pay him and incurred his enmity, which led to a lot of difficulty with all the Indians later on. When the first payment became due, Montford sent E. B. to his bank in Sherman, Texas, for seven thousand dollars in cash. E. B. returned to Pond Creek with the money, gave it to his wife, Mollie, who put the money in a diaper bag, loaded her young daughter, Veta, into the buggy, and drove to Montford's home on Beaver Creek where she gave the money to him.

The first difficulty with this lease arose over two separate and inconsistent positions that the federal government took concerning the leasing of Indian lands. In an opinion of the attorney general dated July 21, 1885, he stated that Indians were not capable of leasing their reservation lands for grazing purposes and that the president or secretary of the interior did not have authority to approve such leases, if made. The commissioner of Indian affairs, however, authorized or acquiesced in the leasing of lands by Indian agents under the following conditions:

1. The Indians, whose lands were to be grazed, must first consent to the leasing of their lands.
2. Such grazing permits were to be given only to actual settlers residing in the neighborhood, who understood the Indians, and only for the settler's livestock.
3. No responsibility for the livestock should be in any way attached to the United States government.
4. No exclusive privilege of grazing rights should be given on the reservation.
5. A fair compensation should be paid for the grazing privilege.

The chiefs with whom Montford made his lease were his neighbors and friends, and they went beyond the authorization given by the commissioner in that they gave to him the exclusive grazing rights and he was to be protected from intruders and depredations. It was also understood that the lands were to be surveyed, which was never done, but Montford built a three-wire drift fence along part of the south line to keep out the cattle from the Kiowa and Comanche reservation, part of which had been leased to Texas cowmen. There was no reason to fence the east side, which joined his home range, although he constructed a horse pasture eight miles square and enclosed it with a four-wire fence that extended along the South Canadian River to the mouth of Deer Creek. He established his headquarters in a dugout on a spring creek that ran into Deer Creek a couple of miles east of the present town of Hydro and a half mile south of the old Highway 66.

The rest of the South Canadian River was unfenced as far west as where Weatherford is today. There was a drift fence of three wires extending twelve miles south of the river. The rest of his country was open, and he expected his line riders to keep the cattle thrown back on his lease and off of the Cheyenne and Arapaho reservations.

E. B. objected to this move because it was too near the Cheyenne and Arapaho Indians who, in 1885, had given the cowmen so much trouble on their reservation that the government had canceled the leases before winter began. Also, with Montford in declining health, he was unable to properly look after this new venture along with his recently expanded operations around Pond Creek. E. B. told his father that he would help him shape up his herds, help move his cattle, and help him in any way that he could, but he did not want any part of the move into this distant and potentially dangerous western lease.

As soon as the horse pasture near Deer Creek was built, they moved a large part of his horses. He left at his Beaver Creek headquarters one hundred head of his best thoroughbred race mares and stallions, and at Whorley Creek, a few miles east of Silver City, about six hundred of his best stock horses. This herd that they moved up the Canadian River to their new range consisted of Cleveland Bay, Kentucky Whip, and Wagner breeds of horses. They weighed between one thousand and twelve hundred pounds and were faster and more serviceable than the Texas or Indian ponies. Montford had been improving the quality of his horses for twenty-five years, and you could tell a Johnson horse by his conformation and action without even looking at the brands. In crossing the river with this herd of horses, the trampling of their feet helped settle the quicksand and improved the crossings for the cattle herd that was to follow.

When E. B.'s crew arrived at the fenced-in pasture, two men were left in the dugout camp on Cedar Creek Canyon to look after them. E. B. returned home and started gathering the cattle to be moved. After one herd was shaped up, Montford and his misfit outfit showed up to take them over and move them. In E. B.'s opinion Montford's foreman, Thornton Downing, was lazy, high-tempered, overbearing, inexperienced, and to make matters worse, he had hired a crew of Caddo and Wichita Indians who were poorly mounted on their own ponies. E. B. turned over a couple of wagons to haul the weakest and youngest calves, and after shaping up the herd, removed his steers and cattle that he had been gathering. He then turned the remaining outfit over to his father and his foreman. E. B. offered to help hold the herd the first night because it looked like a storm was coming up, but Montford said that it would be a good time to try out his new Indian helpers.

That night a hard-blowing rainstorm hit the herd, which Montford and his Indians tried to hold instead of just letting them drift with the rain. E. B. and his crew had learned a long time before that when lightning begins popping and jumping across the horns of a herd, and a hard wind and rain hits them on the bed-ground, they stay together much better if they are turned loose and allowed to drift with the storm. When the storm has passed, they usually bed down again, and the herd can be found the next morning almost intact. The inexperienced Indians tried to hold Montford's herd, and small bunches broke away and disappeared in the night, while the main herd drifted far enough to drop off into a deep canyon.

The next morning when E. B. rode over to see how the Indians had withstood the hard night, he could hear cows bawling and he knew that they were in trouble. He found the canyon full of milling cattle, but by some good fortune only a few were killed. This presented quite a problem, because in the herd were cows that had lost their calves and calves that had lost their mothers. These cows and motherless calves kept trying to break back and each time one would break out of the herd, every cow, thinking the running motherless calf was hers, tried to break back, too. They ended up hiring some experienced Negro cowboys to help them move this awkward herd. When Montford finally reached his horse pasture, he dropped out these troublesome cows and calves where his four-wire fence would hold them until the cows and calves were weaned.

Montford's foreman, Downing, took the second herd of eighteen hundred head, and E. B. and his crew took another herd of about the same number. All of those cows were mixed Durham and Hereford breeding and of excellent quality. E. B. and his men returned home while Montford and his Indians started branding the late calves. After branding about eight hundred, Downing persuaded Montford to let the rest go until the next spring branding. Montford was worn out with his poor help and gave in to Downing and returned home. He left six men to patrol the unfenced range and to keep the cattle on his leased lands and off the other reservations.

He had just about reached home when they started having trouble. The Cheyenne and Arapaho Indians were always prowling around and crossing his range on some pretext or other. They often dropped by his camp and ate up all the food left for his men. When his line riders caught them or stopped them, they would claim that they were hungry and were hunting game or looking for lost ponies. The line riders even caught them driving some of his cattle across the river and onto the reservation. Sometimes the older men got the cattle back, but sometimes the Indians made threatening gestures with their rifles, and the men just let them go. The Indians soon proved able to run their bluff on Montford's best men; although partially out of necessity due to meager and shrinking food allotments, they had become quite accomplished in their thievery.

At this particular time there were several things happening in the lives of these half-wild Indians that made them much more difficult to deal with. There was a religious craze that swept the reservations. The missionaries and religious agents had taught the Indians just enough religion to make them believe that the immediate and second coming of the Messiah was at hand. During the fall and winter of 1889, a rumor spread from the Shoshone Agency in Wyoming that Christ had returned and was living just about two hundred miles north of the Shoshone Agency.

In November 1889 Porcupine, a Cheyenne medicine man, took off for the Shoshone Agency in search of Christ. His search led him to Wovoka, a son of the renowned Paiute shaman, Tavibo. When Porcupine returned from his journey to Nevada in the spring of 1890, he claimed that he had seen Him.[1] Porcupine said that Christ was scarred on the wrist and face. He said that Christ told him of the crucifixion, taught him a religious dance, counselled love and kindness, foretold the resurrection of the noted Indian dead, the renewal of youth for all good Indians, the enlargement of the earth, the return of the buffalo, and the restoration of all their land in its original state. Then on August 20, 1890, Porcupine declared that he, himself, was the New Messiah. He decreed a dance, the Ghost Dance, which was to start at the beginning of every new moon and was to last six days and nights to please the Great Spirit.

The Arapahoes, greatly excited by all these rumors, raised enough money to send some of their tribesmen to Wyoming to check into Porcupine's claims. Lieutenant Black Coyote of the agency police and Sergeant Washee, an Indian scout, were sent on this pilgrimage. They were gone two months, and upon their return reported that they were unable to get through the deep snow to reach the Messiah, but that the Shoshones had assured them that the reports were all true. The Cheyennes, skeptical, sent two of their own delegates, Little Chief and Bark, to further investigate these wild claims. Their report reinforced the earlier stories and the Ghost Dance movement grew in intensity.[2]

The Indians stopped all work and gathered themselves together in large religious meetings to prepare themselves for the coming of Christ. Drums, rattles and musical instruments were forbidden, because the report was that the New Messiah did not approve of such noises. Preaching, singing, and dancing met with his approval. At the meetings an Indian would rise and exhort the wonders that Christ was going to perform for them. The rest of the Indians would get up, begin circling around, singing, crying, and dancing until they worked themselves into a frenzy and fell, exhausted.

These dances continued to grow in fervor and frequency, reaching a climax in September 1890 when a great Ghost Dance was held on the

Cheyenne-Arapahoe camp near river, around Fort Reno, 1890–1891. Courtesy, University of Oklahoma, #40 Shuck Collection, Western History Collection.

Canadian River about two miles south of the agency at Darlington. It was estimated that some three thousand Indians were present, including nearly all of the Arapaho and Cheyenne, with many Caddo, Wichita, Kiowa, and others in attendance. This dance was highlighted by the participation of Sitting Bull, who had come down from the northern Arapaho to instruct the southern tribes in the doctrine and ceremony of the Ghost Dance.[3] The Indian agents ordered these meetings to stop, but the Indians became so wrought up that they offered to die in defense of their new faith, and the agents left them to their own devices.

Late in the spring there came another rumored report that the Christ had written to the president in Washington granting him two years to remove the white people from the Indian country. If they were not removed by then, they would be destroyed. The Indians truly believed that all the white people were going to be wiped off the earth and all their lands restored to them. Since they knew that they were going to have a wonderful time at the coming of Christ, it seemed reasonable to the Indians that they should eat, dance, and be merry in preparation for the great event.

As their dancing increased they became gay, carefree, and reckless. For these celebrating Indians to really enjoy themselves, they had to

Group of Indians posed at Fort Reno, Indian Territory, Troup C, 5th Cavalry, August 14, 1890. Courtesy, University of Oklahoma, #39 Shuck Collection, Western History Collection.

have plenty to eat. Montford's cattle, ranging just across the river, being far superior to the cattle issued by the agency and seemingly placed there for them to plunder, became the base of supplies for their feasting.

During this same time period, another circumstance happened by the order of Agent Ashley that encouraged the raiding and killing of Montford's cattle. The agent ordered all rations withheld from those families who had children of school age and refused to send them to the agency school. To check the Indians on this order, Ashley required the head of each family, when he presented a ticket for rations, to also present a certificate from the school superintendent stating that all of his family of school age were attending school. Whirlwind and several other Indians notified the agent that this action was forcing them to go on the warpath. As each Indian's rations were refused, they had little choice but to kill Montford's cattle to take the place of their withheld rations, and they were soon caught at it.

Agent Charley T. Ashley was a new man, and the Indians soon learned that they could fool and hoodwink him. When they ignored his order to stop their Ghost Dances celebrating the coming of the Messiah, he returned to his agency, and the Indians were practically out of control of any kind. They had a few burned-up corn patches that they reported to the Indian Agent and claimed that Montford's cattle had eaten. Although the Indians themselves had driven most of these cattle across the river onto their reservation, they continued to harass the Indian agent until he was foolish enough to tell the Indians that if Montford did not keep his cattle off the reservation, the Indians could butcher them. They had, of course, been butchering them all along, but now that they had the approval of their agent, the sky was the only limit in the number that they butchered.

During the fall of 1889 John H. Sams, who was working for Colonel D. R. Fant, sent word to Montford that he had found several places on the Cheyenne reservation where the Indians had butchered his cattle. At this time Sams was driving a herd to Darlington from Camp Supply and had watered his herd on Twelve Mile Creek, which was at least twelve miles north of the river and north of Montford's range. After watering his herd, the cattle got a whiff of the freshly killed beef, ran to the point where they had been slaughtered, and bawled and bellowed. While trying to drive his cattle from the spot, Sams found six heads, six sets of feet, and the contents of the paunches and entrails. This was typical Cheyenne butchering. The ears on the heads were both cropped and the right one was split, which was Montford's mark. Another time, Sams had turned his herd south to skirt a Cheyenne village of about two hundred tepees that had assembled for the Ghost Dances, when he found another slaughtering spot. There were twenty head of Montford's cattle at this place, which was near Fort Reno.

On December 24, 1889, Charley Ashley, the Indian agent, wrote Montford a letter in which he stated that a Cheyenne Indian named Whirlwind had rounded up a band of cattle that had wandered off Montford's Caddo lease. He also complained of similar occurrences in August in which the cattle destroyed small patches of corn belonging to the Indians. Montford ignored the letter, because he knew that the Indians had driven the cattle onto the reservation so that they could complain to the agent.

On Christmas Day 1889 the Indians set fire to Montford's range along the South Canadian River, and Montford's line riders caught them in the act. But the fire had already put on a big head fire, and it was too late to head it off. After setting fires, the Indians rounded up about three hundred head of cattle, crossed the river with them, and headed them north toward one of their encampments. Tom Smith and Jake Moran, two of Montford's line riders, overtook the herd, which was being pushed along by twelve Indians. When the line riders approached, the Indians threatened them with their guns, and they were forced back south of the river. After the range was burned, many of Montford's cattle, in search of grass, drifted or were driven by the Indians to the north side of the river.

Under the direction of an Indian scout, the Cheyennes rounded up over fourteen hundred head of these cattle and herded them for a short time on the flats west of Fort Reno. The Indian scout claimed that he was holding them for the dollar-a-head trespassing fee, which was allowed by an act of Congress. When Montford heard that the Indians had burned his range and were holding his cattle for this trespassing fee, he decided the best thing to do was pay the fee and leave the cattle there until spring. He sent Henry McLish to Fort Reno to get an accurate count of the cattle. Meanwhile, the Indians continued to raid his range. The line riders caught them in the act and sometimes recovered the bunch that they were stealing, but the Indians would return after the line riders had passed and steal another bunch.

In April 1890 Henry Belton "H. B." Johnson, another son of Montford's, and six men started at the Darlington Agency and worked both sides of the North Canadian River and the Cheyenne Reservation to Cantonment for Montford's livestock. Out of the fourteen hundred head of cattle that Henry McLish had counted at the first of the year that the Indians were holding for a fee, they found about one hundred and fifty head of cattle and horses and one mule. The brands on the horses had been disfigured by burning, but the old brands were easily recognized. As the riders prowled through the reservation, they found the heads and feet of Montford's cattle everywhere. Outside of many of the tepees, hides with Montford's brand on them were hanging to tan. Many of the hides that had been tanned were made into trunks, bags, and moccasins. When Montford met H. B. and his men at Deer Creek, he was terribly disappointed in the small number of cattle that had been recovered.

He decided to start branding all the calves at once. In spite of much of the range burning and the loss from Indian raids, the remaining cattle had done exceptionally well. The calves that had not been branded in the fall were almost as large as their mothers, and the male calves had necks like bulls. Shortly after they started branding, the spring rains set in, which held up their work and many of these freshly castrated calves developed screwworms. They were having a very difficult time, and finally out of desperation Montford sent a messenger to E. B. and asked that he bring his wagon crew and a lot of screwworm medicine to help him out because there was still a lot of work to do.

E. B. called in his crew, picked up a month's supply of food, bought two new coils of rope, bought all the screwworm medicine that he could find in Silver City and Fort Reno, and headed out to assist Montford. When E. B. arrived at the Deer Creek camp, Montford was sick; Downing, the foreman, was at his wits' end and ready to give up. Also at the camp, sitting around the branding corrals, were about fifty Cheyenne and Arapaho Indians. When E. B. asked Montford what part these Indians played in this situation, he said that they had been trying to help with the branding, but due to the large size and meanness of the calves, the Indian helpers had their clothes literally torn off of their backs. They had now become afraid to get into the pen with the calves, so they just stood around, looked on, and ate. It took a beef each day to feed them. E. B. insisted that these extra Indians be fired so they would not have to keep feeding them.

First on the agenda was rounding up the cattle to doctor those with a case of screwworms. The infested calves hid out in the tall grass and cedars and were most difficult to catch. When they did find them, they killed the screwworms, doctored the sore with cresylic ointment, and painted a spot on their backs to show that they had been treated. Montford had already branded about five hundred calves, so after doctoring nearly two hundred and fifty more, they decided that they had gotten most of them, and began branding again in earnest. When they had rounded up part of the country, they held the herd under guard near the pens and cut off a number each day that they thought they could handle. After penning the cattle, they separated the calves from the cows and got to work branding. E. B., after looking the situation over had first put two large elm posts in the branding corral. He then used two ropers; one caught the calves by the head, tossed the rope over one of the forked posts, and pulled the calf's front end off the ground. While he was doing that, the other roper heeled him, then they eased the calf back to the ground as the men got on top of them and held them in place. The rest of the crew worked on the ground, holding, branding, castrating, and swabbing. The ropers kept changing to fresh horses often because these big calves jerked the horses as much as a big steer. Even though they developed an efficient system and branded rapidly, it still took them about six weeks to get the whole job completed.

In June they moved fifteen hundred head of three- and four-year-old steers to the Wichita lease. By fall most of these steers had fattened up nicely. They shipped five hundred head of these cattle to market, straight off of the grass, and placed another five hundred in the feedlots at Montford's headquarters to finish them out on corn.

During 1890 Montford had a lot of trouble over this Wichita lease. He had been promised exclusive use of these lands, but found that other cowmen had moved herds onto the Wichita reservation. On July 2, Charles Adams wrote to him and requested the June rental payment and referred in the letter to Herring and Stinson, who were grazing the south end of the Wichita and part of the Kiowa reservation. In Montford's reply he noted that Herring and Stinson were on part of his range and, in addition, that he had talked to Mr. Baker, foreman for the Marshall

Cattle Company, which was also encroaching on his country. He inquired of Adams if Baker and these other cowmen had made a new lease on his lands with the Indian agents. On July 22, Adams answered his letter and demanded that Montford pay his rental according to the terms of the lease without any reference to the arrangements made by the other cowmen.

Since it looked as if Montford was going to have trouble over his lease, he consulted some lawyers. They examined his lease and the treaties made by the government with the Chickasaws. They discovered under the Treaty of 1855 that the Choctaws and Chickasaws reserved the right to settle on this leased district, which was part of the Wichita reservation and included the lands that Montford had leased.

In September Adams wrote to Montford again, saying that Sergeant Tom, an Indian scout, and some other Indians had reported to him that Montford did not intend to pay any more rent because he was a Chickasaw and that he could keep his cattle there as long as he desired. Montford consulted the governor of the Chickasaws, who then appointed a commission to discuss the status of the Leased District and the rights of the Chickasaws thereon. A joint committee of Chickasaws and Choctaws was formed, and a meeting date was set to meet with a commission of the United States government. The government commission, learning of the subject to be discussed, failed to appear and informed the joint committee that it was not necessary to negotiate over the Leased District because the government by the Treaty of 1866 already owned the lands.

In a letter of October 1890, addressed to the governor of the Chickasaws, the joint committee reported, as follows:

The special committee on the part of the United States Government failed to meet us at Atoka, as was expected and informed Governor Smallwood of the Choctaw Nation that they would not negotiate for lands already belonging to the Government, meaning the lands west of the ninety-eighth degree west longitude if the Choctaws and Chickasaws desired. This information, of course, created some surprise with the joint committee, as this was the first time or intimation that the Government ever claimed absolute title to said lands.

Our joint committee was called together with the Chairman, and the matter was thoroughly discussed, after which it was agreed by the joint committee that each commission inform its Chief Executive of the situation of affairs, which was promptly done and resulted in the special session of the legislature of both Nations; and the passage of an act giving additional powers to the Commissioners and to the Chickasaw delegates in Washington, to act with each other in the defense of our title to the aforesaid lands. The Chair-

man of our commission proceeded to Washington at once and met
the special committee of the U. S. Government, along with the
Chickasaw and Choctaw delegates. The special committee of the U.
S. held that by cession, made by the Choctaws and Chickasaws in
the Treaty of 1866, amounted to entire relinquishment on the part of
the Choctaws and Chickasaws, and that the title was in the Government absolutely. This was the beginning of a hard fight, but feeling
confident that our cause was just, we resolved to fight it through to
the bitter end. We engaged able, experienced lawyers on treaties,
etc., and with them and the valuable aid of General Paine, our
Chickasaw attorney, we succeeded in establishing our title to the
leased lands and had the matter of the sale of said lands to the
United States Government referred to a committee to frame a bill
providing for the purchase and payment of the same at an early date
as possible. We would also state that the report of our per diem and
mileage will show on the certificate given by the Chairman; all of
which we respectfully submit.

Chairman on part of Chickasaws,
B. C. Burney

The bill that was passed was for the purchase of the Leased District,
which was occupied by the Cheyenne and Arapaho Indians, but did not
affect the Wichita reservation where Montford had his livestock.

In October, the same month that the committee made its report,
Montford decided to make a lease direct with the Indian chiefs of the
Wichita reservation. He followed his old policy, which he had used with
the Cheyenne and Arapaho Indians in 1885. He made this lease to keep
the friendship of the Indians on the Wichita reservation, although he
believed that he was under no obligation to pay anything. On October
17, 1890, he made this new lease with the chiefs of all the remnant tribes.
His son H. B., acting for him, got each chief to sign this lease by mark. It
provided for the payment of fifty cents a head for all livestock on the
reservation. The payment was to be made at the end of the year, and the
money was to be paid direct to the chiefs and not to the Indian agent. An
army officer supervised the payment and made a per capita settlement
with the Indians.

In November 1890 Captain A. E. Woodson, in command at Fort
Reno, wrote to Montford that a delegation of Cheyenne Indians had
reported to him that many of Montford's cattle had drifted onto their
reservation west of his Deer Creek camp. The Indians claimed that they
had reported this to their agent and that their agent, Ashley, had told
them that they might kill these cattle if they were found on their reserva-

tion. Captain Woodson urged Montford to get his cattle off the reservation at once or expect to take a serious loss from the killing of his cattle by the Indians. Since this part of the Leased District was south of the South Canadian River and was part of the lands under the Treaty of 1855, Montford felt that he had the right to pasture these lands until the U.S. government paid the Choctaws and Chickasaws for the land.

Montford's line riders could not keep the cattle off of the Cheyenne and Arapaho reservations because the Indians rounded up small bunches and drove them onto their reservation. Then they could claim that the cattle were trespassing and that they could butcher them. Indian treacheries of 1885 on the Cheyenne and Arapaho reservation were swiftly duplicating themselves on these lands on which the Cheyenne and Arapaho had no right to trespass.

On February 27, 1891, Montford answered a letter from the agent, Ashley, who had ordered Montford to remove his cattle, in which Montford stated that it would be destructive to move his cattle at this time of the year and that unless he had a direct order from the president of the United States, he would not move them. Shortly after this letter was written, fires were set all along his range and his wire fence and drift fences were cut about every forty feet. This wire became a total loss. Many of the horses and cattle were caught in the path of this fire, which had been set by the Cheyennes and Arapahoes, and burned to death. The rest of the cattle drifted into canyons and crossed creeks and the South Canadian River. This fire was a duplication of the fires of the year before, but it was much more serious. Soon after the fire there came a heavy snow that forced the surviving animals to scatter in every direction in search of food. The Cheyennes and Arapahoes assisted the cattle and horses to grass by driving them onto the reservations where Agent Ashley had given his consent to the butchering of the trespassers. There was no one to question the right of the Indians to eat the cattle and steal the horses. Admitting the inevitable, the cowboys abandoned this ranch south of Deer Creek.

About a week after the fire, E. B. learned about the catastrophe. Although the weather was very cold, he rode to Montford's headquarters and offered to do what he could to recover many of the cattle. Montford had heard that the Indians were holding a bunch of about a thousand head near Fort Reno and that they were butchering them every day. E. B. offered to recover these cattle, but Montford said, "No, if we enter the reservation and meddle with the Indians, it will jeopardize the claim I intend to make against the government. We had better keep hands off." His attorney had advised him to do nothing except send formal notice to the commander at Fort Reno that he expected the government to pay for everything that the Indians destroyed.

With the coming of spring and the start of new grass, Montford asked
E. B. to send a crew of his men to the Wichita reservation to salvage what
he could from the previous winter's destruction. When the fences were
cut and the fires set, part of his horses headed south and, along with
many of his cattle, mixed with Caddo Bill Williams's and other Caddo
Indians' herds. They recovered about two hundred and fifty head of
horses and five hundred head of cattle in that part of the Wichita country. They heard of many horses on the Cheyenne and Arapaho reservations, but the Indians kept them hidden and passed them around from
one to another so that the cowboys never caught up with them. Everything that they found they returned to Montford's range around his headquarters at Beaver Creek. Of the fifty-five hundred head of stock cattle
that were taken to the reservation in 1889, they recovered three thousand. When you take into consideration the calf crop of 1889 that was
taken to the reservation and what the calf crops should have been in
1890 and 1891, you can realize what a terrific loss he had taken. Of the
five hundred head of steers left out of the fifteen hundred taken up there,
none of those were recovered. The fences were a total loss because the
wire had been cut into so many small pieces that it was not worth splic-
ing and rolling up.

Montford's attorneys advised him not to try and recover all his losses,
but to confine his claim to depredations that he could prove were committed by the Cheyenne and Arapaho Indians. At a brief hearing before
the agent, who denied the claim, certain losses for which the Cheyenne
and Arapaho Indians were responsible were definitely established. Upon
the basis of this evidence, a petition was filed in the Third Judicial District on January 17, 1894.

The losses Montford had suffered were not of the kind that used to
be expected by cattlemen from the wild Plains Indians. The Cheyenne
and Arapaho Indians had been on the reservation for twenty-two years.
A younger generation had grown up. The Indians had been educated at
the agency schools and spoke excellent English. The teachers had tried
to teach the Indians the white man's ways and had found the Cheyennes
and Arapahoes apt pupils. Just a year after all their depredations against
Montford, in April 1892, they agreed to take separate allotments and
their surplus lands were opened for white settlement. It seemed to
Montford that the Cheyennes knew better than to make raids and steal
and that, in learning the white man's ways, the honor and integrity of the
old Indian chiefs, his friends, had completely disappeared.

In the agent's report of 1892, he gave an entirely different opinion of
these Indians. He stated that these Indians were the first of the wild,
blanket Indians to take allotments and assume the role of neighbors and
citizens with the white homesteaders who had surrounded them. A few

years before they had roamed unhindered over the continent. Now they found themselves shut in and circumscribed, subject to the white man's laws. The agent rejoiced that all these changes had been brought about peaceably and without bloodshed. When Montford heard of these reports, he remarked that the Indians were so full of his beef that their blood would have flowed very freely if they had been stuck anywhere.

Montford's petition, listed as Indian Depredations No. 9975, which he filed in the Third Judicial District of Indian Territory in the December term of 1893, stated that he was the sole owner of the following described property, which was taken and destroyed by the Cheyenne and Arapaho Indians during the fall and winter of 1890–1891 and stated its value:

25 head of good, well bred stock horses, all branded valued at $50.00–$1,250.00

600 head of stock cattle, well graded, all branded valued at $20.00–$12,000.00

1700 head well graded stock cattle and young steers with same brands as above, valued at $20.00–$34,000.00

200 head of three and four year old steers, all branded valued at $30.00–$6,000.00

Total Claims–$53,250.00

This petition was filed in accordance with the act of Congress passed March 2, 1891, providing for adjudication and payment of claims arising from Indian depredations. The claim was turned down because the loss did not occur from hostile invasion or from aggression on the territory of the Chickasaw Indians, as provided in Article 14 of the Treaty of 1855 and reaffirmed in Articles 10 and 45 of the Treaty of 1866. The judges' opinion quoted Article 14 of the Treaty of 1855, which provided that:

The United States shall protect the Choctaws and Chickasaws from domestic strife, from hostile invasion, and from aggression by other Indians and white persons not subject to their jurisdiction and laws; and for all injuries resulting from such invasion or aggression, full indemnity is hereby guaranteed to the party or parties injured, out of the Treasury of the United States, upon the same principle and according to the same rules upon which white persons are entitled to indemnity for injuries or aggression upon them committed by Indians.

The court did not pass on whether or not Montford was on Chickasaw and Choctaw land when he was occupying the Leased District. The court assumed that he, as a Chickasaw, was illegally on a reservation occupied by other Indians, although the Treaty of 1855 provided that the Chickasaws might settle on what became known as the Leased Lands. As to the lease that Montford obtained from the Wichita tribes, the judges held that the government did not authorize Indians to lease their lands for grazing purposes, nor did they approve of such a lease. Montford discovered that he was dealing with a different branch of the government from the one that had approved his first lease, which was made in 1889. Since his losses resulted from the trespassing of his cattle and horses on the lands of the Cheyenne and Arapaho Indians and not on Chickasaw lands, his claim was disallowed, although it was proven by the evidence that the Cheyennes and Arapahoes were either directly or indirectly responsible for the trespassing of his livestock.

The five hundred big steers that he returned from the Wichita reservation were first turned out into the cornfields and were permitted to hog it down or eat it off the stalk. Montford contracted these fields from renters and other farmers by counting the ears on a few scattering rows, then estimating the amount of corn in the field. After the steers had eaten the cream out of the cornfields, they were moved to his feedlots and finished. The cows and calves were wintered on what remained, along with some prairie hay that was cut and stacked by his renters in the summer after their crops were laid in. These stacks were measured and the hay estimated. The average price in the stack was two dollars a ton. Fireguards were plowed around the stacks. The stock cattle wintered in excellent condition, and in the spring of 1892 Montford began liquidating his cattle interests so as to fit the number that his range would carry in the Chickasaw country. He also sold and traded many of the horses that he did not need.

Four years after Montford's death in 1900, depositions were taken at El Reno for the Court of Claims, Indian Depredations, No. 9775, *Montford T. Johnson vs. the United States et al.* Depositioners were Henry B. Johnson, Ben H. Clark, Thomas Smith, John H. Sams, George Bent, Jacob Horn, Henry McLish, Mike Balenti, J. T. Stibbins, Charles B. Campbell, and E. B. Johnson.[4] Numerous times during the early part of the 1900s bills were put forth in Congress to reimburse Montford's estate. In 1910 Oklahoma representative Scott Ferris submitted a bill in Congress, House Bill 17192, to reimburse Montford's estate for the loses suffered during these depredations. Nothing ever came of these claims; none of the loses were ever recovered.

After years of litigation, the Choctaws and Chickasaws finally established their ownership to the rest of the Leased District. On March 3, 1891, Congress acknowledged the fact that the title to the Leased District was still in the Chickasaw and Choctaw tribes and passed a bill providing money to purchase that part of it occupied by the Cheyenne and Arapaho Indians. The appropriation at that time was $2,991,450, but it still took decades of legal action before the matter was settled. Therefore, Montford's position was vindicated but his claims were never refiled.

Notes

1. Mooney, James. [1896] 1996. *The Ghost Dance*. North Dighton, MA: JG Press, p. 181.
2. Ibid., p. 257.
3. Ibid., pp. 296–297.
4. Johnson, E. B. 1950. E. B. Johnson Collection, Western History Collection, University of Oklahoma at Norman. Box #18, Folder #2.

Half Moon Ranch

ontford removed all his cattle from the Wichita reservation in 1891. One year later the Cheyenne and Arapaho Indians took allotments in severalty and opened the surplus to white settlement. In June 1892, the Wichitas agreed to do the same in their reservation, and the government began clearing their country of open-range ranchers. The land-hungry settlers were closing in on Montford from all sides.

Caddo Bill Williams, Montford's old friend, who with his wife and children had run their ranch in the Wichita reservation since 1878, were also notified that they had to take allotments in severalty and remove their cattle and horses from the open range. Caddo Bill ran the Half Moon brand and his livestock was always of excellent quality. C. B. Campbell, Montford's nephew, had married one of Caddo Bill's daughters, Maggie. C. B. had increased his herd of the 7BC brand to about a thousand head and his range was just east of Caddo Bill's and along the western border of the Chickasaw Nation. C. B. had always had the horse-racing fever, and after he married Maggie, Caddo Bill encouraged him to raise racehorses. He had by this time accumulated a very large and fine bunch of horses.

Around 1890 Caddo Bill got hit with "gold fever" and set up an office in Yuma City, Colorado, near Cripple Creek. He plunged everything he had into his mining business, but within two years he had lost it all. With their spirits crushed and financially destroyed, Bill and Annie returned to Indian Territory to sell off their beloved Half Moon ranch. Annie, her heart and spirit drained, died soon after their return in 1893

W. G. "Caddo Bill" Williams and family, November 30, 1887. Courtesy, University of Oklahoma, #189 Munn Collection, Western History Collection.

and was buried on their ranch at Verden. The following year, Bill married Susan Romick, but she was never accepted by the family, and they were later divorced. Bill also tried to drill the first oil well in Grady County in 1898, according to the book *History of Minco*, but abandoned the project, unable to keep his modest drilling apparatus operating. He was later proven right, as the land now stands with many producing rigs.[1] Bill eventually returned to Minco where he lived with his daughter, Maggie, and C. B. Campbell, his son-in-law, until his death in 1913.

E. B. at this time had charge of the Salt Creek ranch, which was just east of C. B.'s range. C. B. wrote to E. B. that Caddo Bill had to move and sell off his cattle and suggested that they go in together and buy him out. Caddo Bill priced his Half Moon brand and cattle as follows: cows at twenty-five dollars a head, two-year-old steers at eighteen, and yearlings at twelve. He offered to take one-third cash, one-third in six months, and the final third in one year without interest. C. B. and E. B. bought him out and moved the cattle to their range on Salt Creek. Caddo Bill wanted to sell his horses, too, but E. B. had just had his expensive and bad experience with Sly Burr in trading off his surplus horses and did

not want more than they could use. E. B. and C. B. did buy twelve of
Bill's best cow horses.

At first E. B. and C. B. intended to keep their private brands on Salt
Creek separate, because E. B. planned on moving thirty-five hundred
steers from the blackjack country where they had wintered. C. B. saw
that E. B. was going to have the advantage of the range so he offered to
sell his 7BC brand at the same price that they had paid for Caddo Bill's.
He gave E. B. his note through the bank that they'd started at Minco, on
the basis of thirty-five dollars a head for E. B.'s steers, so they became
partners in the Half Moon ranch. They established their headquarters
just west of the present town of Pocasset, where they built good corrals
and pens. On the west side of their range was an old drift fence along the
ninety-eighth meridian that they repaired and used. On the east was the
right-of-way fence of the Rock Island Railroad that by 1891 had been
built as far south as Chickasha. They put Willis West, an experienced
cowhand who had worked a long time for C. B., in charge as foreman.
At the end of the first summer this partnership had shipped enough
calves, dry cows, and other cattle from Pocasset to meet their expenses
and payments to Caddo Bill.

In mid-April 1893 E. B. shipped a bunch of his fed, fat steers to
Kansas City, Missouri, and went along with the cattle. When he returned
to Norman on April 26, Norman was in a turmoil of excitement over the
cyclone that had struck west of Norman in the Chickasaw country the
day before. Some friends told E. B. that his home and headquarters at
Pond Creek had been destroyed and several persons had been killed,
which gave him one of the worst frights of his life. He hired a horse and
made a dash for home. After he crossed the South Canadian River, he
found the roads blocked by torn and twisted trees. When he reached
higher ground, he could see that his house was still standing, and when
he reached the Clifford place, which was near his home, Mr. Clifford
told E. B. that his wife and children were safe, but some of his men had
been killed. Those two men were Bill Chidister and Will Love, who had
been boarding with the Clifford family. They had refused to go to the
cellar, saying, if their time had come, it had come; they were not afraid
of any cyclone. When the cyclone hit, it lifted the house into the air.
Then it exploded as if a bomb had gone off inside. Bill Chidister was
killed immediately; Will Love was found with his hat still on his head.
His pockets were jammed full with corn cobs, his eyes were knocked out,
and his body was terribly beaten and bruised. In spite of all his beating,
he was still alive when they found him and lived long enough to tell
them what had happened.

When E. B. reached home, Mollie and his men told him what had
happened there. That day, before the cyclone struck, the men were

working a herd in the blackjacks to the west when they saw a very black cloud rushing toward them from the northwest. They soon heard a loud roar as if a train was going over a bridge, and they knew from experience that a big hailstorm was coming. They turned the herd loose and rode to a small gully. They dismounted quickly, unsaddled their horses, and pulled their saddles over their heads. The banks of the gully and the saddles protected them from the enormous hailstones. Many of the stones had frozen into clusters, and some of these were too big to go into the top of a regular-sized water pitcher.

The day of the storm was hot and very still. The clouds were red and green in color and seemed to boil like water in a kettle. There were long streaks of lightning that were followed by terrific crashes of thunder. About five o'clock a funnel-shaped cloud dropped out of this boiling mass. E. B.'s family and their hired men, who had been watching the clouds, ran for the only cellar that they had, a half-basement under the boys' bunkhouse. As they watched the approaching storm, birds, rabbits, and coyotes ran ahead of it. Then as the storm was about to strike, they closed the cellar door and watched it from a window on the south side of the cellar. After the first blast was over, they saw the suction from it lift the porch from the main house and dump it against the bunkhouse.

After the storm had passed, they came out to view the wreckage. A granary full of shelled corn had been lifted from its foundation; fences were torn down, the posts and wire a tangled mess. At the Clifford place the horses were plastered with mud, a few chickens walked around, stripped almost clean of all their feathers. In the rest of the neighborhood many freakish tricks were played by the storm. At a nearby house, the suction pulled out all the upper windows and sash and all the contents of the upper room that could get out of the opening. Several days after the storm, a clock from this upstairs room was found in a cornfield and the clock was still running. Cora Hayes, another neighbor, had purchased ten yards of satin to make a dress. After the storm the cloth was found wrapped around the belly of a horse, as if a nurse had placed it there as a bandage. E. B.'s ranch suffered considerable loss of improvements and crippled livestock, but he felt lucky after observing some of the destruction that his neighbors' properties suffered.

The storm next crossed the Canadian headed east and north, apparently joined up with another funnel cloud on the east side of the river, and raised additional havoc on the northern part of Norman. According to the *Norman Transcript*, April 28, 1893, eight members of the O'Connor family and three of the Maloney family were killed along with Miss Ann Heddens, who had been teaching school in the neighborhood. She was killed by flying crockery. Since there was not yet a Catholic church in Norman, twelve wagons lead the funeral procession carrying these twelve

The Norman Transcript.

A LIVE REPUBLICAN NEWSPAPER—DEVOTED TO THE BEST INTERESTS OF NORMAN AND SOUTHERN OKLAHOMA

NORMAN, OKLAHOMA TERRITORY, FRIDAY, APRIL 28, 1893.

TERRIBLE DEVASTATION.

Three Cyclones of Tremendous Force and Large Proportions.

VISIT CLEVELAND COUNTY.

A Swath Cut Through Fine Farms on three Sides of Norman.

TWO CYCLONES MET.

Their Force and Fury doubled And Destruction Terrible.

PASSES TO THE NORTHEAST,

Its Track a Veritable Desert, Leaving Death in Its wake.

"Terrible Devastation" and "Two Cyclones Met." Norman Transcript, Norman, Oklahoma Territory, April 28, 1893. Courtesy, Oklahoma Historical Society, Newspaper Archives.

Catholics to Purcell for burial. The only surviving child, George O'Connor, later returned to Norman as its first homegrown Catholic priest.[2] All in all, over thirty people were killed and more than a hundred were injured by that tornado.

On November 1, 1893, a storm cloud of a different kind appeared on the horizon of the Chickasaw Nation. On that date, President Cleveland appointed the Dawes Commission to negotiate with the Five Civilized Tribes for the purpose of securing their agreement to take allotments in severalty and to give up the privilege of maintaining separate Indian governments. The commission proposed that each member of the Choctaw and Chickasaw tribes be allotted three hundred and twenty acres, with the residue of their lands not allotted to be sold at auction, and the proceeds distributed by per capita payments to the members of the two tribes. Although the Chickasaws had never adopted their Negro freedmen as set out in the Treaty of 1867, it was proposed that each Negro living in the Chickasaw Nation should receive forty acres of good land. The commission further proposed that it be unlawful for an Indian to buy, enclose, or hold in his possession in any manner, directly or indirectly, more land in value than that of three hundred and twenty acres of average allottable lands. This last provision absolutely prohibited a Chickasaw from buying any of the surplus lands belonging to the Chickasaw and Choctaw Nations. However, there were no restrictions whatsoever placed on the amount of land a white man could buy.

The recommendations of the Dawes Commission seemed to Montford nothing short of treachery. He was distressed by the fact that his old friends, the Cheyennes and Arapahoes, could no longer be trusted and, especially, when he found out that the white man's government had no intention to grant his claims for the depredations that that had been committed and almost encouraged by the attitude of the government's Indian agent.

At a general convention of the Chickasaws in 1896, the Chickasaws presented, by resolution, what effect these recommendations would have on their system of community property and upon their government. It meant that the tribal government would be entirely abandoned. Since the allotments were to be made on surveys based on section lines, the houses, homes, and other improvements made by the Chickasaws would have to be either moved or unjustly divided because the Chickasaws, in building, had paid no attention to section lines. Orchards, water supplies, and other immovable improvements could not be allotted to their rightful owners. Each Indian would be forced to fence his individual allotment. Hogs that had run wild and fattened on the mast in the forests would have to be penned and fed in closed lots. The established roads along the ridges would have to be abandoned and new roads built along section lines, no matter what the terrain happened to be. The right to use the open range by purchase, lease, or tribal grant would cease.

When Montford and E. B. looked at these proposals from their own personal point of view and interest, the proposals meant the end of the

Chickasaw Rancher. During the period between 1893 and 1896, after the wild Plains tribes had accepted allotments, conference after conference was held between the Dawes Commission and the Chickasaws and Choctaws. The commission stood fast by their original proposals. They visited different sections of the Indian Nations and discussed the proposals with most of the leading citizens. At every Indian gathering some member of the commission addressed them on the subject. In spite of all the high-pressured salesmanship on the part of the government agents, the tribes refused to negotiate, and at an international convention, unanimously refused to approve the proposals. Sentiment against the proposals of the Dawes Commission became so strong that on November 5, 1895, the Choctaws passed a bill, with but one dissenting vote, making it treasonable for any member of the Choctaw Nation to influence the people against the Choctaw government. The bill further provided that any person twice convicted should be sentenced to death.

Still the commission persisted. Their attitude was that the Indians were sentimental about their homes and hunting grounds, that they were slow in understanding propositions made to them, and that they were consequently cautious about accepting any changes in their affairs. The truth was that the Choctaws and Chickasaws understood all too well what the federal government was endeavoring to do to their nations and country. The government was determined to destroy their tribal governments and force the Indians to give up their large common domain and accept small individual allotments.

In addition to bombarding the Indians with propaganda, the government permitted white men to overrun the two nations and did nothing about it. In permitting this intrusion of white settlers, the government violated every treaty that they had made with the Indians, but the government saw in this procedure of harassing the Indians a way to gain their end. What the government could not accomplish by reasoning with the Indians, they hoped to accomplish, as they had always done in the past, by making conditions so unpleasant for the Indians that they would have to give in.

This attitude was very different in Washington than it had been in 1834 when President Jackson had told the chiefs of the Chickasaws, "Sell your lands east of the Mississippi and find a new home in the west. I pledge to you as chief representative of the white man's Government of these United States of America that this new home shall be Indian country so long as the grass shall grow and the water shall run." The difference in the attitude was only superficial; the white man had, once more, caught up with the Indian. Except this time, there was no place left to remove the Indians to.

Notes

1. Robbins, Virgil A., ed. 1990. *History of Minco.* Published by the Minco Senior Citizens, Minco, OK.
2. Womack, John. 1976. *Norman–An Early History, 1820–1900.* Self-published, p. 139.

Montford's Death

ontford was ill in spirit and had been in poor health for many years. He suffered from recurring attacks of malaria. His teeth became infected and a dentist in Kansas City finally pulled all of them out. This dentist made a set of false teeth for him out of gold, even including the plate. At first he was very proud of his new teeth, and one day down in his orchard he plucked a ripe apple from the tree, bit into it, and chewed it up to show how well they worked. Later, however, the plate began to rub and irritate his gums, which became infected. In his last few years Montford made a number of trips to Eureka Springs for his health. The letters he sent home always seemed to find him in good spirits, but he did mention some of the strange assortment of medicines he was taking for his dropsy, including sulphur, zinc, cream of tartar, castor oil, and various roots. He also pointed out to his wife Addie, in one of these letters, his concerns for their young childrens' education and the cost of boarding them at Meta Chestnut's school. Montford's declining health finally forced him to turn over the active management of all his affairs to his son, E. B. He managed one last trip to Eureka Springs in September 1895.[1]

After a final very severe attack of all his ailments, which had confined him to his bed for many months, he passed away at three in the morning on Monday, February 17, 1896. Tuesday morning found every business house in Minco closed to show their respect for Montford. "A Good Citizen Gone" was the heading of Montford's front-page obituary in the *Minco Minstrel*, dated Friday, February 21, 1896. He was referred to as a "sturdy citizen of the territory, progressive, and a pushing business man; a leader in the upbuilding and advancement of his community, having figured in nearly all enterprises of importance in this part of the territory for many years."

Montford's father, Boggy, shortly after learning of his son's death, wrote a note of thanks to the community that was printed in the *Minco Minstrel* a few weeks later. Boggy died within a year and a half of Montford, apparently from complications brought on to this active man after having broken his hip. Montford was only fifty-two years of age, and Charles "Boggy" Johnson was in his late seventies when he died in New York, although the Memphis *Weekly Commercial Appeal* placed Boggy in his early to mid-eighties.

Living close to nature, Montford, like most Indians, believed in the Great Spirit whom he recognized as God. In his dealings in this world he attempted always to live up to the rules of good living that he had inherited from his Chickasaw traditions. The key words of Chickasaw ethics were honesty, hospitality, morality, and generosity. Montford's simple philosophy of life was based on the idea of the brotherhood of man. The fearless Indian chiefs, the lowly Indian in rags, the Negro freedmen, the renegades, the poor whites, the frontier military leaders, officers of the law and judges, the outlaws and distinguished leaders among the whites all called him friend.

He accepted Christianity and attempted to bring up his children in the faith of their mother, Mary Elizabeth, who was a Catholic, but he was never formally accepted into any church. During his last illness, his sister, Adelaide, urged him to join the Campbellite or Christian Church and to undergo their baptism by immersion. She suggested that he could be immersed in a bathtub. He told Adelaide that if he got well enough to be baptized in a pond or creek, as was the custom in that locality, that he would be baptized. He said to immerse in a bathtub is cowardly and an admission of fear of death and the hereafter.

Montford made every effort to take care and provide for his large new family that had resulted from his second marriage. At his death, all of these children were minors. He had insured his life for fifty thousand dollars and arranged with E. B. to be the guardian of his minor children. After providing for his family, he looked about him and saw very little in the future that might encourage him to continue to live. He had played his part in the development of the Chickasaw Nation. He saw nothing now but the continued encroachment of the white settlers, who seemed determined to destroy the way of living that he and his friends had worked so hard to develop.

As the sun sank into the west with its rays glistening on the waters of the South Canadian River, which ran just north of the burial ground at

Silver City Cemetery, burial place for many pioneer families, including Johnson, Campbell, Bond, Tuttle, Cochran, Herman, Fryrear, McLish, and others. Neil Kingsley Collection.

Silver City, this Chickasaw Indian was lowered into the ground from whence he came. He had never been privileged to enjoy health or his wealth or to have any honors conferred upon him. He had lived on rough and sometimes scanty fare; the palms of his hands were calloused by years of toil, his legs were bowed from the years spent in the saddle, and his lightly bronzed skin had been turned to copper by the scorching rays of the prairie sun. So this Chickasaw rancher took the solitary road to the Happy Hunting Ground.

Excluding E. B., the names of the other surviving children from Montford's first marriage were Henry B., Robert, Tilford T., Fannie, Stella, and Benjamin F. Johnson. They all lived and took their places in the different communities in the Chickasaw Nation.

The will of Montford T. Johnson appointed his son, E. B., and his nephew, C. B. Campbell, administrators of the estate and named Edward B. the guardian of his minor children from his second marriage. The names of these children were Gettye, Ira M., James W., Charles B., Norma, and Vivian, who was just a baby. E. B. cared for and saw to the education of all these children.

Acting in accordance to his father's requests before he died, E. B. agreed to turn over his Pond Creek place to his younger brothers, Robert

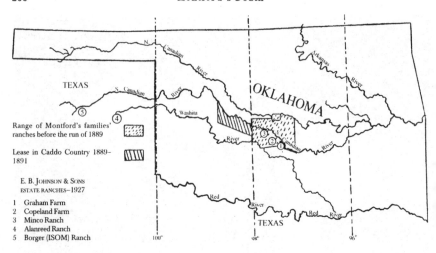

Map of Montford Johnson's ranches circa 1890 and E. B. Johnson and Sons ranches circa 1927.

and Tilford. Montford had also bought out Hy Downing's improvements for Fannie and the L. Faubion place for Stella. Montford's second-oldest son, Henry B., continued successfully the ranching business that he and Montford had been engaged in for many years.

There were some other problems with this disjointed second family of Montford's. The most noticeable was the troubled teenage years of James Wolf Johnson, who, besides writing some bogus checks around the area, was caught in Mustang by the sheriff trying to sell a team of mules and a wagon he did not own under a false name. E. B. drew up an agreement with James that he was to live with Uncle Jim Bond and Montford's sister, Aunt Adelaide. James, facing a trip to reform school, agreed to living and working under Uncle Jim's supervision. In this agreement it also stated, "I will not use any tobacco or whiskey in any form or any bad language. Further, I will apply myself at least three hours daily to some literary work and will not read any trashy novels. At the expiration of this time, I agree to go to a good business college for at least six months or till I graduate."[2] Uncle Jim, E. B., and James all signed the agreement. James did eventually straighten himself out, but not without a great deal of help from the Bonds, especially his Aunt Adelaide.

Soon after Montford's death, his two daughters by his first wife, Fannie and Stella, died. Stella, married to Doctor P.K. Connaway, died four months after her father of peritonitis at the age of twenty-four. Fannie, a former student at Meta Bond College and recently married to James A. Tolbert, died at the age of twenty in October 1898. Norma, a daughter from Montford's second marriage, also died shortly after his death, from pneumonia. Addie, Montford's second wife, became an invalid after suffering a nervous breakdown shortly after his death. Her mother filed suit in 1898 to declare her daughter insane and to be appointed her guardian. Addie was confined to a private ward in the sanitarium in Norman until her death in April 1905. E. B. continued to take care of all her bills and made the arrangements for her to be buried next to Montford in the old Silver City cemetery.

Notes

1. Johnson, Montford T. 1950. Letter from Montford. E. B. Johnson Collection, Western History Collection, University of Oklahoma at Norman.
2. Johnson, James Wolf. 1950. E. B. Johnson Collection, Western History Collection, University of Oklahoma at Norman.

E. B. Moves His Family to Norman

The primary task that faced E. B. and all the Chickasaws was to protect themselves from the plan of the Dawes Commission to force the Chickasaws to take allotments in severalty. In 1896, the year of Montford's death, Charles Curtis introduced a bill in Congress that required the Dawes Commission to proceed at once to hear and determine the application of all persons who might apply for citizenship in the Five Civilized Tribes. It provided further that it should be the duty of the United States to establish a government that would rectify the many inequalities now existing in the Indian Territory and afford needful protection to the lives and property of all the citizens and residents. When the general public learned that the Dawes Commission had been empowered to enroll citizens, thousands of people, especially from bordering states and territories, poured into the Indian Country and endeavored to place their names on the tribal rolls.

To protect themselves against persons trying to get on the rolls illegally, a Chickasaw Commission entered into an agreement on April 23, 1897, with the Dawes Commission. This was known as the Atoka Agreement, but when it was submitted to the popular vote of the Chickasaws to be approved, it was defeated. The following year, in June 28,1898, Senator Charles Curtis introduced another bill, which provided for the dissolution of the Indian tribal governments and the acceptance of allotment in severalty. That is, it would destroy the tribal government and break up the commonly held land, making each individual responsible for his or her own little acreage—divide and conquer, leaving no room for the Indian way of life. Most of the previous stipulations from the Atoka Agreement were included within the Curtis Act.[1] The Choctaw and Chickasaw freedman and their descendants would also receive the land allotments that had been stipulated in Article 3 of the Choctaw and Chickasaw Treaty of 1866. Their just rewards came in the form of forty-acre allotments, the smallest acre allotments of all the tribes to their respective freedmen. One possible reason for this discrepancy was that the number of freedmen registered on the final Chickasaw rolls in 1906 outnumbered the full-blood Chickasaws by a count of 4,670 to 1,538.[2]

Although these freedmen had to wait some forty years before they received any kind of recognition in the Indian territories, they had an even harder go of it on the "civilized" side of the river. Many Negro men met violent deaths in the Oklahoma Territory at the hands of riotous lynch mobs in many of the new towns. The local and national newspapers reported many scenes of mob violence in these frontier towns following the "Run of '89." In fact, Norman, often referred to in local newspapers of the times as the Athens of the Plains because of its university community, was a "sundown town," meaning that no Negro was welcome in town after sunset. Negroes were not allowed to attend either the University of Oklahoma or Oklahoma State University until well after World War II.[3] According to a *Norman Transcript* article dated February 16, 1997, Norman's first Negro homeowner was Professor George Henderson and his family in the mid-1960s.

The Curtis Act also provided for the liquidation of the tribal trust funds and the termination of all tribal governments as of March 4, 1906. Like most Chickasaws, E. B. was adamant in his dislike for both the Atoka Agreement and the Curtis Act, although he did think that the Atoka Agreement was the lesser of two evils. In a speech he had written shortly before the tribal voting, E. B. stated that "both bills were bitter medicine," and would be eventually found unconstitutional. He spoke for their mutual rejection at the polls.[4] Unfortunately, the Chickasaws seeing no other options, approved the Curtis Act on August 24, 1898.

Since there were so many questions and claims to be settled in connection with the dissolution of the tribal government and the allotment of lands, the Indian Department appointed some committees to work out these details. E. B. Johnson was appointed by the Indian Department to serve on the appraisal committee, which had to appraise all Chickasaw lands prior to allotment. E. B. spent nearly a year, half of which was in the field, starting in May 1899. In November 1902 the Dawes Commission was ready to complete its action on the appraisals that E. B. and Hampton Tucker had submitted as the Chickasaw and Choctaw representatives, respectively, and to prepare the schedules. On December 5, 1902, the commission adopted the complete schedule of the

Chickasaw and Choctaw appraisal. The prices ranged from $6.50 per acre for the best land, down to $.25 for the least desirable.[5] E. B. also served on a finance committee to settle all differences and accounts between the Chickasaws and Choctaws. Later, Chickasaw Governor D. H. Johnston asked that he serve on several committees that appeared before Congress, trying to get a settlement from the government on the Leased District and the sale of the Indian coal lands.

Like the majority of Chickasaws, E. B. bitterly opposed the Dawes Commission, but when they moved in and took charge of the Chickasaws' affairs, he decided that since they could not beat them that he had better join them. He served on various committees and became a warm friend of Tams Bixby, the active head of the Dawes Commission. Bixby was sympathetic to the problems confronting the Chickasaw Indian ranchers, and when the commission decided upon the removal of the Choctaws and Chickasaws that had remained in Mississippi and planned to enroll them as citizens of the Indian nations, he advised E. B. to take advantage of the situation. Since the government and some individuals were shipping in these Mississippi Indians by the trainloads and enrolling them as citizens, Bixby urged E. B. to enroll and allot a group of these Indians on lands that were located in his ranges and pastures.

Many Indians were in prison and they, too, were eligible for allotments. The commission offered E. B. the exclusive right to get allotments for these penitentiary Indians. The plan was, that after the Indians had been allotted the lands, E. B. might make five- or ten-year leases with each allottee and continue to operate his ranches as they had in the past. This was contingent on the possibility of getting around the ruling that no Indian could control more than three hundred and twenty acres.

E. B. was still in partnership with C. B. Campbell in the Half Moon ranch. Six square miles of this ranch was fenced off, maps were prepared, and the job of getting allotments and leases for this enclosure was turned over to C. B. Meanwhile, E. B. was busy disposing of improvements that had reverted to him from lands that in the past had been leased to white settlers, and allotting the minor children for whom he was guardian, his own children, and the penitentiary Indians. The allotments of Montford's minor children and family were on Montford's old headquarters on Beaver (now Snake) and Boggy Creeks. E. B.'s own family were allotted lands that had been improved by his father-in-law, Robert M. Graham, and by Ike Harness; the penitentiary Indians were allotted lands adjoining or near these lands.

After getting his work of allotting these different groups well under way, E. B. inquired of C. B. how he was getting along with the allotments and leases on the Half Moon ranch. He was surprised to learn that C. B. had turned this work over to his foreman, Willis West, who had

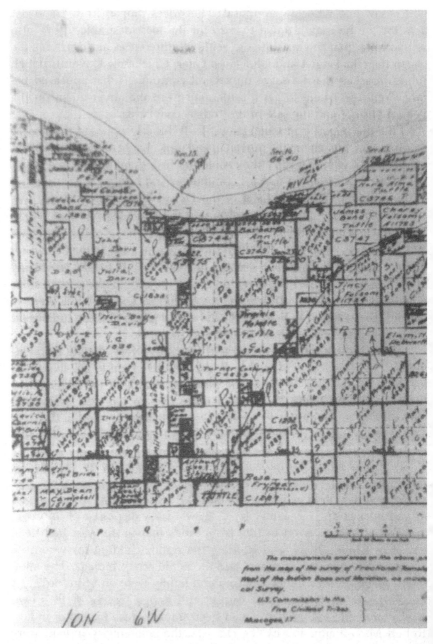

Chickasaw allotment assignments in Tuttle, Oklahoma, and former Silver City, Indian Territory, area. Courtesy, Chickasaw Nation Tribal Library, Ada, Oklahoma.

done practically nothing about it while C. B. was traveling around the race circuits with a band of racehorses. What E. B. saw as C. B.'s inattentiveness to solving these allotment problems, and other misunderstandings the two were having in handling their jointly owned ranch, was making E. B. very nervous about their partnership. E. B. soon sold his interest in the Half Moon ranch to C. B.

C. B. Campbell continued to enlarge his ranching and racehorse operations. In 1920 he moved to Chickasha and purchased a fine three-story brick home at 1428 Kansas Street, which is now known as the Campbell-Richison Bed and Breakfast. Years later, both C. B. and E. B., independent of each other, got into some business deals with E. B.'s brother, Ben Johnson, and a Mr. J. D. Sugg. Both of these deals eventually went sour, and both C. B.'s and E. B.'s families nearly lost everything. Much of each family's land holdings had been put up for collateral in these business deals. C. B. was hurt the most and lost much of his holdings, but kept his new home, which was held in his wife's name. The stress and strain of the lawsuits that consumed these business deals finally took their toll on C. B., and he had a stroke that left him partially paralyzed. In the year before he died in 1925, he also lost both of his daughters to illness. The sole bright spots during this period for C. B. were his wife's tireless devotion and the victory of one of his stable's horses, Black Gold, in the Kentucky Derby in 1924, then owned by the Hoots family. Black Gold was the offspring of Black Toney and the mare U-See-It, which E. B. and C. B had named after seeing a sticker on the bottom of a bottle at a drinking fountain in their Minco bank.[6]

During this same time period, E. B. was tied up with similar troubles. His business deals with his brother Ben and J. D. Sugg came very close to destroying everything that Montford and E. B.'s family had built up over the previous fifty years. Fortunately for E. B., he had started to accumulate ranchland for his cattle business in the Texas Panhandle beginning in the early 1900s. By the time the financial problems with Ben and Mr. Sugg peaked with the crash of cattle prices in 1922, E. B. and his sons were finally starting to lease much of their Texas land for oil and gas exploration. E. B. sold off approximately 50 percent of these mineral rights to save his family from this impending financial ruin. These legal problems dragged on well into the late 1920s. [Although some family members have asked in retrospect why E. B. did not help C. B. out of his financial problems, they were simply unaware of the almost identical and equally bad fix E. B. was in at the same time. E. B. discussed them in his memoirs, but Neil Johnson never mentioned them in his original edition of this book.–C.N.K.]

Soon after this breakup with C. B., E. B. began having trouble with his own allotting. Two men, Trueblood and Hocker, filed a complaint

against E. B. as an excessive holder of allotted lands on which they wanted
to file. After numerous lawsuits, E. B. lost control of part of the land that
he had been holding to allot his penitentiary Indians. As soon as
Trueblood and Hocker had filed for their Indians, E. B. finished filing
for the Indians he represented. Several years later, E. B. bought out the
allottees of Trueblood and Hocker, which enabled him to include most
of his land in one solid block.

The enrolling and allotting by the Dawes Commission lasted a period of seven years. While this work was going on and after the rolls had
been closed, there were a large number of newborn children. Since there
was a surplus of land, the rolls were reopened to enroll these newborn
children. E. B.'s youngest son, Edward Jr., was in this group. E. B. filed
for him on a tract near Walnut Creek and in the center of a tract that had
been blocked out by W. N. Rucker, a merchant in Norman. When the
rolls were closed again, there remained a surplus of lands to be sold. To
circumvent the ruling of the Indian Department that no Indian could
control but three hundred and twenty acres of land, E. B. persuaded
many of his friends and business associates in Norman to purchase lands
adjoining the allotment of his young son, Eddie. Through these men, E.
B. made all the payments and used these lands until many years later
when the unfair ruling against the Indians was done away with, and E. B.
purchased or had these lands transferred directly to him. This small ranch
that was assembled was operated in connection with his Minco and Graham farms, and he called it the Copeland ranch. It was named after Ed
Copeland and his wife, the former Miss Annie Andrews, who ran the
ranch for many years. The headquarters of the Copeland ranch was located about one-half mile southeast of the intersection of Highways 9
and 62, about four miles south of Newcastle.

In 1898 E. B. and Mollie decided it was time to move their growing
family to a town where they could send their children to school. E. B.
purchased from Sol Owens three hundred and forty acres of land lying
just north of the Norman Sanitarium for five thousand dollars. The sanitarium had originally started out as a Methodist College, but after a brief
stint as High Gate College in 1894, the buildings were sold to the Norman
Sanitarium Company. With the assistance of his friends and neighbors,
E. B.'s family loaded twelve wagons with all types of implements, including their piano, and in one day moved the entire family and all their
possessions from the Pond Creek (Newcastle) ranch to their new home in
Norman. The trip was basically a straight shot eleven miles east of the
Pond Creek ranch, crossing the river at Downing's Crossing, on the sec-
tion-line road that would later be called Robinson Street. [The Pond
Creek ranch house was located in the western part of Section 15, T9N,
R4W, just west of the Newcastle High School football stadium.–*C.N.K.*]

First Norman home of the E. B. Johnson family, located where Griffin Park is now off of East Robinson Street, circa 1903. Courtesy, Mary and Dick Clements.

E. B. added on to the house to the east and built a cistern to accommodate his growing family. They had an orchard north of the house with many different fruit trees, including peaches, pears, apricots, plums, and apples. There was also a grape arbor that grew over the walk that went to the outhouse. Northwest of the main house was a smokehouse, which was about twenty by forty feet in its dimensions. The meats were salted down and cured for about two weeks, and then they would be smoked by an applewood fire. Two hundred yards to the east was a big red barn with a hallway through the middle. There were five or six stalls on the east side, with a saddle and harness room and oat and corn bins on the west side.

Also, in the spring of 1898, E. B. had the Johnson Building built, a fifty-by-eighty-foot brick building on Main Street on the corner east of the central block. The McCall's Store was an early client. Their advertisements proudly told of their many electric light fixtures that made the store appear as bright as day even at night.

About once a year, after they moved into Norman, a band of absentee Shawnee Indians would come in from their settlement near Little Axe. Their chief, Big Jim, and his son, Little Jim, who had helped bring in those cattle from Tecumseh a few years earlier, were good friends of E. B., and every year they would load up about a dozen wagons and

E. B. Johnson family in the front yard of their first home in Norman, circa 1907. Back row (left to right): Ina, Veta. Middle row: Montford (Hap), E. B., Mollie, Neil. Bottom row: Eddie, Arline, Froma, Graham. Courtesy, Phyllis and Ron Murray.

come into town for a visit. They would camp in the horse lot and in the front yard. Mollie was not very happy with these gatherings on her yard and would fuss at E. B. for allowing this group to stay with them. E. B. would give them a full beef and tell them they were welcome to stay until the food was gone. Big Jim and about a hundred other Shawnees had settled on Little River around 1885. He died in October 1900, three weeks after contracting smallpox while in Mexico. He had long sought a new place to resettle his band, according to Dave Wildcat, his interpreter.[7] Years later, when Mollie was recuperating from cancer surgery, she would hallucinate about those Indians and in her delusion chastise E. B. until he'd promise to get those Indians out of her backyard.

To the north of the house about a half mile was a large shallow pond that would freeze over quite easily in the winter. The boys and their friends would play ice hockey using tin cans for pucks and broken tree limbs for sticks. At night they would often have groups of students from the university come out for skating parties. It was quite common to see twenty or thirty boys and girls at the pond with a big bonfire blazing away to keep off the winter's chill.

During this time period, E. B. finally got all his family's allotment business straightened out. There had been challenges made on members of his family and some on Montford's second family too. Fortunately, Montford had made out his will detailing how his estate was to be divided between all his family members. His will was the proof that these children from his second marriage needed to qualify them for enrollment on the allotment rolls.

E. B. also had a very serious accident while driving his buggy in town. One morning, while rushing his friend John Q. Adams to catch a train, E. B. caught a wheel on an old rotted-out culvert, which promptly sent the buggy crashing upside down. John landed on E. B.'s right knee, dislocating it and bending it back against his body. John and the horses were all right, but the buggy, like E. B., was pretty well torn up. A few weeks later while he was about to get off the crutches, a two-bit pony kicked him in the shin, which developed into blood poisoning. Doctors Bobo and Davis had to lay open E. B.'s leg from knee to ankle, scraping out all the infection to save his leg from amputation. This kept him laid up for almost four months, perhaps teaching him to take things a little easier.

Almost every summer the family would take a trip down to Sulphur Springs to visit their uncle, Perry Froman, and bathe in the healing sulphur springs. It was quite a chore loading the wagons with tents, cooking utensils, bedrolls, and groceries. The boys would ride their ponies while the girls and Mollie rode in the buggies. In addition to E. B.'s immediate family, they often had Mollie's parents and E. B.'s half brothers and sisters. Some of the children suffered from the "itch," or impetigo as it was commonly known. It usually took three or four days to make the sixty-mile trip to uncle Perry's. The kids loved every minute of these camping trips, for to them it was just a big adventure. Unfortunately, it certainly wasn't as much fun for the adults, especially Mollie and the older girls, who had to cook and clean for all that bunch in the great outdoors. Besides Perry Froman's house, E. B. and Mollie's sister, Callie Graham, both had cabins by the springs. E. B.'s cabin had two rooms, helping to ease the workload, and he would rent a cookstove to help consolidate the cooking chores for that big crew. Feeding that bunch was nothing but hard work.

In 1902 a 640-acre tract was ceded to the federal government for twenty dollars an acre at the springs. The government then proceeded to buy up all these cabins, tear them down, and turned Suphur Springs into Platt National Park. E. B.'s cabin must have been in fairly good shape since the government, according to records in the Platt National Park archives, paid him four hundred dollars for his and two hundred and seventy-five dollars for cousin Callie's. The majority of cabins owners

E. B. Johnson family at Uncle Perry Froman's place near Sulphur, Indian Territory, where the Chickasaw National Recreational Area is now, 1898. Adults (left to right): Celeste Froman, Stella Johnson, E. B. Johnson, Mollie Johnson, Perry Froman, Adelaide "Addie" Johnson (Montford T. Johnson's widowed second wife), Sally (Humphries) Campbell (Addie's mother), Frances Johnson, and probably "Granny" Vicey Harmon. Children (left to right): Veta Johnson, Hap Johnson, Neil Johnson, Charles Boggy Johnson, blurred girl, Ina Johnson, unknown, baby Graham Johnson, and Vivian Johnson. [Another version of this photograph appears in Oklahoma Oasis *by Palmer H. Boeger, showing also, Perry Froman's wife along with Marylis and Robert Graham–C.N.K.] Courtesy, the family of Robert A. Johnson.*

received one hundred dollars or less for their cabins. The park is currently known as the Chickasaw National Recreational Area.

After moving to Norman, Mollie remarked on her pleasure in having a telephone and electric lights. She could now call or visit her parents at their home, which E. B. had gotten for them less than a mile south of Mollie and E. B.'s first Norman house at 503 South Carter. Since her parents preceded Ed and Mollie's move into Norman, Mollie would have to take a buggy across the river from the Pond Creek ranch to visit her mother and her father, who still suffered greatly from the injuries he sustained in that long-ago prairie fire. Mollie's sisters, Callie and Hattie, were also living at the Carter Street address in 1908, along with two of Montford's children, Vivian and Charles Boggy. Now they were close at hand by buggy or telephone. Ed and Mollie's family lived at their first Norman home for eleven years. The sight is now the eastern part of Griffin Park, off of east Robinson Street.

It was at this home where E. B. and Mollie reared their family of four boys and four girls: Veta, Ina, Neil R., Montford T. "Hap", Graham B., Froma, Arline, and Edward B. Jr. While living here, he continued to operate the farms that he and his children had been allotted. As Montford's second set of children came of age, they generally sold their allotments and E. B. purchased those, until he owned most of the lands in and around Montford's old home by Minco. He also operated the Copeland ranch and the Graham farm. In addition, E. B. was a major stockholder in a few of the local banks and helped organize banks in Minco, Anadarko, Chickasha, Purcell, and Norman.

E. B. always had a fine buggy team and a light single-seat buckboard. He could usually make the circuit between the three farms in three or four days. Hap remembered coming home with his father on one occasion when the banks of the Canadian River were full and the current was running fast. E. B. said, "Whatever you do Montford (Hap) hang onto the arms of the buggy, as I will be busy with the horses." The horses were as anxious as they were to get home, so they did not hesitate entering the swift river. The team swam well, but due to the swift current, the buggy ended up about a quarter of a mile downstream when it finally reached the other side.

On another occasion, at this old homeplace in Norman, brothers Neil, Hap, and Graham and cousin Boggy had driven a team of mules down to the Graham farm to pick up a load of apples. On the way home, they had to pass by the asylum. There were a bunch of inmates out in the yard, and as the boys drove by, five or six of the inmates made a run at the fence and crawled out. The boys thought that these inmates were after them and started to whip the mules, hoping to outrun the escapees. Neil was driving the team with the rest of the boys in back, throwing apples at the approaching inmates. Neil wheeled the mules around just about the time the tallest inmate grabbed the end of the wagon. The boys thought he was going to crawl up with them, but once the inmate realized that the wagon was headed back to the asylum, he turned loose of the wagon and ran off to the north. Later, as the scared boys were turning the mules loose in the pasture at home, the guards, having caught up with the tall guy, brought him back by the four boys on the way back to the asylum. He hollered at them that he had had no intention of hurting them, but the boys remained unconvinced.

1902 found E. B. in the hotel business when he purchased the Hoover House, formerly the Victoria Hotel, on the northwest corner of Main and Webster, and renamed it the Arline Hotel after his youngest daughter. He hired his sister-in-law, Ms. Callie (Clara) Graham, to run the Arline. They added a second floor porch that wrapped around the front of the building and set the hotel up to be a rooming house for female college students. Unfortunately, the streets from the university remained unpaved during this time and few girls were interested in walking those four or five blocks when the streets were muddy. The First Christian Church used the hotel for the next few years. A January 1909 *Norman Transcript* article reported, "E. B. Johnson traded the Arline for some two sections of land in Gray County, Texas, and considerable livestock." It had a number of owners over the next twenty years until it fell into disrepair in the 1930s and was torn down. McCall's Grocery Store then was built on that lot. [As of 2001, it was Dodson's Nutritional Food Center.–*C.N.K.*]

Callie Graham, after running her own millinery shop, joined up with her sister Hattie (Harriet) Graham and moved to Arizona, where they taught at an Indian school for many years. Hattie's doctors had recommended a drier climate for her, so she and her sister went out to Arizona and lived a fairly austere life on the reservation. Their humor always remained high, as one could see from their photos in which they were usually hamming it up. All their pets and barnyard animals had names, most of which were named after other Graham and Johnson family members. Callie certainly had plenty of drive. She had shown over the years that she could do anything she put her mind to as a surrogate parent with Montford's second family, teacher, and business manager in Oklahoma. Her sister Hattie, a bit quieter, was quite a fine artist and painter.

Once again the U.S. government tried to mess with the Indians. This time the United States Congress in 1908 passed a bill that would allow states to tax individual Indians through their allotments. It added over 12 million acres to the tax rolls in Oklahoma.[8] One organization formed to fight this intrusion by the Choctaws and Chickasaws was the Treaty Rights Association. They filed suit against this act of Congress. Chickasaw governor Douglas H. Johnston was the chairman of this committee and attorney J. Frank McMurray headed up the legal team. Four years later in 1912, the United States Supreme Court struck down this act in the case of *Chaote v. Trapp*, deciding "that tax exemption was a vested right and that the attempt of Congress to abrogate it was a violation of the Fifth Amendment to the Constitution," stating that it was in conflict with the Atoka Agreement passed in 1898.[9] The Treaty Rights Association with Governor Johnston and E. B. in attendance, along with a large crowd of Chickasaws and Choctaws, posed happily for a group photograph in Ardmore after the positive decision.

E. B. Johnson and family with Mollie's parents, Marylis and Robert Graham (seated on bench) under the brush arbor at the Graham farm. E. B. is holding the horse at right with his son Neil sitting on it, 1898. Courtesy, Phyllis and Ron Murray.

In 1909 E. B. purchased the fine brick home of Sam Renner and some twelve surrounding lots that were just west of the campus of the University of Oklahoma at 538 Elm Street. Their only neighbor at the time was Bennie Owen, Oklahoma University's football coach, and his family, who lived directly north of them. In 1910 E. B. and his family moved to this new home, where his children entered into the life of the university as soon as they were eligible to enter. E. B. and his sons got to work on their new home to prepare it for this large family. They brought in a gentle mule team from the Graham farm and dug out a full basement under their new home, adding a furnace and coal bins. They also had a large concrete barn built out in back by a Mr. Christensen, with four stalls for horses, two mangers for cows, and space for buggies or cars. There was also a small corral and a small hogpen out in back. They generally kept two milk cows on hand for the family's needs.

Arline and Eddie were the youngest of the eight children, and they became great friends. They would walk down to the candy store and buy jelly beans together and then dispense them to each other, one jelly

Treaty Rights Association (formed by Chickasaws and Choctaws), Ardmore, Oklahoma, November 30, 1912. Photo by Ram Webb. Front row, as located by the arrows (left to right), Chickasaw governor Douglas H. Johnston, and E. B. Johnson. Courtesy, Oklahoma Historical Society, #21676.1R, Neil Kingsley Collection, Archives and Manuscripts Division.

bean at a time, when they got home. Eddie would walk with Arline to school and carry her books even though he was two years younger. Arline regarded her older sisters more as beautiful mothers, since they were up to twelve years older than she was.

In the summers, once Neil, Hap, and Graham were old enough to work on the farms, E. B.'s youngest son, Eddie, was responsible for taking care of some of the in-town chores. He would hook up his mother's gentle horse, Pearl, and drive a wagon over to their old farm on the north side of town. There he would milk the cows, collect the eggs and vegetables, and bring them back to the Elm Street house. Another less frequent job of Eddie's was to take their old milk cow, Peg, when she was in heat, over to the asylum where there was a good jersey bull to mate her with. Eddie would tie a rope around her neck, tie it to the back of his car, and then slowly start out across the campus and by all the college shops. The students would all want to know why he was pulling this cow across campus. They knew, of course, and everyone had a good laugh about this little parade that would ultimately give the Johnsons a fine Jersey calf.

Norman street scene, Main Street and Peters Avenue, southeast corner, April 1909. [Author Neil Johnson, slightly left of center in white hat, under the "u" in the "Fatigue" sign–C.N.K.]. Courtesy, University of Oklahoma, #82C, Cleveland County Collection, Western History Collection.

E. B. also bought ten acres that were south and west of the house on Elm Street and put in a fine apple orchard. The children would gather the apples and run them through a press, filling several fifty-gallon drums with apple juice. Some of the resulting cider was siphoned off by students from the university before it turned to vinegar. These ten acres soon had homes and a few fraternity and sorority houses built on them as Norman and the university continued to grow. E. B. used another twenty acres as a feedlot for some of his cattle that were nearly ready to ship. This acreage was southwest of town to keep the smell out. That lot started at the southwest corner of Lindsey and Berry Roads in 1908. Hap thought that his father located this lot so close to town to take advantage of the inexpensive cottonseed hulls from his friend Mr. Ambrister's cottonseed mill to augment his other cattle feed. From there, the cattle had only to driven about two miles to the Santa Fe Railroad's stock pens.

E. B. never allowed any whiskey, except for a small bottle of rye for medicinal uses, to be kept in the house. Eddie recalled a time when he and his brothers and sisters, fully grown with their own families, were in Norman for an O.U. football game. Eddie said that late in the evening they moved upstairs to have a cocktail. Soon E. B. appeared and said, "Let me see what you are drinking." He shook the bottle, looked at the head, poured some on his hands, and rubbed them together. He said, "That is good stuff." Then for the first time, he told them about his life in New York when he was going to school and selling liquor for his grandfather, Boggy. He said he quickly became disgusted with whiskey and drunks as he called on saloons and other whiskey dealers. He promised himself he would not allow this to happen to his family.

This also brought to mind another incident involving alcohol. In 1914 or 1915, E. B. killed a beef and invited all the neighboring ranchers on McClellan Creek, out in the Texas Panhandle, for a barbeque; he even built a platform for dancing. The cowboys were told not to drink whiskey, but in the cool of the evening two of the cowhands were getting pretty tight. Before sundown, E. B. walked up to the two and said, "Alright boys, that's it!" and turned the dance floor over. That was the end of the dance. The next morning these two cowboys showed up at church. Right in the middle of the morning's sermon, a big commotion erupted in the back of the church where the two drunk cowboys were starting to raise a little hell. Mollie calmly got up, walked to the back of the church, took each of these boys by the arm, and took them to sit by her. They were so scared, they didn't utter another sound during the rest of the service. Her own children were amazed at their mother's composure. Having never had whiskey in their house, they wondered how she knew so much about handling drunk cowboys. After church Mollie stated in a matter-of-fact way, "I have been with drunk cowboys all of my life, and they do not faze me in the least."

E. B. was definitely the disciplinarian in the family. Whenever the children got into mischief or acted up in a way that did not meet with his approval, he would grab the guilty party by the ear and pull up on it until the offending party was high on their toes. Mollie disapproved of this treatment wholeheartedly and would give E. B. "thunder," as the children called it. Mollie laid down the law on another occasion when E. B. had shorn off Montford's (Hap's) baby curls without discussing it with her first. Mollie admitted that she put on the worst pouting spell of all time, telling Ed, "If I were a man, I would whip you for that." E. B. got the message, so when Graham arrived with his light curly locks, E. B. waited for the word before he rid Graham of his Little Lord Fauntleroy hairdo.

After the killer 1893 tornado, Mollie was always uneasy anytime storm clouds started to build. Whenever any dark clouds approached, she would herd everyone down into the storm cellar, which was located about one hundred feet northwest of the house. She made sure that lanterns and an axe were always kept down there. The axe was to chop away the cellar door if any debris prevented it from being opened after a storm had passed.

Mollie was an original member in a number of social clubs in Norman. She was a member of Social Hour (later, the Old Friends Club), the Old Regime, and the Merry Makers. She also served on the Ladies' Aid Society for over twenty-five years. She and E. B. were also instrumental in getting an organ for their church, the First Christian Church in Norman.

Notes

1. Gibson, Arrell M. 1971. *The Chickasaws.* Norman: University of Oklahoma Press, p. 304.
2. Ibid., pp. 306–307.
3. Teall, Kaye M. 1971. *Black History in Oklahoma.* Oklahoma City: Oklahoma City Public Schools, p. 276.
4. Johnson, E. B. 1950. E. B. Johnson Collection, Western History Collection, University of Oklahoma at Norman. Box 18.
5. Brown, Loren H. 1944. "Appraisal of the Land for the Choctaws and Chickasaws by the Dawes Commission." *Chronicles of Oklahoma*, Oklahoma Historical Society. Vol. 22, pp. 182–191.
6. Crozier, W. E. 1983. "Minco: History of a Town." *Newcastle Eagle*, January 26.
7. *Cleveland County Genealogical Society Newsletter*, January 1995. Unidentified newspaper clipping from October 12, 1900. Vol. 15, no. 1.
8. Debo, Angie. 1968. *And Still the Waters Run.* Princeton, NJ: Princeton University Press, p. 180.
9. Ibid., p. 29.

Hat Brand Expands into Texas

eil and Hap, being the two eldest sons, became very competitive with each other since their early days. By 1908 when they were fifteen and thirteen years old, respectively, they were often pulling stunts on each other or fighting over one thing or another. During that summer the two of them were working for Mr. Reece out at the Alanreed ranch. One morning Mr. Reece told Neil to take a team of mules and a wagon to Clarendon to pick up some supplies. Hap got to stay on horseback, riding the fences. Later that afternoon when Neil returned with the supplies, Hap was waiting for him and laid in with as many mule-driver insults as he could come up with. Neil, after six hours in the wagon, quickly had enough of his younger brother's lip, stopped the mules, tied them up, and challenged Hap to a fight. A few hours later, around dinnertime, Mr. Reece, knowing that the boys should have long ago come in for dinner, saddled up and headed out in search of them. Shortly before sundown he came upon them, each one sitting under a separate mesquite tree, nursing their respective wounds. They had spent all afternoon fighting and wrestling around in the dirt, stopping only long enough to catch their breath before starting up again. Mr. Reece ordered them to quit it and to get along home.

A few years previous to this last incident, Hap, feeling that E. B. was partial to Neil, decided to run away from home. Hap and his good friend, "Dad" Martin, jumped the train in Norman and headed to Pauls Valley to join the circus. After spending all night in the train, they arrived in Pauls Valley and went looking for the circus and their new careers. Much

Hap Johnson, Alanreed ranch foreman Mr. Montgomery, and Eddie Johnson at the ranch house, circa 1912. Courtesy, the family of Robert A. Johnson.

to their dismay, they were immediately turned down in their attempt to get a job, so they just hung out, wondering what they should do next. Having brought only enough money for breakfast, the two of them were getting a little worried as the day wore on. That second night they slept on hay bales down by the railroad tracks. The next morning, before the day was very old, an angry-looking E. B. showed up just in the nick of time, as the boys were thinking about jumping the train again. Hap was feeling very good about having told his younger brother, Graham, about the plan to join the circus before they jumped the train.

In 1908 W. H. Johnson and Morgan Crow, who owned a ranch in Hutchinson County, Texas, became financially involved with the bank in Norman and E. B., after inspecting the ranch, bought a third interest. It became known as the Johnson, Johnson, and Crow ranch. Their brand was a Bar N on the left shoulder. After E. B. bought in with them, they bought out numerous small adjoining landowners until they assembled about twenty-five thousand acres. This property initially became known as the Isom ranch and later the Borger ranch.

While in Norman during one Thanksgiving holiday, Mr. Crow was invited to stay for the traditional turkey dinner. The children, under E. B.'s strict rules of behavior, dressed up in their Sunday best, and sitting at attention for their guest, broke into nervous laughter after Mr. Crow blew his nose on Mollie's finest table linen. Totally unnerved by the event, Ina, while assisting Mollie with the serving, asked Mr. Crow if he would like seconds of anything, saying, "Mr. Turkey, would you like some more crow?" Needless to say, that misspoken comment brought down the house and everyone had a great laugh, including Mr. Crow.

In 1909 Sol Owens, from whom E. B. had bought his first Norman home, was shot and killed at a gate in the southwest corner of his pasture, near the town of Jericho, Texas. At the insistence of Sol Owens's widow, E. B. finally purchased this ranch near the town of Alanreed, Texas. He traded a lot of his Norman property, including the Arline Hotel, for these Texas lands until he had assembled about twenty-five thousand acres. This became known as the Alanreed ranch. He also acquired some farmland, about a thousand acres, just south of Amarillo. E. B. was definitely back in the ranching business.

Also around this time, E. B. built a new house at the Graham farm. It was a large two-story home with fourteen rooms in it, large enough to accommodate his whole family. E. B. built it for his family, knowing that if the economy ever went bad again, they could always move back to this, their allotted farm, and survive. Fortunately, E. B. and Mollie's family residence remained their Elm Street home for the rest of their lives.

All of the boys had successful football careers at the University of Oklahoma—Neil, Hap, and Graham in the teens and Eddie in the early 1920s. Eddie grew to be over six feet tall, but the other three were well under that measure. The *Daily Oklahoman* ran an article on them in the 1916 Christmas Eve edition with the somewhat needling headline, "Trio

Graham farm with farmhands assembled for harvest, circa 1902. Two miles west of Noble in the Chickasaw Nation. Neil Kingsley Collection.

of Midgets Make Name of Johnson Famous in Soonerland; Fourth Coming." They listed them by name: Neil (Rip), Montford (Hap), Graham (Fat), and Eddie (Kid), reporting that the biggest of them was only five feet eight inches tall and weighed one hundred forty pounds. Eddie was barely in high school at the time, and he grew to be over six feet tall. The article went on to praise their Indian ancestry and the athletic prowess of both their father and grandfather. Occasionally Graham, who at the time was O.U.'s quarterback, was not allowed into the locker room before a game because the attendant thought him too small to be on the team. O.U.'s coach, Bennie Owen, had to come out of the locker room to convince the guard to let Graham in.

During World War I the three oldest boys went into the services. Hap and Graham were finishing up their undergraduate work, while Neil was finishing up law school. Being in their last semester, both Neil and Hap were allowed to graduate early because they were going directly into the service. Neil and Hap joined the army and Graham, not to be left out, went into the navy. Neil and Hap headed to the front in Europe, but fortunately for them, the armistice was signed two days after they arrived in France. Hap and a friend managed to slip out of camp the night the armistice was signed and jumped a truck into the town of Brest. There they joined in the celebration with the French people who had jammed the streets, singing their national anthem, the "Marseillaise," as they rambled around the town. About two in the morning they decided to get back to the base before they were caught AWOL, so they hopped aboard another truck and got back into the camp without being missed. After just a few months in France they headed back to the United States.

Back in Oklahoma, between 1915 and 1918 the Chickasaws had sold off all the rights to their coal and asphalt properties. Along with the sale of other landholdings and townsites, the tribe ended up with over 19 million dollars in proceeds. According to the Atoka Agreement, this money was to be shared equally between all enrolled tribal members. Between 1916 and 1925, each enrolled Chickasaw received approximately one thousand seventy-five dollars.[1] Neil, Hap, and Graham put some of their money into their fraternity's building fund. William C. Levere, the national leader of the Sigma Alpha Epsilon fraternity, upon his visit to the Norman chapter, made these observations in his report from February 1917: "Just at this time the United States government came along and paid the Indians for land the government had taken over, some two hundred dollars apiece. Neil Johnson, the Eminent Archon of the chapter has two brothers in the chapter and on receipt of the two hundred dollars, each of the three promptly paid it over to the chapter house." The brothers also talked their youngest brother, Eddie, and their two younger sisters into donating their funds, through their father, E. B., to the building fund. Levere further commented on his visit,

> The chapter has quite a number of Indians in its membership. There
> are Choctaws, Cherokees, Chickasaws and Osages. The second
> night I was there they staged an Indian "Stomp Dance" for me and
> it was a weird, hilarious ceremony they made of it. I can now give
> an Indian yell that will make the hairs of the Supreme Council stand
> on their ends. I was adopted as a member of the tribe, and had my
> picture taken with them, wearing full Indian headdress, blanket, etc.[2]

The three partners in the Hutchinson County ranch did not get along very well, so W. H. Johnson and E. B. bought out Morgan Crow; then Ben F. Johnson, E. B.'s youngest brother, bought out W. H. on the condition that E. B.'s sons could buy Ben's position out when they returned from World War I. A year later, with the boys now out of the service, they bought their Uncle Ben's interest and entered into a partnership with their father. Now that Neil and Hap were out of the army, they began taking over the responsibilities of running the farms and ranches from E. B. Both the boys were for the most part through with their school and military obligations, so they could now devote their full attention to the family businesses.

In that same year a good friend of E. B.'s, Charles Gould, a professor of geology at the University of Oklahoma, conducted a geological survey of the Texas Panhandle. Professor Gould told E. B. and a number of other Texas cattlemen that someday a world of gas and possibly oil would be found in Hutchinson County. The boys took this potential into account when they bought out their Uncle Ben and paid him more than the grassland alone was worth. One Panhandle cattleman remarked after hearing Professor Gould's predictions, "I couldn't decide whether you all was a might smart man or a damn bluffer."[3] Gould was indeed correct; shortly thereafter they drilled a successful natural-gas well. The Johnson land was soon leased to George E. Montgomery to explore for oil and gas. In 1918, gas was discovered on the Masterson ranch, which was across the Canadian River from the Johnson interests. However, due to the lack of pipelines and processing plants, major oil production did not really gear up until the middle of 1926 in the Panhandle. This newly found income from royalties and leases enabled the family to liquidate their most pressing financial obligations and keep the family farms and ranches out of harm's way.

In the spring of 1926, while Hap was riding fence on the Isom ranch, he came across a survey team in the adjacent pasture of John Weatherly. Ace Borger, a local promoter, had bought a quarter section from John Weatherly to start a town. A number of oil wells had been completed recently, and the oil boom was on. The Johnsons leased out a tract of their land, too. This street became Dixon Street, and although they put a clause in the agreement that no illegal businesses could be operated there, in a short time bootleggers and prostitutes were widespread. Their lessee apparently didn't think that these particular activities were illegal. On one occasion, Hap was propositioned on the front porch of his ranch house by one old cowboy's wife. Stunned, he declined her offer, finding out later that she had been a "sporting girl" at the Elk's Hotel in Borger until her recent marriage to this cowhand. The population of this new town of Borger exploded, and within six months there were about twenty-five thousand people living there. The sheriff himself was a convicted felon. Finally the state government decided to bring in the Texas Rangers to get a little law and order in the town. Just before the real law arrived, a stranger arrived at Hap's place and begged him to store a few barrels of whiskey in his cellar for a spell after the news of the approaching Rangers got out. Hap received a five-gallon keg of corn whiskey for his troubles, which he remarked was quite good.

Also during this time period in the mid-1920s the Johnson's leased some of their Isom ranch to the Phillips Company, among others, who eventually used some of their lease for a refinery. The Johnsons had an agreement with their neighbors, the J. A. Whittenbergs, not to graze these particular sections, so this lease that Hap worked out with Phillips turned out to be a real bonus for the Johnsons. There were also two townsites established within these leases, Phillips and Electric City. They would eventually merge into the growing Borger township.

In 1927 E. B., his wife, and his four sons pooled all their lands and cattle and organized a common-law trust known as the E. B. Johnson and Sons Estate. As soon as the stock was issued on the basis of what each put into the trust, E. B. and his wife, Mollie, transferred all of his stock to his children. He gave $341,000 worth of stock to each of his four daughters, and $87,032 worth to each of his four sons. The reason for the difference between the amounts given to the boys and the girls was that the boys owned individually a half interest in the Hutchinson County ranch, and they waived their interest to shares in the half interest that E. B. owned. The boys had also contributed the value of their allotments and received stock in return for it. The girls did not contribute anything in creation of the trust. E. B. served as its president on a salary and directed its policies until his death.

In 1934 the E. B. Johnson and Sons Estate bought and leased a ranch of one hundred thousand acres near the town of Navajo, Arizona. First they hired Gordon Grimes to build a large water tank and install a pump. Then they shipped about five miles of two-inch pipe to run a waterline up to the mesa. Neil brought in his water-witch man, who had found some good wells on the Minco farm; unfortunately, he only found dry holes in Arizona. A geologist friend of Hap's eventually suggested some other possible locations that did make productive water wells.

Even with their water problems figured out, they realized that the unpredictable weather and the short grazing season were not very good for a cow-and-calf operation. After two years, they sold the ranch to an Arizona cowman named Roy Adams and moved their cattle back to Texas. They had originally invested about $30,000 plus the improvements and sold out for over $100,000. The boys felt that it had not been such a bad deal after all. E. B. visited this ranch one time. The high altitude was not good for his high blood pressure, and it made him irritable and very nervous. He just didn't like the quality of the cattle he saw there. In the end, everyone was happy to be rid of that distant Arizona property. E. B.'s sons could now go back to concentrating on their Texas and Oklahoma operations.

Eddie joined the family business in the late 1920s, after college and an undefeated year as Norman High's football coach, beating the best in

Oklahoma and Texas. He first learned and eventually took over the accounting duties from an outside firm, saving the Johnson businesses a good deal of extra expense. In March 1933, he and his wife, Juanita, with their two children, Eddie and Elaine, moved to the Alanreed ranch and ran it. They moved the Johnsons' business office there too, so Eddie could keep taking care of the books. In 1936 they bought a house in Amarillo on South Hughes Street, where they had another daughter, Nita.

Eddie and his friend Jay Taylor later bought out the old Amarillo stockyards and formed their company, the Western Stockyard Corporation. Eddie and Jay worked hard for many years to make this business a huge success, allowing them to invest in many other businesses over the years.

Graham, never interested in a ranching or farming life, went into the banking business after his college and navy years and ended up as a partner in the Norman Savings and Loan company. He married Genevieve "Jimmy" Farrar and had two children, Jere and Graham B. They built their home on the northwest corner of Parsons and College, across the street and west from Neil and Florence Johnson's home with their four girls, Elise, Janet, and the twins, Jean and Joan. Across the street south of Neil's was Phil and Ina (Johnson) Kidd's house, with their children, Phillip Jr. and Mary Lelia. Hap and and his wife, Magaret, had one son, Montford T. "M. T." Johnson Jr. Veta married Carl Giles, having a son, L. C., who died as an infant, and a daughter, Elizabeth. Froma married Roy Johnson (no relation), having two sons, Bob and Bill, while Arline married Leroy C. LeFlore, having two children, Louis and Mary.

In 1933 the Dust Bowl drought was taking its toll of farms in the Midwest. Conditions only got worse in 1934, 1935, and 1936. During that period, the dust storms were at their worst. One evening near Borger, Texas, Hap and his wife, Margaret, were driving over to their friends the Oles' house for dinner when a dust storm hit. It was so black outside that they had to pull off the road. They could not even see their own headlights. The dust was so thick it was difficult to breathe. After thirty minutes or so the storm began to lessen, and they drove on slowly to the Oles'. At the Oles' house and back at their own home, the dust had come in through even the smallest cracks, making every room a complete mess. It was a very tedious clean-up job.

At the beginning of the Christmas holidays in 1935, E. B.'s family had gathered at his home in Norman for the customary reunion. E. B. complained of a sore throat, but his condition did not seem serious. After being ill for a few days, however, the infection from his swollen throat spread through his whole system. Reports varied on his actual cause of death. Some thought it was a heart attack, but one newspaper account and Mollie's nurse, Maude, stated that he died of erysipelas, the

E. B. Johnson, sixty; Adelaide (Johnson) Bond, eighty-three; Neil Johnson, thirty; and his baby daughter, Elise. Four generations of firstborn children, 1923. Neil Kingsley Collection.

E. B. Johnson and Gordon "Pawnee Bill" Lilly, posing for photograph at Pioneer Day in either Newkirk or Pawnee, Oklahoma, 1934. Courtesy, the family of Robert A. Johnson.

same illness that had taken his mother, Mary, some fifty-five years earlier. Edward Bryant Johnson passed away on Christmas Day 1935. He was seventy-two years old.

Up until his final illness E. B. had been able to continue the active life that had been his good fortune to have from early boyhood. In his very early childhood and up to young manhood, he had ridden the ranges of his father with the best cowboys in the country. He gave up this rough life for a brief time, at the request of his father, and went to school in New York to learn the white man's ways. When he returned from school in New York, he became a ranchman again and played an important part in helping his father and his friends adapt themselves to the rapidly changing conditions of life in the Indian Territory.

He was a firm believer in the necessity for a good education for success in modern living, which was one reason why he moved to Norman to be near the schools and the University of Oklahoma where all of his children were educated. He always took a leading part in the affairs of his community. His name usually led the list of contributors to church and city projects. He was member of the Chamber of Commerce, the Kiwanis Club, a thirty-second degree Mason, an Elk, an Odd Fellow, a Shriner, a Woodsmen of the World, and the first president of the University of Oklahoma's Dads Association. All during his life E. B. had worked with and had charge of large groups of men. It was a byword with the men who worked for him that he never ordered them to do a task while he stood idly by and watched. He always took the lead with an encouraging, "Come on, boys."

When his children began entering the university, E. B. took great pleasure in visiting with the many young people who stopped by his home. Most of these students always ditched their cigarettes before leaving the campus because he was very much opposed to cigarette smokers and would not hire a man who smoked, if he knew it.

He was a very devoted husband and father, and even a more devoted grandfather. One of his greatest pleasures was sitting at the head of the table and being the bountiful host to his family and friends. This was especially true on holidays and reunions. To the outside world he was known as a fair trader, a lifelong Democrat, and was fond of saying that there were no bad Democrats. Many friends and relatives remembered his vitality, with some of them having ridden the ranches with him just a few months before his death. He and Mollie worked hard to pass this fine heritage down to their children and grandchildren. Mollie continued her long involvement with her charities and social groups. She lived in their Elm Street home until her death in 1949.

Their old Elm Street home was thereafter used by the university's music department for a practice hall, and the barn was utilized as a storage

E. B. (Ed) Johnson and Mollie Johnson with their children and some of their spouses in the front yard of their 738 Elm Street home in Norman, Oklahoma, October 1935, for E. B.'s seventy-second birthday. Back row (left to right): Florence and Neil Johnson, Veta E. and Carl L. Giles, Froma A. and Robert A. (not pictured) Johnson, Ina and Phil C. (not pictured) Kidd, Edward B., Jr. (Eddie) and Juanita Johnson, and Montford "Hap" and Margaret Johnson. Front row (left to right): Graham B. and Genevieve "Jimmy" Johnson, Edward B. and Mollie Johnson, and Arline and Leroy C. Leflore. Neil Kingsley Collection.

facility for the drama department to store theatrical props and scenery. Finally, in 1965 the house and barn were torn down to make room for a parking lot. That lot as of 2001 was a multilevel parking garage for the university's Catlett Music Center.

Notes

1. Hale, Duane K., and Arrell B. Gibson. 1991. *The Chickasaw.* New York : Chelsea House Publishers, p. 94.
2. Tucker, Charles. 1959. *History of Oklahoma Kappa of Sigma Alpha Epsilon.* Norman: University of Oklahoma Press, pp. 75–76.
3. Gould, Charles N. 1960. *Covered Wagon Geologist.* Norman: University of Oklahoma Press, pp. 193–194.

Epilogue

The Johnson family farms and ranches comprised over sixty thousand acres of leased or owned land, including the Copeland, Minco, and Graham properties in Oklahoma, the two ranches in the Texas Panhandle near Alanreed and (Isom) Borger, and the Amarillo farm. Along with their oil and gas revenues, this family-run cattle and farm business thrived until its final dissolution in the early 1980s. In 1941, the E. B. Johnson and Sons Estate was dissolved and E. B.'s eldest sons, Neil and Montford (Hap), who were already running the businesses, reorganized as Neil R. and Montford T. Johnson, Agents. In 1958 Hap's son, M. T. Johnson Jr., took over the chief operating officer's position. Then in 1968, the Johnson Land and Cattle Company was organized as a limited partnership with M. T. Johnson Jr. as president, working in conjunction with the general partners who represented the rest of the family (limited partners). M. T. was joined by his son, Monty, in the mid 1970s, until the partnership was finally dissolved in the early 1980s. That story will require its own telling.

As for the Chickasaws, it was a slow climb back out of their legislated demise. Although some larger families like the Johnsons managed to hold on to their landholdings and even acquire more, after the acreage restrictions were lifted in 1908, many other Chickasaw allottees were duped or swindled out of their land.

The federal government was also slow in selling off the 3 million acres of tribal land that had not been allotted. The townsites weren't sold off until 1915, followed by the timberlands in 1916 and the coal and asphalt lands in 1918. This money, some $19 million, was distributed to members of the tribe after rejecting many new applicants for tribal membership who tried to get on the tribe's rolls, hoping to share in this extra money. Between 1916 and 1925, each enrolled Chickasaw received a little over a thousand dollars. Unfortunately, the vast majority of Chickasaws were extremely poor and this situation only got worse during the Depression in the 1930s.

Slowly, the Bureau of Indian Affairs began launching a few programs to benefit the Indians. They inaugurated the Indian Credit Association to help Indian farmers get their farms up and running; they passed the Oklahoma Indian Welfare Act in 1936 that, among other things, allowed Chickasaws to obtain loans for college.

Douglas H. Johnston had been the Chickasaw governor from 1909 until his death in 1939, and although he had been a presidential appointee, he filed a number of lawsuits against the federal government on behalf of the tribe. Some of these lawsuits were not settled until the administration of Floyd E. Maytubby in the late 1940s. The most significant ones involved the unsold mineral reserves and the tract of land known as the Leased District. In 1949, Congress agreed to purchase the reserves for $8.5 million. The tribe, unhappy with that settlement, sued the government through the Indian Claims Commission and received an additional $3,489,843 in compensation.

At the same time the tribe was having these victorious court decisions, the U.S. government was developing a new policy for the Indians known as "termination." In order to save federal funds, the government wanted to renege on all their ties to the tribes and cease living up to any of the treaties made with the Indians. Fortunately, a bill to terminate the Chickasaws and the other members of the Five Civilized Tribes was not drafted until 1958, and due to the disastrous results from some earlier attempts at tribal terminations, Congress voted the bill down.

In the 1960s and 1970s, the federal government began giving tribes more input into their dealings with the United States. In 1971, for the first time in over sixty years, the Chickasaws were permitted to elect their own governor, Overton James. During Governor James's administration the Chickasaws started a tribal newspaper, organized community meetings, and persuaded the federal government to establish an Indian Housing Authority in Oklahoma. The Indian Self-Determination Act was passed in 1975.[1]

Bill Anoatubby succeeded James as governor in 1987, and within a year the tribe approved a new constitution. Once again the Chickasaw Nation had become a real political entity. Governor Anoatubby's administration has started up many new programs and Chickasaw-run businesses to strengthen the tribe's position. A number of educational and health programs have also been established for tribal members.

The tribe moved its headquarters to Ada in the 1980s. There, in their complex of buildings, are all the administrative offices, along with a library, museum, and the community center. In Sulphur, along with the Chickasaw National Recreational Area, the tribe operates the Chickasaw Motor Inn, a seventy-two room motel and restaurant. They also operate numerous bingo halls, smoke shops, and, most recently, two large truck stops in the northern part of the Chickasaw Nation, with a third one just north of the Red River opened in 1998.

The most recent annual meeting of the tribe, which was held in Tishomingo in October 2000, was attended by well over a thousand people. The meeting is held on the front yard of the old tribal headquarters building, which is in the middle of a complete restoration. The tribe also maintains a museum and genealogical library on the property.

As the executive and legislative branches struggle for equilibrium, this government, like any other, must be viewed as a work in progress. The news from within the tribe appears wholeheartedly positive, showing gains in the businesses and growth in the service areas for tribal members. According to the Chickasaw Nation's annual report, total assets have grown from less than $20 million in 1987 to an estimated $156 million in 2000. News from the federal government, however, is usually mixed, with a number of congressional legislators, some from Oklahoma, still trying to push the Indian tribes back toward nonexistence. The chiefs of the other Five Civilized Tribes were also there to show their support as all Indian tribes continue to struggle for survival in a continuing hostile environment.

The interaction with the various European and American governments helped destroy the Chickasaw's spirit and traditions long before their removal to Oklahoma, and their decentralized and impoverished conditions in the Indian Territory only helped in the continued deterioration of the tribe for many years to follow. Fortunately, there were still many families who kept up the traditions as best they could and passed their heritage on to their children and grandchildren, planting the seeds for the tribe's continuing resurgence.

Those Chickasaw traditions, once so strong and essential in Montford Johnson's life, slowly eroded with subsequent generations. E. B.'s generation grew up proficient in both the Indian and white man's worlds. Montford made sure his children received the best education he could afford, realizing full well the difficulties they would face in this changing society. Subsequent generations became less and less involved with their Indian roots, growing up outside the Chickasaw Nation. All of E. B. and Mollie's children were on the Chickasaw rolls and remained proud of their Indian heritage, but as time and generations passed by there was understandably little or no interaction with any of the federally appointed tribal leadership. The federal government had all but extinguished any real tribal government until the election of Overton James in 1971.

Only recently, like the slow but steady resurgence of the Chickasaws, interest in Native Americans and their histories and traditions is also on the rise. Hopefully, there is much we can still learn from each other, leaving the ignorance and prejudice of those earlier times far behind where they belong. Perhaps we can still live in an America that can come to understand and respect the truths that our Native American ancestors embraced about the earth, family, faith, and tradition centuries before the Europeans arrived on this continent, claiming it as their own.

Note

1. Hale, Duane K., and Arnell M. Gibson. 1991. *The Chickasaw*. New York: Chelsea House Publishers, pp. 93–103.

Appendix

Names of Silver City Pioneers, first settlement in the Chickasaw Country 1873–1891

Names were taken from plaque in Tuttle, Oklahoma, presented by the Daughters of the American Revolution Committee and the Executive Committee of Pioneers in 1931.

W. G. (Caddo Bill) Williams
Montford T. Johnson
Edward (E. B.) Johnson
James H. Bond
C. L. Campbell
C. H. Campbell
B. P. (Bud) Smith
Reford Bond
James H. Tuttle
Ben Pikey
Thomas E. Waldon
Rev. G. W. Larrimore
Rev. C. P. Kelly, M.D.
P. A. Smith
Charles Brown
Lon Gray
Mark Brittain

Lizzie Davis
Joe Lindsay
Mary E. Johnson
Sallie Campbell Minter
Mary Leslie
Fannie J Worley
Burrel Fryrear
Robert M. Graham
John Davis
Charles Rider
R. M. Clopton
Martin Colbert
Zan (T. A.) Leslie
Lum Adkins
Reese Barton
Bill Perdeer
Frank Foster

Peter Krey

John Worley

Rube Jennings

John Beard

Tom Ellison

Cass Wantland

W. R. Leeper

Sophia Waldon

Carrie Tuttle

Martha Smith

Jane Shirley

El Meta Chestnut Sager

Jane Bond

E. B. Parish

Anna Dark Brown

Marielas Graham

Frances Schrock

Stella Johnson Connaway

Nora Bond Tuttle

Emma Lee Downing

Minnie Pikey

Sarah McKinney Atkins

Ella Rider

Lovica Colbert McBride

Callie Graham

Sarah Shinn Kelly

Lucinda Brittain

Adelaide Bond

Mollie Cornett

(Uncle) Jimmy Wright

Jas. Campbell

Joe Kirkendall

Ben Goode

Oscar Davis

Bill McClure

Theo. Price

Hy Downing

Owen Hennessy

Jim Morrison

C. M. Roundtree

Wm. Moncrief

Charles Snyder

Charles Ryther

Hosea Waldon

Henry McLish

Margaret W. Campbell

Ida Ledford Smith

Abigail Wright

Mollie Graham Johnson

Cora Caruth West

Vicey Harmon

Mary E. Lindsay

Effie Johnson

Fannie Johnson Colbert

Minerva Ward Leeper

Rosie Fryrear

Susie Clopton

Annie Williams

Nancy T. Wantland

Cowhands for the Johnsons and customers of the Silver City Store 1882–1888 and Hat Ranch hands during 1885–1887* (some names appear on both lists)

Phillip Cross*

Charles Brown*

Don Harris*

R. L. Wood*

W. F. Goldsby*

Jim McLaughlin*

Lon Gray*

W. S. Green*

T. W. Folsom*

Isaac Thomas

Charles Thomas

G. W. Gordon

H. B. Johnson

George Graham

R. J. Thompson

W. O. Parker

Andrew Karohoi

John Stroud

Lawrence Lane*
John Billbrey*
Edmund Pickens*
Will Johnson*
Rube Jennings*
J. L. Rushing*
Ike Jones*
Jim Kay*
Leck Lee*
Lon Lee*
Jap Green*
J. W. Lawson*
Colbert Carter*
Limon Leeder*
Andrew Langdon* (cook)
Henry Peuden
Jesse Carter
Dave Duff
John Davis
A. Ward
S. Blundell
Walter T. Goldsby
Isaac Thomas
Alert Reed
Naith Harris
L. C. Wantland
William Ellison
C. B. Camden
James H. Bond
James Swalley
W. L. Wilson
Mannie Parker
Walnut Creek Place
Omer Jones
J. P. Cushman
Smith & Forsyth
Charles Parker
Haswell Brothers
Nash Potter
Tom Smith
Charley Davis
Milus Bedenfield
Mexican McGill

Bill Anderson
Henry Rowe
Fred Wait
Jake Horne
Rob Seaton
H. Bersheres
Dave Bumgarner
John Bonett
Dug Gibbens
James Horbolt
George Horbolt
R. S. Bean
Dick Colbert
J. N. Snider
A. J. Shepard
R. J. Phillips
D. Donald
Tom Elis
Bob Wilson
Tom Bush
A. L. Wood (cook)
Ellis Johnson
Charley Thomas
Isaac Ward
Thomas Eoff (cook)
Oborne & Walker
    (purchase 543 cattle)
John C. Worley
Charles W. Morrison
Williams Raines
Fort Reno Beef Contract
Chas Carson
Greasy Valley Place
Douglas McPeek
Nin Miller
Walters & Lappin
M. B. Cook
Robert Seaton
_____ McMorris
George Charley
Theodore Reed
J. E. Barrow
Jim Naro

Mack Carter
Harry Kelley
John Jones
Mexican Houston
Thomas Hardy
Lem Blenng
George Fowler
_____ Hays (cook)
Joe Patterson
George Elliott
Boley Brothers
John &William Miles
Charley Petty
Lin Love
Love & Ness
John Stibben
George Love
Clate Love

South Texas Lumber Co.
Samuel Biles
W. P. Jones
Wm. Ness
M. J. Lawrence
Dock Turnbull
Lee Wilson
A. E. Winkler
Joe Stephens
Deer Creek Acct.
Townsend & Picket (bought cattle)
Jim Downing Place
Arch Strapps
Frank Lewis
Smith & Kelley
Owens Smith & Co.
E. M. Yates
T. A. McCauley

Index

Page numbers in italics indicate illustrations.

Made in United States
Orlando, FL
18 July 2022

19920785R00192